JOURNAL FOR THE STUDY OF THE OLD TESTAMENT
SUPPLEMENT SERIES
308

Sheffield Academic Press

Victim and Victimizer

Joseph's Interpretation
of his Destiny

Yiu-Wing Fung

Journal for the Study of the Old Testament
Supplement Series 308

Published by
Sheffield Academic Press Ltd
Mansion House
19 Kingfield Road
Sheffield S11 9AS
England

Typeset by Sheffield Academic Press
and
Printed on acid-free paper in Great Britain
by Bookcraft Ltd
Midsomer Norton, Bath

British Library Cataloguing in Publication Data

A catalogue record for this book is available
from the British Library

ISBN 1-84127-103-9

CONTENTS

Victim and Victimizer

PREFACE

This study began as a methodological inquiry on biblical charac-terization. A great portion of my research was spent in reading current literary theories, which did enhance my literary sensibility, but their complexities hinder rather than help my original attempt to devise a clear methodology in analysing biblical characters. At the end, I find the effort in acquainting myself with literary theories is well spent as it eventually enables me to offer a new perspective in reading a familiar character in a well-read story.

I am greatly indebted to Professor David J.A. Clines for the direction and encouragement he provided me during my research. Over the years, Alliance Bible Seminary has been generous in granting released time and financial support. Gratitude is also due to my colleagues and students for their prayerful support. Finally, I thank God and my wife, Lena, for their presence and comfort when, at times, I thought this research would never end.

ABBREVIATIONS

AB	Anchor Bible
AV	Authorised Version
BI	*Biblical Interpretation*
Bib	*Biblica*
BN	*Biblische Notizen*
BibRes	*Biblical Research*
BR	*Bible Review*
BT	*The Bible Translator*
BTB	*Biblical Theology Bulletin*
BToday	*The Bible Today*
BZAW	Beiheft zur *Zeitschrift für die alttestamentliche Wissenschaft*
CBQ	*Catholic Biblical Quarterly*
CBQMS	Catholic Biblical Quarterly Monograph Series
ExpTim	*Expository Times*
HBT	*Horizons in Biblical Theology*
HTB	*Harvard Theological Review*
HUCA	*Hebrew Union College Annual*
IB	Interpreter's Bible
ICC	International Critical Commentary
Int	*Interpretation*
ITC	International Theological Commentary
JBL	*Journal of Biblical Literature*
JJS	*Journal of Jewish Studies*
JNES	*Journal of Near Eastern Studies*
JQR	*Jewish Quarterly Review*
JSOT	*Journal for the Study of the Old Testament*
JSOTSup	Journal for the Study of the Old Testament Supplement Series
NICOT	New International Commentary on the Old Testament
NovT	*Novum Testamentum*
NRSV	New Revised Standard Version
OTG	Old Testament Guides
P(ST)J	Perkin's (School of Theology) Journal
RB	*Revue Biblique*
RSV	Revised Standard Version
SBLSP	SBL Seminar Papers
TD	*Theology Digest*

TOTC	Tyndale Old Testament Commentaries
VT	*Vetus Testamentum*
VTSup	Supplements to *Vetus Testamentum*
WBC	Word Biblical Commentary
ZAW	*Zeitschrift für die alttestamentliche Wissenschaft*

INTRODUCTION

The purpose of my thesis is to investigate how a reader constructs a portrait of Joseph in the book of Genesis. Characterization in narrative theory suggests that a portrait is constructed primarily 'through the character's action, speech or external appearance'.[1] The description of external appearance is rarely given in Hebrew narratives; most readers therefore focus on Joseph's actions and speeches as a basis for their perception of his image. Joseph is one of the best-known biblical characters and, understandably, every detail of his actions and speeches has been closely scrutinized. Generally, his various speeches (e.g. to Potiphar's wife when he expresses the fear of God against sexual temptation; to Pharaoh and his two officers when he asserts that God is source of the authority of his interpretation; to his brothers when he declares God's intentions in his suffering inflicted by them and his destiny) tend to elicit positive responses from readers concerning his moral character and faith in God. In contrast, his actions provoke more diverse and even contradictory responses. For example, the reporting of his dreams to his brothers in his youth and his long trial imposed on them later after the fulfilment of his dreams yields different portraits of him for readers. While some readers see him as an insensitive and cruel person, others consider his actions betray his innocence and caring attitude.[2] The ambiguity of these dual images results mainly from readers'

1.   Shlomith Rimmon-Kenan, *Narrative Fiction* (London: Routledge, 1983), p. 67.
2.   There are already two morally opposite evaluations of Joseph's portrait in the early Jewish literature—Philo, Josephus, the Testaments of the Twelve Patriarchs, *Genesis Rabbah* and the Targum. In this early period, Joseph had already been praised as an upright hero as well as condemned as a devious brother. Maren Niehoff in her book, *The Figure of Joseph in Post-Biblical Jewish Literature* (Leiden: E.J. Brill, 1992), gives an excellent survey of Joseph's portraits in this literature. See also Earle Hilgert, 'The Dual Image of Joseph in Hebrew and Early Jewish Literature', *Journal of the Chicago Society of Biblical Research* 30 (1985), pp. 5-21. James L. Kugel, 'The Case against Joseph', in Tzvi Abusch, John Huehn-

different evaluations of his behaviour, which still attracts scholarly scrutiny.[3]

My aim in this thesis is to provide a portrayal of Joseph from a different perspective by scrutinizing his speeches (rather than focusing mainly on his actions) in order to expose the problematic nature of his ideology. I suggest that his ambiguous behaviour stems from his belief. For example, I will attempt to establish a link between his claim of domination in his disclosure speech (45.5-11) and his subsequent policy of mass enslavement of the Egyptians (47.13-26). His treatment of foreigners has received severe criticism but his claim of domination over Egypt encounters little or no objection. This is one of the examples to support my contention that his speeches are not given proper examination by other readers in constructing his portrait. Besides the relationship between his speeches and actions, an important part of my study will focus on the interrelation between his various speeches about God's intentions and actions. I will try to demonstrate that the more he speaks of God, the more his speeches become incoherent. As a result, each of his claims of God's specific action, although if it stands alone it can be reasonably justified, becomes highly problematic in the context of the rest of his claims.

One of the important factors that influence readers' perception of Joseph's character is the narrator's repeated description that 'the Lord was with him' (39.2, 3, 21, 23).[4] It is generally assumed that the pres-

ergard and Piotr Steinkeller (eds.), *Lingering Over Words: Studies in Ancient Near Eastern Literature in Honor of William L. Moran* (Atlanta: Scholars Press, 1990), pp. 271-87, documents the negative portrayal of Joseph in this early literature.

3.   E.g. Mark A. O'Brien, 'The Contribution of Judah's Speech, Gen. 44.18-34, to Characterization of Joseph', *CBQ* 59.3 (1997), pp. 429-47 (444-45), paints a negative image of Joseph due to his harsh test on his brothers. He considers that Judah's speech and 'radical gesture [to offer him as a slave in place of Benjamin] unintentionally challenges Joseph's own desire to be in control and to have Benjamin regardless of the consequence'.

4.   Claus Westermann, *Genesis 37–50: A Commentary* (trans. John J. Scullion; Minneapolis: Augsburg, 1986), p. 253, points out that there is a long tradition of Christian teachings from the Fathers to the nineteenth century referring to Joseph as 'the type of Christ' due to his virtue and his rise to power after suffering for others; Aubrey W. Argyle, 'Joseph the Patriarch in Patristic Teaching', *ExpTim* 67 (1956), pp. 199-201 (199), surveys this interpretation in Christian writings of the second century; Charles T. Fritsch, 'God Was With Him: A Theological Study of the Joseph Narrative [Gen 37–50]', *Int* 9 (1955), pp. 21-34 (24), a modern reader,

ence of God with Joseph is proof of Joseph's moral excellence. Ackerman for example, describes this link thus:

> But a recurring motif is God's presence with Joseph in Egypt, whether
> he is in Potiphar's house or in Pharaoh's prison. The reader notes with
> satisfaction that Joseph's rise to power in Egypt results from a combina-
> tion of pious behaviour, divine help, and his wise advice at court.[5]

Joseph's rise to power is related to divine help and his wise advice to
Pharaoh. But there may not be a direct connection between his pious
behaviour and divine presence, unless one regards his pious behaviour
as the cause of divine presence, as if it somehow deserved divine help.[6]
Joseph's refusal of sexual temptation may be seen to be connected with
the divine presence with him. But God is first with Joseph before the
temptation, and the sequence of events does not suggest that Joseph
merits God's favour because of his morality. It can be argued that the
bracketing of the temptation scene with this phrase, 'the Lord was with
Joseph', is a narrator's device to indicate that God's presence with
Joseph is related to his moral excellence. But the divine presence in
previous instances in Genesis indicates only divine assistance and does
not have direct connection with the morality of the persons involved.

reaffirms the same understanding: 'As the ideal man of God, Joseph points beyond
himself in the history of redemption to the One who was altogether perfect, and
who, by his perfect obedience, brought salvation to the world.' However, Henry
Morris, *The Genesis Record: A Scientific and Devotional Commentary on the Book
of Beginnings* (Grand Rapids: Baker Book House, 1976), p. 535, argues against this
interpretation on the ground that 'the New Testament nowhere speaks of Joseph as
a type of Christ'; W. Lee Humphreys, *Joseph and His Family: A Literary Study*
(Columbia: University of South Carolina Press, 1988), p. 91, also suggests that the
contrast of 'stark villains and unsullied heroes' resulted from this kind of 'interpretative strategies' does not do justice to the 'full characters in the Joseph novella'.
    5.   James S. Ackerman, 'Joseph, Judah, and Jacob', in Kenneth R.R. Gros
Louis and James S. Ackerman (eds.), *Literary Interpretations of Biblical Narratives*, II (Nashville: Abingdon Press, 1982), pp. 85-113 (86). Fritsch, 'God Was
With Him', p. 27, also stresses Joseph's merit: 'After long years of trial and tribulation, Joseph finally receives his well-earn reward. His enduring faith and loyal
obedience win for him the highest office in the land of Egypt.'
    6.   Niehoff, *The Figure of Joseph*, p. 32, is more cautious in ascribing this per-
sonality trait to Joseph because of this phrase, but she considers that Joseph
deserves God's protection: 'One important conclusion may nevertheless be drawn
with regard to the protagonist. He is considered sufficiently important by the narrator to be presented as a type who deserves God's explicit protection.'

God is with Ishmael (21.20), Abraham (21.22) and Isaac (26.3, 24, 28). But none of these passages is concerned with the character's morality. All speak of God's assistance and protection of the characters. The Canaanite king Abimelech detects a link between the prosperity of the patriarchs, Abraham and Isaac, and the divine presence with them (21.22; 26.28). He recognizes divine assistance but not any virtue in Abraham and Isaac. In the Joseph story, both Potiphar and the keeper of the prison favour Joseph because God causes him to prosper in whatever he does (39.4). They mention no virtue of Joseph. Pharaoh later recognizes that God's Spirit is in Joseph, but this is because of Joseph's wisdom in interpretation of dreams, not his morality (41.38). The narrator also narrates God's promise to Jacob to be with him (28.15), but that comes after his cheating his brother and father. Worst of all, he deceives his father with an untrue assertion about God's help (27.20). It is obvious that Jacob does not merit God's presence with him. Nevertheless, God promises to be with him immediately after his wrong action. Therefore when one comes to Joseph, the next person who enjoys the divine presence, it is difficult to assume automatically that he is morally good just because God is with him.[7]

There is also a close parallel between God being with Jacob and God being with Joseph. Both of these occurrences take place after the conflicts with their brothers. Both characters enjoy prosperity after God is with them (Jacob in Laban's house and Joseph in Potiphar's house). Both stories report the cause of the conflicts as the younger brother provoking his older brother's anger. Jacob does it secretly by cheating his brother of his father's blessing, promising lordship over his brother (27.29), while Joseph twice openly declares face to face his desire for lordship over his brothers through his dreams.[8] Using Jacob as an analogy does not necessarily prove Joseph is as bad as he is. But the phrase 'the Lord was with Joseph' should not be seen as a seal of approval for Joseph's moral excellence. He is portrayed as better than Jacob not because of the divine presence, but because he rejects sexual temptation

---

7.   John Holbert, *The Storyteller's Companion to the Bible*, I (Nashville: Abingdon Press, 1991), p. 174, rightly comments, 'God is with Joseph, but that does not prevent Joseph from being pictured as a complex human being'.

8.   Peter D. Miscall, 'The Jacob and Joseph Stories as Analogies', *JSOT* 6 (1978), pp. 28-40 (32), also gives a rather negative view of Joseph when making a comparison with Jacob's story. See also Laurence A. Turner, *Announcements of Plot in Genesis* (JSOTSup, 96; Sheffield: JSOT Press, 1990), p. 158.

and he forgives his brothers. However, this phrase in Gen. 39.2, 3, 21, 23 has been an important factor in shaping readers' assessments of Joseph's character. Because of the divine presence with Joseph, many readers tend to assume that God, as well as the narrator, sanctions his actions and words. But if this phrase is correctly interpreted, Joseph's portrait and his assertions about God's intentions will be judged on their own merit more carefully.

At the beginning of the story, Joseph's dreams of domination over his brothers provoke angry responses from them and result in his subsequent enslavement. Afterwards, his suffering as a slave as well as his fulfilment of his dreams are declared by Joseph in his disclosure speech (45.5-11) to be part of a divine providential plan. At the end of the story, the initial hostile reaction to his dreams by his brothers becomes complete acquiescence when they all come to bow down before him and offer to be his slaves (50.18). Does the shift of attitude on the part of his brothers take place because they are convinced by Joseph's explanation of a divine plan? Or is his brothers' submission merely due to his present power and their fear of his revenge? Joseph himself undergoes a radical shift of attitude too. He has tried hard to forget his past suffering as a slave, but later he comes to acceptance of it as a necessary means for salvation in God's plan. Surprisingly, he not only accepts slavery for himself but also carries out an incredible scheme of mass enslavement of the Egyptians. The plot of this story is about a slave making a nation of slaves (chs. 40–47) as much as it is about fraternal strife (chs. 37–45, 50). The overlapping of these two story lines indicates that there are important interactions and interrelations the narrator may want to establish. The new insight Joseph proclaims in his disclosure speech is not only relevant to define and settle the stormy relationship between the protagonist and his brothers, it is also important to explain his intraction with his newly adopted country. Therefore, I examine Joseph's justification of his domination over his brothers as well as over Egypt and provide a challenge to his claim.

In Chapter 1, I expose the problematic nature of the hierarchical oppositions behind the idea of divine providence implied in Joseph's disclosure speech. If the idea of divine good overriding human evil can be proved problematic, his justification of his domination will become more difficult to sustain. In Chapter 2, I will discuss some of the reasons that may explain why his claim is so persuasive. Then, I will argue that Joseph's claim of a divine plan is a case of self-delusion with the tragic consequence that the protagonist repeats his brothers' evil which he has condemned through his test. Readers may not find the protagonist's ideology pertinent today, but the common assumption is that his ideology is the same as that of the narrator. It is this assumption of the coalescence of the perspective between the narrator and the protagonist that I will set out to call into question in Chapter 3. The question I will ask in this chapter is: Is Joseph's justification of the dreams of domination for salvation (45.8b-11) qualitatively different from Judah's excuse of opting for slavery in order to save his brother (37.26-27), especially in the light of Joseph's repeated assertions of the God-sent famine in his interpretation of Pharaoh's dreams (41.25, 28, 32)? This question exposes the problem of the incoherence of Joseph's various speeches, because he is claiming that God has planned both the destruction and salvation. The examination of this problem will have serious consequences on one's opinion of Joseph's credibility as a mouthpiece of the narrator. The last two chapters will document the different responses made by readers, especially concerning their acceptance (or avoidance) of Joseph's claims of domination and divine favouritism.

My approach follows the basic principles of narrative theory in constructing a portrait from the textual elements. A number of articles and books have been specifically devoted to employing narrative theory in reading the Joseph story. I am greatly indebted to their methodological insights, but my interaction with them in this work is primarily on our different assessments of Joseph's portrait.[9] I also borrow two concepts

9.   Humphreys in his book *Joseph and his Family* provides a concise survey of various aspects of narrative theory (characterization, plot and other rhetorical techniques) and applies them to the study of this story. Niehoff, *The Figure of Joseph*, also has a chapter on the characterization of Joseph before examining his portraits in the works of Philo, Josephus, and *Genesis Rabbah*. The following works (or part of their contents) employ different aspects of narrative theories to interpret the Joseph story. On plot and narration—Laurence A. Turner, *Announcements of Plot in Genesis*, pp. 143-73; Robert Alter, *The Art of Biblical Narrative* (New York: Basic Books, 1981), pp. 155-77; Meir Sternberg, *The Poetics of Biblical Narrative: Ideological Literature and the Drama of Reading* (Bloomington: Indiana University Press, 1985), pp. 285-308; George W. Coats, *From Canaan to Egypt: Structural and Theological Context for the Joseph Story* (CBQMS, 4; Washington, DC: The Catholic Biblical Association of America, 1976). On repetition—James S. Ackerman, 'Joseph, Judah, and Jacob', pp. 85-113; Donald A. Seybold, 'Paradox and Symmetry in the Joseph Narrative', in Kenneth R.R. Gros Louis, James S. Ackerman and Thayer S. Warshaw (eds.), *Literary Interpretations of Biblical Narratives*,

of Derrida's complex philosophical enquiry in illustrating my observation of certain curious aspects in the Joseph story (the problematic nature of hierarchical opposition in Chapter 1 and the idea of *pharmakon* in Chapter 5). I benefit greatly from his theory, but I do not claim that there is a methodological and thematic correlation between Derrida's discussion of these two concepts and my use of it. My discussion is not a direct application of deconstruction, and a systematic analysis of his theory is beyond the scope of this work.

Unless otherwise stated, the English translations of the Hebrew text which occur in this thesis are taken from the RSV.

I (Nashville: Abingdon Press, 1974), pp. 59-73; Miscall, 'The Jacob and Joseph Stories as Analogies', pp. 28-40; Donald B. Redford, *A Study of the Biblical Story of Joseph* (VTSup, 20; Leiden: E.J. Brill, 1970). On characters' speech—Mark A. O'Brien, 'Contribution of Judah's Speech', pp. 85-113.

Chapter 1

THE PROBLEMATIC NATURE OF JOSEPH'S CLAIM
OF DIVINE PROVIDENCE

Overview

The Joseph story is well researched in studies of biblical narrative, especially with regard to the method of New Criticism. This literary approach enables readers to appreciate the artistry of the biblical text and to understand its structure, plot, character, point of view and themes. However, the basic moral and ideological stance of literary scholars[1] towards the text does not differ much from those of historical-critical scholars.[2] Joseph remains as an example and a spokesman of God's divine providence. In the light of recent developments in the application of literary theory to the biblical text, the Joseph story and its interpretations will be revisited to see whether or not a more radical portrayal of Joseph will emerge.

Binary Oppositions in the Joseph Story

Among the many facets of the deconstructive approach to reading, I restrict myself to focusing on the unsettling effect of its deconstruction of binary opposition. Jacques Derrida demonstrates that prior meta-physical, epistemological and ethical systems have been constructed on the basis of conceptual oppositions such as original/derivative, central/marginal, internal/external, transcendental/empirical, universal/particular, good/evil, self/other, and presence/absence. One of the terms in each binary opposition is privileged and the other suppressed or excluded. By analysing the denigrated or marginalized terms and the nature of their exclusion, Derrida's strategy of reading is to prove that such preference for one term over its opposite is ultimately untenable. The

---

1. E.g. Robert Alter, Meir Sternberg, Jan P. Fokkelman, Shimon Bar-Efrat, Adele Berlin, Eric I. Lowenthal.
2. E.g. Gerhard von Rad, Samuel R. Driver, John Skinner, Ephraim A. Speiser.

privileged term can always be found to depend on and be invaded by its ostensibly excluded opposite. In other words, the privileged term is constituted by what it suppresses, and the latter returns to haunt it. Thus the privileged term never achieves perfect identity or conceptual purity; it is always already parasitic on or contaminated by the marginalized term. Derrida's aim is not simply to reverse the opposition but to problematize such a hierarchy of binary opposition. The above description of Derrida's deconstruction of binary opposition is best summarized in his interview with Jean-Louis Houdebine and Guy Scarpetta in his book *Positions*.[3] Below is a concise description of the deconstructive approach, and its aim, as employed by biblical scholars:

> A text typically sets forth or takes for granted some set of oppositions, one term being privileged over its partner; but in so doing it cannot help allowing glimpses of the impossibility of sustaining those oppositions. In deconstruction it is not a matter of reversing the oppositions, of privileging the unprivileged and vice versa, but of rewriting, reinscribing, the structures that have previously been constructed. The deconstruction of texts relativizes the authority attributed to them, and makes it evident that much of the power that is felt to lie in texts is really the power of their sanctioning community.[4]

A deconstructive reading of Joseph's portrayal will find no better starting point than his final theological claim within his reassurance and comfort to his brothers:

---

3. Jacques Derrida, *Positions* (trans. Alan Bass; Chicago: University of Chicago Press, 1981), pp. 37-96. Derrida's deconstruction is first meticulously argued in his three books published in French in the same year (1967) and further expounded in another three books published in 1972: *Of Grammatology* (trans. Gayatri Chakravorty Spivak; Baltimore: Johns Hopkins University Press, 1976); *Writing and Difference* (trans. Alan Bass; Chicago: University of Chicago Press, 1978); *Speech and Phenomena* (trans. David B. Allison; Evanston: Northwestern University Press, 1973); *Dissemination* (trans. Barbara Johnson; Chicago: University of Chicago Press, 1981), pp. 61-172; *Margins of Philosophy* (trans. Alan Bass; London: Harvester Press, 1982); *Positions* (trans. Alan Bass; Chicago: University of Chicago Press, 1981). The translators, Gayatri Chakravorty Spivak (*Of Grammatology*) and Barbara Johnson (*Dissemination*), give readers two good introductions to Derrida's complex thought. The three interviews in *Positions* provide a concise summary of Derrida's deconstruction.

4. J. Cheryl Exum and David J.A. Clines, 'The New Literary Criticism', in J. Cheryl Exum and David J.A. Clines (eds.), *The New Literary Criticism and the Hebrew Bible* (JSOTSup, 143; Sheffield: JSOT Press, 1993), pp. 11-25 (19-20).

> But Joseph said to them, 'Fear not, for am I in the place of God? As for you, you meant evil against me; but God meant it for good, to bring it about that many people should be kept alive, as they are today. So do not fear; I will provide for you and your little ones.' Thus he reassured them and comforted them (50.19-21).

Joseph's concise summary of the past, his intricate interaction with his brothers and God's relation with them, centres on two obvious pairs of oppositions: divine intention/human intention and good/evil ('You meant evil against me; but God meant it for good'). Any portrayal of Joseph will not be complete without confronting this claim and its implied oppositions. There are other series of binary oppositions intertwined with these two pairs within the narrative and its interpretations by many historical-critical or literary scholars. The prominent ones are lord/slave, life/death, brother/foreigner, and knowledge/ignorance.[5] Under close scrutiny of the text, these oppositions do not provide a sustainable and authoritative anchor for the argument within the narrative. As a result, interpretations relying uncritically on these oppositions will soon be found wanting. Deconstruction warns us that one always undermines what one has affirmed due to unexamined hierarchical oppositions. This chapter will chart this process of self-undermining in Joseph's famous theological dictum.

Joseph's dreams about his brothers and parents bowing down before him predict a relationship of lord/slave (or lord/servant, to use a less severe term) between them. The brothers plot to murder him in order to frustrate any chance of his dreams being fulfilled. Judah successfully persuades the brothers not to kill their own brother but to turn this master of dreams into a slave by selling him to foreigners. Instead of being a lord over his brothers, Joseph begins a downward turn from Canaan to Egypt, from being a favoured son to a slave in a foreigner's house and finally a slave in a prison. However, his ability to interpret dreams, at first for Pharaoh's two officers and later for Pharaoh himself, reverses his descent and finally helps him to rise from the position of a foreign slave in prison to be the lord over Egypt, second in power only to Pharaoh. Joseph's own dreams come true (at least partially) when his brothers come to bow down before him in their trip to Egypt to buy

---

5.   Frederick E. Greenspahn in his book, *When Brothers Dwell Together: The Preeminence of Younger Siblings in the Hebrew Bible* (Oxford: Oxford University Press, 1994), offers an extensive discussion on the opposition of younger versus elder in Genesis.

food during the famine. Hiding his identity, Joseph begins a series of accusations of spying and of theft against his brothers until Judah offers himself as a slave in place of Benjamin. Joseph then reveals himself and reassures them with two famous theological declarations in 45.5-8 and 50.19-20, which most readers (ancient or modern, historical-critical or literary scholars) consider as the governing centre for interpreting or uniting the whole Joseph story, a centre upon which a doctrine of divine providence is firmly grounded.[6]

The portraits of Joseph given by readers, ancient or modern, are obviously not homogeneous. Despite the diversity of opinions on various details of Joseph's words and deeds, favourable and positive evaluations of his character on the whole outnumber negative ones. Those who are well aware of human complexity and prefer a more rounded figure would nevertheless tend to consider his vices in the end to be overshadowed by his virtues. While the time he spends in years of captivity (chs. 39–41) generally elicits admiration from readers for his

---

6.   E.g. Walter A. Brueggemann, *Genesis* (Interpretation; Philadelphia: Westminster Press, 1986), p. 290, considers Joseph's claims in these two passages as 'the major theological statements which interpret the entire narrative', and he also makes it clear that the narrator shares Joseph's viewpoint, 'In these two places only does the narrator make obvious the programmatic claim that God's leadership, though hidden, is the real subject of the narrative'; Westermann, *Genesis 37–50*, p. 251, 'Joseph's words…meant to bring together the whole event from the beginning to end. It is God's action that gives unity to the whole course of happenings. All passages…are to be brought into synthesis under this key sentence… [which] covers the whole structure that determines the Joseph narrative'; Robert E. Longacre, *Joseph: A Story of Divine Providence* (Winona Lake, IN: Eisenbrauns, 1989), pp. 42-43, deduces from Joseph's remarks here a macrostructure, 'the overall plan and global purpose of a story', which in this case is the divine providence revealed by Joseph that can serve as 'an (explanatory) control' in the composition and interpretation of the Joseph story; Gerhard von Rad, *Genesis: A Commentary* (trans. John H. Marks; London: SCM Press, rev. edn, 1972), p. 438, 'It is true that the passages in which Joseph really speaks about God have programmatic significance for the interpretation of the narrative as a whole'; Coats, *From Canaan to Egypt*, pp. 90-91, considers that Joseph's statement of God's purpose to preserve a remnant for his brothers not only explains the tragedies within the Joseph's story, but goes beyond it to the entire Pentateuch and 'ties directly with the promise to the patriarchs for a great progeny'; Seybold, 'Paradox and Symmetry', p. 71, remarks that 'the controlling deep structure of the entire narrative' is, as revealed by Joseph, 'the whole paradoxical purpose of his "death" as God's way of preserving the family'.

integrity and endurance, his behaviour towards his brothers both at the beginning of the conflict (ch. 37) and in the long and tortuous test (chs. 42–44) casts a shadow on his portrait. But for some readers his final disclosure of identity without exacting revenge mitigates, if not obliterates, the impression of his previous harsh treatment of the brothers. And his consolation of his brothers' fear with the revelation of divine providence also gives an impression of his growth in maturity and sensitivity. Whatever defects (real or apparent) Joseph previously had, his reconciliation with his brothers and his recognition of divine providence in their shared past seems to give him a favourable portrait in the end.

Divine Intention Overriding Human Intention

The overall and final evaluation of Joseph's character hinges crucially on the responses of readers to his final theological claims in 45.4-8 and 50.19-20. The final portrait of Joseph will be utterly shattered if his claims can be proved to be problematic in the light of the textual evidence in the narrative. While other details of his words and behaviour are constantly subjected to questioning, his claim of divine providence has never been seriously challenged in a detailed way. John Rogerson in his article 'Can a Doctrine of Providence be based on the Old Testament?'[7] begins his discussion by quoting Joseph's words and then he moves on to argue against the view that 'God is believed [by the Old Testament writers] to be leading all history to a definite goal according to a fixed plan.'[8] In his view, Joseph's words here have been seen as the 'classical' passages for a belief in divine providence. However, after his initial quotation, his discussion makes no attempt to study Joseph's claim within the context of the Joseph story.

---

7.   John W. Rogerson, 'Can a Doctrine of Providence Be Based on the Old Testament?', in Lyle M. Eslinger and Glen Taylor (eds.), *Ascribe to the Lord: Biblical and Other Essays in Memory of Peter C. Craigie* (JSOTSup, 67; Sheffield: JSOT Press, 1988), pp. 529-43.

8.   Rogerson, 'Can a Doctrine of Providence Be Based on the Old Testament?', pp. 529-43 (535). According to Rogerson, this notion of divine providence has been held in Old Testament scholarship since the first half of the nineteenth century when the concept of 'history as an organic, unfolding process directed by God towards a goal' (p. 537) has been commonly accepted. But Rogerson thinks that the Old Testament writers 'could not have had a conception of history as a totality or as a process' (p. 541).

Donald Redford stages a more direct assault on Joseph's claim of an underlying divine plan. Joseph's claim of divine 'preconceived design' is accused of rendering human motivation 'trivial', human effort 'needless' and human passion 'pointless'. Apart from his sarcastic remark that 'God had manipulated the principals of the drama like so many marionettes', Redford has not contested Joseph's claim in any details.[9] W. Lee Humphreys counters Redford's version of the Joseph story as a 'grand puppet show staged by a divine puppeteer' by affirming that the 'claims of God's providential design working around and through the tug and pull of the life of this family are not allowed to blunt human freedom and responsibility for the exercise of that freedom in this novella'.[10] Therefore, the usual reaction to Redford's charge of God's manipulation of human affairs is to insist that Joseph's claim does not exclude human freedom and responsibility. Gordon Wenham emphasized that the relationship between the two is a 'theological mystery' and 'ultimately beyond human comprehension', but both are true and strongly affirmed by the Joseph story and the rest of Scripture.[11]

For many readers, Joseph's poles of divine providence and human action are constantly in tension. They are, in von Rad's words, 'ultimately very unyielding side by side'.[12] Neither of them can be excluded or neglected. However, they are not on equal terms. The former is always privileged over the latter.[13] This hierarchy is easily detectable in

9.   Redford, *Biblical Story of Joseph*, p. 74. Redford considers Joseph's claim (both in 45.5-8 and 50.15-20) as 'denigrating to the story as a whole' (see pp. 74, 104). Gerhard von Rad, 'The Joseph Narrative and Ancient Wisdom', in E.W. Trueman Dicken (trans.), *The Problem of the Hexateuch and Other Essays* (Edinburgh: Oliver & Boyd, 1965), pp. 292-300 (298), also considers that Joseph's claim poses a danger in portraying 'the purposes of God as altogether hidden, incomprehensible and unfathomable'.

10. Humphreys, *Joseph and his Family*, p. 128. Coats, *From Canaan to Egypt*, p. 90, interprets Joseph's word not as saying that 'God pulled the string for the brothers' plot against Joseph', but rather as relating all those past tragedies to the coming event of preservation of Jacob's family.

11. Gordon J. Wenham, *Genesis 16–50* (WBC, 2; Dallas: Word Books, 1994), p. 432.

12. Von Rad, *Genesis*, p. 432.

13. Derrida, *Positions*, p. 41, states: 'in a classical philosophical opposition we are not dealing with the peaceful coexistence of a *vis-à-vis*, but rather with a violent hierarchy. One of the two terms governs the other (axiologically, logically, etc.), or has the upper hand.'

the words used by many readers to relate these two poles. For example, 'God's overall action has *subsumed* the brothers' evil action';[14] 'God's *overruling* of human affairs';[15] 'The *overriding* power of God's rule'.[16] This concept of God's overriding power tries to maintain both God's ultimate power and human responsibility. But the former always easily overpowers the latter. Von Rad is aware of this danger. He comments, 'This rule of God for the salvation of men continuously permeates all realms of life and *includes* even man's evil by making the plans of the human heart serve divine purposes, without hindering them or excusing them.' By his phrase, 'without hindering or excusing' human evil, von Rad asserts human responsibility. But immediately, he confesses, 'this all-sufficiency of divine sovereignty makes human action almost irrelevant'.[17] The human action becomes insignificant before the privileged divine one. The divine sovereignty will inevitably swallow the human action without a trace. Therefore, Brueggemann declares, 'the ways of God are at work, regardless of human attitudes or actions... This story takes a high view of God, so high that human action is declared irrelevant', 'God's way will triumph without the contribution of any human actor, including even Joseph himself.'[18]

Laurence Turner in his book *Announcements of Plot in Genesis* tries to address this problem by emphasizing the human factor. He first gives an insightful analysis of all announcements in Genesis and concludes that most, if not all of them, both during and after Joseph's time, have hardly been fulfilled in a straightforward and literal way as most readers believe. For example, the promise of progeny and nationhood to Abraham does not enjoy spectacular success; by the end of Genesis, the promise of land possession remains a promise; the command to Abraham to 'be a blessing' is an almost unmitigated disaster; and Jacob's

---

14. Westermann, *Genesis 37–50*, p. 251. However, Westermann does not think that Joseph's words explicitly speak of God's providence which 'could only be described as a reflective conclusion from what has been said' (p. 143).

15. Wenham, *Genesis 16–50*, p. 432. Samuel R. Driver, *The Book of Genesis* (London: Methuen, 10th edn, 1916), p. 397, comments that 'he has no intention of exacting vengeance for actions which, however intended, have been *overruled* by God's providence for good' (my italics); John Skinner, *Genesis* (ICC; Edinburgh: T. & T. Clark, 2nd edn, 1930), p. 487, 'Joseph reassures them by pointing out the providential purpose which had *overruled* their crime for good' (my italics).

16. Brueggemann, *Genesis*, p. 294.

17. Von Rad, *Genesis*, p. 438.

18. Brueggemann, *Genesis*, pp. 289, 292.

lordship over his brothers is simply negated.[19] Turner explains the reasons behind the frustration of providence and concludes:

> divine providence is essentially 'reciprocal'; that is, the degree of success it enjoys is related to the type of activity humans engage in when responding to its dictates. While it may succeed in reaction to human opposition, or in sympathy with human inability or despite apathy, it cannot be fulfilled if humanity attempts to take matters into its own hand. Such human strategies lead to the frustration of providence.[20]

It is in expounding the Joseph story that Turner best explains his 'formula' concerning the reciprocal nature of divine providence: 'human attempts to frustrate the Announcements tend to fulfil them; human attempts to fulfil the Announcements tend to frustrate them'.[21] According to his interpretation, in spite of the attempt by his brothers to frustrate his dreams and in spite of Joseph's own 'apathy' towards them, the first dream of his brothers bowing before him comes to fruition. The second dream (the obeisance of his parents) is not fulfilled because 'Joseph tries to make it happen through his playing God with his family'.[22] Human activity plays a part in determining the outcome of the divine plan. Turner, therefore, warns us not to take Joseph's speeches in 45.5 and 50.20 as the 'predestinarian' model, as stating that God's plans succeed regardless of any human activity; nor should it be taken as the 'marionette' model commented on by Redford. Instead of the 'overriding' model of divine providence, Turner offers us a 'reciprocal' model that balances divine providence and human activity. In Turner's view there are three types of action that will affect the outcome of God's plan. Both the attempt to frustrate and apathetic inactivity will bring about (or even will speed) the fulfilment of God's plan. The third kind of action is the attempt to fulfil God's plan. The first action is not recommended, even if it may speed God's plan, because it is an evil action. The third type of action is not good in Turner's view because humanity should not attempt 'to take matters into its own hands' and try 'to force the issue'.[23]

The problem of Turner's proposal becomes evident when he advocates that the proper human attitude and activity in response to divine

19. Turner, *Announcements of Plot in Genesis*, pp. 175-76.
20. Turner, *Announcements of Plot in Genesis*, p. 169.
21. Turner, *Announcements of Plot in Genesis*, p. 179.
22. Turner, *Announcements of Plot in Genesis*, p. 165.
23. Turner, *Announcements of Plot in Genesis*, p. 169.

announcement are 'apathy', 'forgetting', '[being] in a state of not caring', 'unquestioning, passive obedience', 'resigning' oneself, 'apathetic
inactivity', and being in a 'passive' phase.[24] What is apathetic inactivity? Is it really a type of activity? Turner has just demonstrated that
human action can affect the outcome of the divine plan; he then advocates human non-action as the best response to the divine plan. He
condemns Redford's 'marionette' model but his understanding of the
teaching of the Joseph story in effect advises readers to act as marionettes. He is against a 'high view of divine providence' in theory, but
he is for it in practice.[25] The problem of divine providence and human
responsibility remains.

My strategy of reading is via a different route. Instead of discussing
the relationship between divine action and human action, I try to
scrutinize the underlying oppositions (chains of oppositions) behind
Joseph's claim. I want to see whether his claim can be sustained by his
adopted oppositions. When Joseph proclaims, 'You meant evil, but God
meant it for good', I do not confront his claim directly. I will take a
detour through the evil of his brothers to deconstruct his claim about
divine good.

The Pit as a Symbol of Death or Slavery

Once the brothers see Joseph far off, and before he comes near, they are
not only quick in deciding to kill him but the way of the subsequent
cover-up is also already chosen. Their plot to get rid of this master-
dreamer and his dreams involves three stages: killing him, throwing
him into a pit (בור)[26] to hide their crime, and fabricating an accident in
which he is devoured by a wild beast.

Reuben's words, 'Let us not take his life; shed no blood' (37.21-22),
break up the consensus about the killing, and only the second stage—
that of throwing Joseph into a pit—is allowed to proceed. Reuben's
intervention turns the pit into a temporary *refuge* instead of the *grave*
they intended in their original plot.[27] Seybold rightly notes that the pit
serves an important symbolic role: standing 'ambiguously between

---

24. Turner, *Announcements of Plot in Genesis*, pp. 164, 165, 178, 179.
25. Turner, *Announcements of Plot in Genesis*, p. 182.
26. See Gen. 37.20, 22, 24, 28-29.
27. Seybold, 'Paradox and Symmetry', p. 61, describes the pit (later the prison)
as 'a refuge which allows Joseph's life to be preserved'.

freedom and death', it is 'the place where Joseph is both condemned
and saved' and 'becomes a paradox central to the story's outcome and
meaning'.[28] The pit as grave/refuge repeats itself in Joseph's further
descent, as Seybold summarizes:

> The pit itself prefigures his enslavement in Potiphar's household and his
> incarceration in the prison. Both the enslavement and the incarceration,
> like the pit, are first ambiguous and finally paradoxical events. Each step
> is a movement downward in the relative fortunes of Joseph; it is better to
> be the favored son than the favored slave, better to be the favored slave
> than the favored prisoner.[29]

The eldest brother's attempt to save and restore Joseph to his father is
frustrated by Judah. He also appeals to the brothers to avoid murder and
suggests that the selling of Joseph into slavery to the Midianite traders
is a more profitable way to get rid of this dreamer. Joseph then ends up
in Potiphar's house which functions as a pit for him, a place where he
finally escapes fratricide. But the temporary loss of freedom in the pit
becomes permanent slavery in Potiphar's house.

Joseph's downfall continues when Potiphar's wife falsely accuses
him of attempted rape. His master is angry and puts him in another
house, the house of prison (בית הסהר). The seriousness of the crime
seems to demand a more severe punishment than imprisonment. Within
Genesis, the rapist Shechem perishes with all the male population in his
city.[30] The lighter sentence may indicate that Potiphar is not convinced
of Joseph's guilt.[31] As an accused slave, Joseph is unlikely to be able to
defend himself. But his master can be seen to be kind enough to spare
his life.

Reuben, Judah and Potiphar in different ways and in various degrees
help Joseph to escape from death. However, the alternative to death is
the loss of freedom: temporarily in the pit (בור), permanently in Potiphar's house (בית) and finally in the prison (בית הסהר). When Joseph
later pleads with the chief butler to remember to get him out of this

---

28. Seybold, 'Paradox and Symmetry', pp. 61, 64.
29. Seybold, 'Paradox and Symmetry', pp. 62-63.
30. In hearing the news of Shechem's rape, Jacob's sons are also very angry
(חרה, 34.7), the same word used to describe Potiphar's anger (39.19).
31. Cf. Westermann, *Genesis 37–50*, p. 67; Wenham, *Genesis 16–50*, p. 377;
however, von Rad, *Genesis*, pp. 366-67, ascribes Joseph's escape from death solely
due to God's protection, as expressed in the statement 'the Lord was with Joseph'
39.21, 23.

house (בית), he uses the word pit (בור) to describe the prison (40.14-15).[32] The phrase בית הסהר[33] is normally used for prison in this story. But the narrator temporarily adopts Joseph's perception in using the same word בור for prison when he is finally taken out of it by Pharaoh (41.14).[34] The painful experience of being thrown into a pit has a long lasting effect on Joseph's memory. Avivan Zornberg depicts succinctly the experience of the pit as 'the informing image' of Joseph's life: 'For the essential fact of his life is that he is a man who was thrown into a pit, into one of many pits, into more than one.'[35]

The pit prefigures a series of alternatives in the affliction which Joseph suffers under the hand of others: grave/refuge at Reuben's hand, death/slavery at Judah's hand, death/imprisonment at Potiphar's hand. Each pair is imposed on Joseph by others. There are alternatives for him but he has no choice. He is always at the mercy of others' decisions. Joseph is forced to face two equally unpleasant alternatives and this is clearly and explicitly expressed in Judah's persuasive argument to his brothers concerning Joseph's fate:

> Then Judah said to his brothers, 'What profit is it if we *slay* our brother and conceal his blood? Come, let us *sell* him to the Ishmaelites, and let not our hand be upon him, for he is our brother, our own flesh.' And his brothers heeded him (37.26-27).

To slay or to sell: Judah presents two courses of action to his brothers. At the same time he also condemns Joseph to two possible fates: death or slavery. Besides the material gain, Judah has a moral reason to advocate the latter alternative. Judah's mention of concealing blood and of their hand being upon their brother clearly refers to the first murder in Gen. 4.10-11, 'The voice of your brother's blood is crying to me from the ground... which has opened its mouth to receive your brother's blood from your hand.' The shedding of blood is punished by death as required by God (Gen. 9.6). Therefore, murder is to be avoided if at all possible, especially murder of one's own brother.

When Seybold comments that enslavement and imprisonment are 'less destructive than the alternative of death', he may very well be

32. Cf. Westermann, *Genesis 37–50*, p. 88.

33. See Gen. 39.20, 21, 22, 23; 40.3, 5; the other alternative is משמר (42.17) or בית משמר (40.3, 4, 7, 10; 42.19).

34. Cf. Avivan Gottlieb Zornberg, *Genesis: The Beginning of Desire* (Philadelphia: Jewish Publication Society, 1995), pp. 290-91.

35. Zornberg, *Genesis*, p. 290.

reflecting what Judah has in his mind by 'saving' Joseph from death by selling him into slavery.[36] He also reckons that, as a slave, Joseph's 'circumstances and position are quite tolerable'[37] because he is soon promoted to oversee others in Potiphar's house or in prison.[38] But the escape from death does not render the other alternative, that is, slavery or imprisonment, any less painful for Joseph. His years of suffering begin in the pit, stripped of his robe, crying and pleading in distress from below without being heeded by the brothers who can still sit down to eat.[39] The next time he is in the pit (prison), he again pleads in vain, asking the chief butler to get him out. Joseph's descent begins at the pit and ends finally at another pit (prison).

Given the chance to recount his past, he cannot forget the two momentous junctures of his life: 'For I was indeed stolen out of the land of the Hebrews; and here also I have done nothing that they should put me into the *pit*' (40.15). James Ackerman accurately observes that 'Joseph is linking his brothers' betrayal with his imprisonment, so that the memory of his suffering is doubly tied to the pit.'[40] The image of the pit epitomizes the long years of Joseph's enslavement and imprisonment in Egypt. Therefore, Joseph would probably be the first to object to the monstrous and atrocious idea suggested by Judah: better to be a slave than to be slain! In concealing their crime, the brothers lead their father to believe that Joseph has been eaten by an evil beast (חיה רעה) (37.20, 33). They indeed have become evil beasts.

36. Seybold, 'Paradox and Symmetry', p. 63.
37. Seybold, 'Paradox and Symmetry', p. 61.
38. Seybold, 'Paradox and Symmetry', pp. 62, 63, notes that 'Joseph has managed to gain dominance in every situation he had encountered even though his progress has been marked by diminishing freedom from that of favorite son, to trusted servant, to favored prisoner'. And he is seen as 'a favorite of the head of the household (Jacob, Potiphar, prison-keeper) over others like himself, whether brothers, slaves or prisons; and he is in a position of dominance over the others, whether he is checking on his brothers for his father (37.12-14), presiding over the other slaves for Potiphar (39.4-5), or overseeing the other prisoners (39.21-23)'.
39. Robert Alter, *Art of Biblical Narrative*, p. 166, notes this 'delayed exposition' of Joseph's pleading in distress in Gen. 37, revealed to us in Gen. 42.21, is employed to compound the brothers' guilt. I think that the revelation of Joseph's past painful feelings at the beginning of the test also hints at the close relationship between Joseph's bitter memory and the long ordeal he is going to put his brothers through.
40. Ackerman, 'Joseph, Judah, and Jacob', p. 90.

Joseph Repeats What He Has Condemned

Now the famine brings his brothers before him, bowing down with their faces to the ground, as his dreams predicted. His memory of the past resurfaces. Of course he remembers his dreams and 'is struck by the way past dreams have turned into present fact',[41] but the long ordeal he puts his brothers through indicates that he also remembers the suffering inflicted by them.

Whether for vengeance or correction, Joseph's test forces the brothers into a confrontation with their past crime. And in turn it helps Joseph to come to terms with his own past suffering beyond his initial suppression of it. Joseph falsely accuses the brothers of spying and demands of them that they bring down their youngest brother Benjamin. And then he puts them in the prison for three days, 'forcing them to relive two separate experiences from the past: his imprisonment by Potiphar, and his being cast into the pit by his brothers'.[42] This measure for measure already 'elicits the first words of self-reproach' by the brothers (42.21-22).[43] After hearing their expression of guilt, Joseph turns away from them and weeps. But he does not abort the test and reveal himself to them. The demand for Benjamin goes on until they come back with him. And the climax of the test comes when Joseph threatened to retain Benjamin as a slave for the theft of the silver cup.

Realizing that the enslavement of Benjamin will be a fatal blow to his father, Judah steps forward to offer himself in place of Benjamin in order to avoid the certain death of Jacob. Joseph's test ironically forces Judah into the same dilemma—to choose between death or slavery—as he had to ponder 22 years previously when deciding Joseph's fate. In the preceding case, Judah decided on slavery rather than death for Joseph; now he chooses slavery for himself instead of death for his father.[44] The victimizer becomes the victim of his own device. It is not

41. Alter, *Art of Biblical Narrative*, p. 163.
42. Ackerman, 'Joseph, Judah, and Jacob', p. 90; cf. Alter, *Art of Biblical Narrative*, p. 166.
43. Sternberg, *The Poetics of Biblical Narrative*, p. 297.
44. Judah does not focus on the possible suffering of his brother Benjamin as a slave, he rather repeatedly emphasizes the certain death of his father. For Judah, it is then not really a choice between slavery for Benjamin or slavery for himself. Judah's emphasis is a choice between slavery or death, his own slavery or his father's death.

only a retribution for the crime of selling his brother. It is rather an ironic indictment of Judah's rationale behind the crime. Judah's words, 'to slay' or 'to sell' (cf. 37.26-27), are denounced in this reversal of roles brought about by Joseph's test.

Judah's impassioned speech prompts Joseph to reveal himself and gives rise to one of the most important speeches in this story. Joseph declares, 'And God sent me before you to preserve for you a remnant on earth, and to keep alive for you many survivors. So it was not you who sent me here, but God' (45.7-8a). There is no more threat of slavery for the brothers and no more danger of death to the father. Joseph hurries them to bring Jacob and the whole family down to stay near him in Goshen. When Joseph reveals the 'divine providence' after the brothers pass his test, many readers consider that 'the Joseph story has reached its climax and is winding down', and the rest of the text returns to focus on the larger story of Jacob (his move to Egypt, the blessings to his sons and finally his death and burial).[45] Joseph's speech in 50.15-21 only repeats the same claim from a slightly different perspective.[46]

---

45. Ackerman, 'Joseph, Judah, and Jacob', p. 107. Humphreys, *Joseph and his Family*, pp. 52-53, comments, 'The modern reader may find the denouement [45.16–50.22] drawn out, being accustomed to a rapid wind-up once the climactic resolution of a story is reached.' All of the following readers more or less end their discussion of the Joseph story at the point when Joseph reveals himself to his brothers in ch. 45 and some of them may include some comments on 50.15-21 too: Sternberg, *The Poetics of Biblical Narrative*, p. 308; Alter, *Art of Biblical Narrative*, p. 175; Seybold, 'Paradox and Symmetry', p. 72; Miscall, 'The Jacob and Joseph Stories as Analogies', p. 38; Turner, *Announcements of Plot in Genesis*, p. 169; Hugh C. White, *Narration and Discourse in the Book of Genesis* (New York: Cambridge University Press, 1991), p. 271; Coats, *From Canaan to Egypt*, p. 46, also ends the dénouement at Joseph's speech in 45.4-11, but he concludes the story with the discussion of Jacob's move from Canaan to Egypt, the primary structure of the story.

46. Humphreys, *Joseph and his Family*, p. 52, remarks, 'But whereas in chapter 45 Joseph's words centred on his own power and position in Egypt and were at the heart of his words about divine design, this time he clearly acknowledges that he is not in a position he has appeared to assume for some time. He is not in the place of God.' I think that both speeches equally stress the same divine design. When Joseph first reveals himself in ch. 45, he has to explain his role to his brothers in this divine design. When the brothers later are worrying about their evil deed to him, Joseph's speech reassures them of their roles in God's design, 'you meant evil against me, but God meant it for good' (50.20). Joseph says that he is not in a position to return

Judah's speech demonstrates that the brothers have repented and no longer treat their father and his favourite son as they did before. Von Rad gives us an apt description of this speech:

> The way the shadow of Joseph, who no longer lives but is present, lies across the speech and is revealed more and more as the really troubling factor, is particularly moving. Because Joseph is gone, Jacob does not want to let Benjamin go; because Joseph is gone, the loss of the second favourite son would inevitably destroy the father. Again and again the thought returns to this one dark point (vv. 20, 28).[47]

The one who once 'engineered the selling of Joseph into slavery' is now 'prepared to offer himself as a slave so that the other son of Rachel can be left free'.[48] Moreover, the brothers are seen by many readers as finally coming to terms with the reality of their father's persistent favouritism towards the two sons of Rachel.[49] The reconciliation scene ends with a disclosure by Joseph 'that it is God who has singled him out for greatness as the instrument of His providential design to preserve the seed of Israel'.[50] The way Joseph treats his brothers in his test

evil against them beyond God's intention, but he probably does not have any self-doubt about 'his own power and position in Egypt'. It is God who has made him lord over Egypt; his authority is not of his own making, as he claims earlier.

47. Von Rad, *Genesis*, p. 394.

48. Alter, *Art of Biblical Narrative*, p. 175.

49. Sternberg, *The Poetics of Biblical Narrative*, p. 308, remarks 'that the sons of the hated wife should have come to terms with the father's attachment to Rachel ("my wife") and her children is enough to promise an end to hostilities and a fresh start'. And 'it surely manifests nothing short of a transformation from subnormal to abnormal solidarity'; Alter, *Art of Biblical Narrative*, pp. 174-75, gives us a rather peculiar concept of love: 'A basic biblical perception about both human relations and relations between God and man is that love is unpredictable, arbitrary, at times perhaps seemingly unjust, and Judah now comes to an acceptance of that fact with all its consequences... It is a painful reality of favouritism with which Judah, in contrast to the earlier jealousy over Joseph, is here reconciled, out of filial duty and more, out of filial love'; Humphreys, *Joseph and his Family*, pp. 48-49, notes, 'Judah's speech reveals that profound changes have taken place in the brothers, that they have changed in their very acceptance of what will not change and what they cannot change. Their father will love one son more than the other; love is not nicely balanced, and its disproportion can result in pain and insensitivity. But even one who loves in an excess that must result in imbalances and pain can be understood, and must be loved, for through this love runs ties that bind sons to father.'

50. Alter, *Art of Biblical Narrative*, p. 176.

has encountered some criticisms,[51] but his final claim about divine
providence is almost universally accepted.[52]

The brothers have struggled to come to terms with the guilt of casting
their brother into a pit, into an unknown and dreadful fate. Being
uncertain of what the foreign vizier will do to them, they have been
forced to endure the constant fear of death or slavery. Now they have

51. Humphreys, *Joseph and his Family*, pp. 128, 129, remarks, 'The end is a
family preserved alive, but the course was in significant respects brutal' and 'Joseph
need not have…carried tales, boasts of his dreams, let alone toyed with his brothers
later when they in turn fall into his hands.' But later Humphreys argues, on the
other hand, that the 'utter disharmony' among brothers needs 'extreme measures' to
heal it (p. 181); Miscall, 'The Jacob and Joseph Stories as Analogies', p. 34, quoting from Coats, condemns Joseph forthrightly: 'He is a ruthless, arbitrary despot in
this part of the narrative.' Cf. Coats, *From Canaan to Egypt*, pp. 82-84; Coats
accuses Joseph of concerning himself 'to maintain his office of power' in deception
and in moving 'his brothers like pawns on a chess board' (p. 88); Wenham, *Genesis
16–50*, pp. 431-32, dismisses these criticisms and argues, 'though Joseph may have
appeared the heartless foreign tyrant to his brothers, the narrator makes it plain that
this is not the way he views Joseph's actions nor the view Joseph had of himself. In
dealing with his brothers Joseph was deliberately putting on a hard front, which he
could only maintain by sometimes withdrawing to weep (42.24; 43.30), and when
at last he is convinced of their change of heart, he weeps freely over them (45.1-2,
14-15).' Turner, *Announcements of Plot in Genesis*, pp. 158-59, objects not only to
Joseph's manner but to the necessity of his test. He disagrees with Westermann's
claim that a severe long trial is required for true reconciliation. And he argues that
the analogous situation to that of Esau in ch. 33 'shows that testing, trial and confession are not a necessary route to reconciliation. Esau has shown a better way.'
Cf. Westermann, *Genesis 37–50*, p. 107.
        52. Von Rad, *Genesis*, p. 398, also remarks, 'ultimately it was not the brothers'
hate but God who brought Joseph to Egypt and moreover "to preserve life" ';
Ackerman, 'Joseph, Judah, and Jacob', p. 106, notes, 'And the purpose of it all,
Joseph now sees, is "God sent me before you to preserve life." ' See also Wenham,
Genesis 16–50, p. 432; Seybold, 'Paradox and Symmetry', p. 71; John Calvin, *A
Commentary on Genesis*, II (trans. John King; London: Banner of Truth Trust,
1965), p. 379; Skinner, *Genesis*, p. 487; Driver, *Genesis*, p. 361; Eric I. Lowenthal,
The Joseph Narrative in Genesis (New York: Ktav, 1973), p. 104; Westermann,
Genesis 37–50, p. 143, does not think Joseph's word here is speaking directly about
God's providence; Joseph speaks only to calm his brothers' fear. Nevertheless,
Westermann accepts that such an explanation can be derived from what has been
said. The following readers question the way Joseph treats his brothers, but they
have no objection to Joseph's final claim: Coats, *From Canaan to Egypt*, pp. 90-91;
Humphreys, *Joseph and his Family*, p. 125, states, 'this family's story must be
comprehended within a larger divine design, and the design is one that seeks to pre-

repented and Joseph has revealed to them his identity and 'God's providence', that is, God has got him out of the pits and has caused him to ascend to rule over Egypt in order to protect his family and other people from the coming years of famine. The Joseph story comes to an end and no further major complication seems to be forthcoming until we hear the voices of anguish:

> all the Egyptians came to Joseph, and said, 'Give us food; why should we *die* before your eyes?'...
>
> they came to him the following year, and said to him, 'We will not hide from my lord that our money is all spent; and the herds of cattle are my lord's; there is nothing left in the sight of my lord but our bodies and our lands. Why should we *die* before your eyes, both we and our land? Buy us and our land for food, and we with our land will be *slaves* to Pharaoh; and give us seed, that we may live, and not *die*, and that the land may not be desolate.' (47.15-19) (my italics)

What the Egyptians are bawling out to Joseph is loud and clear: death or slavery! The Egyptians offer their bodies for food, their land for seed, their freedom for life, opting for slavery rather than death. Such a dreadful choice has been uttered only twice in this story, both in reference to Judah: his imposition of 'to slay' or 'to sell' upon Joseph in ch. 37; and his imploring, forced upon him by Joseph's test, to take Benjamin's place as a slave to avoid the death of his father in ch. 44.

serve life'; Turner, *Announcements of Plot in Genesis*, pp. 143-69, does not dispute Joseph's claims in 45.5 and 50.20 but argues that they should not be taken as 'predestinarian theologoumena'. He only condemns Joseph's attempt to fulfil God's plan in his own way. Turner is rather happy to see Joseph remain apathetic (p. 164) and let his dreams of the bowing down of his brothers and parents before him be fulfilled in their own way; Miscall, 'The Jacob and Joseph Stories as Analogies', pp. 31, 34, draws a clear distinction between the narrator, characters and the reader and rightly points out that Joseph's claim 'tells much of Joseph's character and his development in theological awareness, but it does not necessarily say that God did actually intervene in the past events'. He further reminds us that neither the narrator nor God appear in the narrative to confirm Joseph's interpretation. However, Miscall does not contest Joseph's claim and later he even indirectly accepts its validity when he stresses, 'the endings are in accord with the divine plan and promises'. Only Redford, *Biblical Story of Joseph*, pp. 74, 104, considers that Joseph's revelation of the underlying divine plan is 'unavoidably denigrating to the story as a whole', making all human actions in the plot of the story 'trivial', 'needless', 'pointless' and 'pitiable'.

The contrast is clear. A whole nation of people is echoing the voice of a single person.[53]

Surprisingly, the voices of the Egyptians have attracted little attention from most readers who have devoted their studies to the Joseph story.[54] Even Ackerman and Seybold, who have specifically focused on the theme of death or slavery in their articles,[55] do not mention the plight of the Egyptians at all. Other readers marginalize this section as a later 'appendage',[56] being 'extraneous'[57] and 'anomalous'[58] to the plot of the Joseph story. Westermann asserts that 'what is narrated here has no function in the narrative span of the story'[59] other than the aetiological

53. Berel Dov Lerner, 'Joseph the Unrighteous', *Judaism: A Quarterly Journal of Jewish Life and Thought* 38 (1989), pp. 278-81 (278), suggests the Torah is critical of Joseph's relief policy to the Egyptians and comments, 'It is with great pathos that the Torah gives voice to the pleadings of the Egyptians.'

54. Discussing the theme of being a blessing, both Clines and Turner have a brief passing comment on the death or slavery alternative to the Egyptians. David J.A. Clines, *What Does Eve Do to Help? And Other Readerly Questions to the Old Testament* (JSOTSup, 94; Sheffield: JSOT Press, 1990), p. 58, notes, 'Joseph's plan is of course a blessing only if one would rather be a live slave than a dead peasant'; Turner, *Announcements of Plot in Genesis*, p. 172, states, 'Joseph's relationship to the Egyptians is more complex. Through his agricultural policy Joseph does save the lives of the Egyptians, but does so at a price—their enslavement (47.13ff.).'

55. Ackerman, 'Joseph, Judah, and Jacob', p. 90, notes, 'the brothers in the prison/pit contemplate the prospect of death or slavery—just as Joseph had earlier sat in their pit awaiting death'. See also his similar remarks, pp. 91, 93, 99; Seybold, 'Paradox and Symmetry', p. 63, states, 'While being a slave or a prisoner is destructive to the individual, each is finally less destructive than the alternative of death which Joseph faces from his brothers and from Potiphar.'

56. Westermann, *Genesis 37–50*, p. 173. I do not object to Westermann's claim that this section may be an independent unit before incorporation into the story; I will only argue against his claim that it has no function in the narrative span of the Joseph story.

57. Redford, *Biblical Story of Joseph*, p. 180, sees this 'Agrarian Reform' (together with the narrative of Potiphar's wife in ch. 39) as 'extraneous to the plot of the Joseph story'; Coats, *From Canaan to Egypt*, p. 53, also remarks that 'the unit appears to me to be isolated and extraneous to the overall story'.

58. Skinner, *Genesis*, p. 499, considers that this section, dealing 'with matters purely Egyptian and without interest for the national history of Israel, occupies an anomalous position among the Joseph-narratives'.

59. Westermann, *Genesis 37–50*, p. 173. Coats, *From Canaan to Egypt*, p. 53, notes, 'This section of narration [an aetiology for a perpetual tax system] makes no real contribution to the Joseph story'; Brueggemann, *Genesis*, p. 356, also remarks,

function[60] about the introduction of the one-fifth tax in Egypt (see 47.26).

Those who are interested in this section focus mainly on Joseph's agrarian policy and tax reform, and the voices of the people are heard but become insignificant. Sometimes the single voice of a protagonist can easily drown the voices of a great multitude of anonymous people. Von Rad best represents this kind of perception as he remarks:

> the narrator's interest is fixed rather exclusively on Joseph and his activity. His partner, the hungering and despairing people, is rather anonymously colourless and becomes concrete for the reader only in so far as it was necessary to clarify a new phase of Joseph's activity against this background.[61]

I strongly disagree that Joseph's treatment of the Egyptians plays no role in the plot of this story. In a larger textual context, this section should be seen as the proper conclusion to Pharaoh's dreams and their interpretation by Joseph beginning at ch. 41. Joseph is appointed to oversee the gathering of food in the good years so that the land may not perish through the famine (41.34-36) as he has advised. And when the famine begins, the people of Egypt and all the earth come to Joseph for food (41.53-57). The narrator then focuses exclusively on Joseph's encounter with his family and the reunion after his test (42.1–47.12). After a long detour, the narrator resumes in order to conclude Joseph's proposed plan of famine relief.[62]

It is the 'unexpected' meeting between Joseph and his brothers that interrupts the narration of his relief programme. Joseph has been very successful in Potiphar's house and the prison house, but no detail of his work is given then. Pharaoh's dreams give us a chance to see how well

'The narrative of 47.13-26 is interwoven with the Jacob materials but has no relation to them.'

60. Coats, *From Canaan to Egypt*, p. 53 states: 'the aetiological character sets the unit apart from the rest of the Joseph story'. Coats has argued consistently for the structural unity of the Joseph story, but he sees the present unit and ch. 38 as exceptions.

61. Von Rad, *Genesis*, p. 409.

62. John H. Sailhamer, *The Pentateuch as Narrative* (Grand Rapids: Zondervan, 1992), p. 227, remarks that 'the writer's strategy in inserting the account of Joseph and his brothers (chs. 42–46) in the midst of the narratives dealing with Joseph's rise to power in Egypt (chs. 39–41, 47)' is to stress 'Joseph's wisdom and administrative skills' in saving his brothers and the Egyptians in both accounts.

he works. What relief programme does he propose? Is it acceptable to
Pharaoh and to the people? Finally, how does it fare in the end? This
section concludes Joseph's relief plan, and it cannot be seen as an
appendage unrelated to the main plot of the story and without consequence to Joseph's portrayal.

In the immediate context, the narrator clearly juxtaposes the opposite
treatments received by Joseph's family (47.12, 27-28) and the Egyptians (47.13-26). Humphreys calls it a 'nice counterpoint';[63] I would
rather call it a stark contrast.[64] Provisions and the best part of the land
are freely given to Joseph's family (47.6, 11), and they become fruitful
and multiply exceedingly (47.27). In contrast, the Egyptians barely survive, and all their wealth, land and freedom are gone forever.[65] Favouring one's own in this story should not surprise us because both Joseph's
test and Judah's response depend on the acceptance of their father's
favouritism towards his two beloved sons. In this aspect, the text has
prepared us well for the way Joseph will behave in human relationships.
Apparently a state of despair provokes the Egyptians to offer slavery
for death. Even if this alarms no one else, Joseph should still be alerted
by such an offer. He has suffered years of affliction because his
brothers decided on slavery instead of death for him. In the recent past,
his test has condemned such an offer by forcing Judah himself to make
such a dreadful decision between the two ugly options. One would then
expect that he would hesitate about the Egyptians' proposal. Astonish-
ingly, he is quick to accept it without showing any sign of discomfort.

63. Humphreys, *Joseph and his Family*, p. 54.
64. Cf. Victor A. Hurowitz, 'Joseph's Enslavement of the Egyptians (Genesis
47.13-26) in Light of Famine Texts From Mesopotamia', *RB* 101.3 (1994), pp. 355-
62 (355).
65. Trevor Watt, 'Joseph's Dreams' in David L. Miller (ed.), *Jung and the
Interpretation of the Bible* (New York: Continuum, 1995), pp. 55-70, 121-122 (69),
contrasts Joseph's preferential treatment of his family to his 'land-grab' policy
towards the Egyptians. Brueggemann, *Genesis*, p. 357, notes an irony: 'Egyptians
suffer in their survival as slaves, Israel pays for its royal position.' The contrast of
treatments has been discussed by many readers, cf. J. Gerald Janzen, *Genesis 12–50*
(ITC; Grand Rapids: Eerdmans, 1993), p. 178; Mary Savage, 'Literary Criticism
and Biblical Studies: A Rhetorical Analysis of the Joseph Narrative', in Carl D.
Evans, William W. Hallo and John B. White (eds.), *Scripture in Context: Essays on
the Comparative Method* (Pittsburgh: Pickwick Press, 1980), pp. 79-100 (96); Joyce
G. Baldwin, *The Message of Genesis 12–50: From Abraham to Joseph* (The Bible
Speaks Today; Leicester: Inter-Varsity Press, 1986), p. 196.

The enslaved becomes the enslaver. He who has been sold is happy to buy others. Joseph is undoing what he has achieved in the long confrontation with his brothers in chs. 42–44. And, in effect, he is duplicating Judah's role in ch. 37 by opting for slavery instead of death for other(s). How is it possible for Joseph to repeat the enslavement he himself has suffered and abhorred? In answering this question, the key speeches by Judah (chs. 37, 44), the Egyptians (ch. 47) and Joseph (ch. 45) will be examined in detail. Close attention must be given to the choice between death and slavery: its emergence, its development and transformation.

Problematic Hierarchical Oppositions in Joseph's Claim

Death or Slavery
The imposition of the choice between death (to slay) or slavery (to sell) on Joseph is made clear to the reader by the narrator's report of Judah's speech to his brothers at Gen. 37.26-27. The eldest brother, Reuben, has also earlier pleaded with them not to kill Joseph. He allows them to throw Joseph into a pit in the hope that he may restore him to his father later. The brothers' original plan is to kill Joseph, throwing him into a pit, and deceiving their father that a wild beast has devoured him (37.20). Reuben's interruption turns the pit from a grave to a temporary prison from where he is 'stolen' into slavery.[66] The alternative between death and slavery can be traced back symbolically to the pit. Does Judah know that when he offers himself as a slave to avoid the certain death of his father, he is falling victim to the same kind of choice he made about his brother 22 years ago? When Judah and his brothers plan to get rid of Joseph, they of course know that it will hurt their father greatly. Nevertheless, it seems to surprise them that Jacob would even refuse to be comforted and say, 'No, I shall go down to Sheol to my son, mourning' (37.35). Now they recognize that slavery for Joseph could mean the death of their father.

Some 20 years later, facing the request to bring Benjamin to Egypt, Jacob reiterates similar words, 'You would bring down my grey hairs with sorrow to Sheol' (42.38). When Joseph threatens to retain Benjamin as a slave, Judah and the brothers this time surely know that it will result in certain death for their father. Judah's pleading to the

---

66. It is not certain who (the Midianite traders or the brothers) draws Joseph out of the pit and sells him to the Ishmaelites (37.28). Cf. 40.15.

Egyptian vizier to let Benjamin go home centres squarely on the certain death of their father. He twice repeats Jacob's words, 'bring down my grey hairs in sorrow to Sheol' (vv. 29, 31). And Judah also twice spells out the consequence bluntly without any figure of speech, 'The lad cannot leave his father, for if he should leave his father, his father would *die* (v. 22)', and 'when he sees that the lad is not with us, he will *die* (v. 31)'. In fact, v. 22 is a recapitulation of the dialogue in their first meeting. Admittedly, there are always many tactful alterations, omissions, and additions in all recapitulations in this story.[67] Wenham asserts, 'Judah slips in more details about the age of Jacob and his attachment to Benjamin. Jacob is "elderly"...and "his father loves him", indeed "will die" if he does not return.'[68]

But it is highly probable that Judah has really told the Egyptian vizier about the threat to Jacob if Benjamin is to leave his father. When the brothers bring Benjamin with them to Joseph in their second trip, the first word of Joseph to them is an inquiry about their father's welfare, 'Is your father well, the old man of whom you spoke? Is he still alive?' (43.27). Here Joseph clearly confirms that they have spoken of his father as an old man, as Judah recapitulates in 44.19. Joseph's concern over whether his father is still alive also gives support to the view that Judah's reminder of his father's frailty without Benjamin is an accurate recapitulation. Furthermore, the whole of Judah's argument is based on a reminder to Joseph that he has been told of the possible danger to their old father if Benjamin is to be separated from him. It is really a kind of rebuke to the Egyptian vizier. Judah's speech can be paraphrased as 'We have told you so, but you do not believe us!' Judah is careful enough to prefix it with a fearful plea to pacify any possible anger. All along he refers to himself as 'your servant', but to express his profound emotion, he leaves out this courteous formula at the end.[69]

---

67. Sternberg, *The Poetics of Biblical Narrative*, p. 297, for example, observes the alterations the brothers made in reporting their first Egyptian trip to Jacob: 'the mass arrest gets elided, Simeon's detention played down...the reappearance of the money in one load wholly omitted'. See similar observations by Alter, *Art of Biblical Narrative*, pp. 168-69; Redford, *Biblical Story of Joseph*, pp. 83-84.

68. Wenham, *Genesis 16–50*, p. 426. Westermann, *Genesis 37–50*, p. 135, also considers that the threat of death to Jacob is an addition by Judah. Judah has made an alteration, i.e. his brother is 'dead' instead of 'no more' (44.20 cf. 42.13); cf. Lowenthal, *The Joseph Narrative in Genesis*, p. 97.

69. Westermann, *Genesis 37–50*, p. 136.

Judah words his argument carefully. Even if Joseph is so absent-minded as to forget this or else does not bother to interrupt Judah's speech at this crucial moment, as Redford has commented, it is still unthinkable for Judah to risk his argument by resting on a lie or a false reminder.[70]

It seems to me that the narrator carefully withholds from us Joseph's knowledge about the death threat to his father. Both the brothers and the reader are aware of the threat. Now the reader is told that Joseph also shares this information all along in his test which requires them to bring down Benjamin and to allow Joseph to retain him as a slave. This explains why Joseph shows a keen interest in their father as he earlier inquires twice, 'Is your father still alive?' (43.7, 27). When he reveals his identity, he repeats the same question, 'I am Joseph. Is my father still alive?' (45.3). This delayed exposition reveals to us Joseph's own consciousness of using the threat of death towards his father in order to confront his brothers. Joseph may not know that the brothers have discussed the choice between death and slavery for him. He also may not be aware of the life-threatening blow to his father due to his own disappearance.[71] But in requesting and retaining Benjamin as a slave, Joseph knows that his test will force the brothers to face the prospect of the death of their father.

Twenty-two years ago when Judah decided on slavery instead of death for Joseph, he belatedly discovered that it almost dealt a fatal

70. Redford, *Biblical Story of Joseph*, p. 157, comments, 'One can appreciate the motive for Judah's falsification in the conversation with his father, but would such falsification, deliberate or not, from the writer's point of view be appropriate when Judah addressed Joseph? After all, Joseph was there; he undoubtedly remembered! He could have cut Judah short by hauling out a transcript and proving that it was the brothers who had, without solicitation from him, given information about themselves. The mere possibility of such an interruption by Joseph is most undesirable from the stand-point of plot development, and even debilitating at this crucial point in the drama. No good author would have introduced an irrelevancy of this magnitude when the resolution of the plot was imminent.' George W. Savran, *Telling and Retelling: Quotation in Biblical Narrative* (Bloomington: Indiana University Press, 1988), p. 137 n. 21, comments on Joseph's omniscience: 'Judah's use of an unverifiable quotation of Joseph's own words in 44.19 further undercuts Joseph's omniscience: suggesting to the reader that Joseph does not remember what he said and therefore does not correct Judah. Here the unverifiable quotation subverts the reliability of the listener, rather than that of the speaker.'

71. Judah repeats Jacob's response to Joseph's disappearance, 'Surely he has been torn to pieces; and I have never seen him since' (44.28). But Judah has not told Joseph about Jacob's mournful desire to go down to Sheol for him.

blow to their father. Now both Judah and Joseph know that retaining Benjamin as a slave will result in death for Jacob. The alternative of death or slavery is a false one. When Judah offers himself as a slave in order to avoid the death of their father, he is undoing his past crime, helping his father and his favourite son to escape from both death and slavery. And he is simultaneously forced to repeat the same decision between death and slavery for himself this time. The narrator presents a situation in which Joseph's test recreates the choice between death and slavery in order to reverse Judah's role from a victimizer to a victim of his past imposed alternative. Once this reversal has served its purpose as a condemnation of the false alternative between death or slavery, Joseph reveals himself and reaffirms their brotherhood. No one is forced into slavery to avoid death any more. Jacob and his family are well provided for in the famine, and they live freely in the best land of Egypt.

However, Joseph's policy to enslave the Egyptians in order to save them forces the reader to re-examine Joseph's attitude to the choice between death and slavery. Both Judah (ch. 44) and the Egyptians (ch. 47) repeatedly lament over the dire prospect of death which forces them to offer themselves as slaves:

Judah's plea in ch. 44:

'his father would die' (v. 22);

'you will bring down my grey hairs in sorrow in Sheol' (v. 29);

'he will die' (v. 31);

'Your servants will bring down the grey hairs of your servant our father with sorrow to Sheol' (v. 31).

The Egyptians' plea in ch. 47:

'why should we die before your eyes' (v. 15);

'Why should we die before your eyes' (v. 19);

'that we may live, and not die' (v. 19);

'that the land may not be desolate' (v. 19).

These two speeches are far apart in the textual order, but their juxtaposition may be justified in chronological order. The sentence in 47.18 makes the time of this section difficult to determine.

And when that year (הַשָּׁנָה הַהִוא) was ended, they came to him the
following year (בַּשָּׁנָה הַשֵּׁנִית) and said to him, 'We will not hide from my
lord that our money is all spent; and the herds of cattle are my lord's.'
(47.18).

If the phrase בַּשָּׁנָה הַשֵּׁנִית (lit. 'the second year'; cf. AV) in 47.18
refers to the second year of the famine, the enslavement of the Egyptians is a year before Judah's speech in which he offers himself as a
slave. Joseph tells of five more years of famine to come when he
reveals himself to his brothers (see 45.11). Therefore, it is possible that
the Egyptians are already enslaved before Joseph announces his
domination over Egypt to his brothers in 45.8b-11. The narrator may
withhold this crucial information at this moment and reveal it only later
in the narrative to create the dramatic effect of sudden discovery in the
reader.[72] But 'that year' (the time that their money and herds are gone)
may not be the first year of the famine.[73] One cannot be sure of the
narrated time order between the speeches uttered by Judah and the
Egyptians. Does Joseph repeat the crime (accepting the Egyptians' offer
to be slaves) which his test previously condemned (forcing Judah to
offer himself as a slave as a denunciation of his past crime)? Or, in the
other order, does he get from the Egyptians' offer the insight to declare
the necessity of his own slavery to avoid the death of many in his
disclosure speech? This uncertain chronological ordering creates an
echoing effect between these two similar speeches. It forces us to
rethink Joseph's exact perception of the choice between death and
slavery.

72. The withholding of an important piece of information that later is strategically revealed is a narrative technique employed to enhance the dramatic effect. For
example, Joseph's pleading for mercy to his brothers at the pit is revealed to readers
only long after the event (42.21). Its dramatic function is described in detail by
Alter, *Art of Biblical Narrative*, p. 166.

73. Nahum M. Sarna, *Genesis* (The JPS Torah Commentary; Philadephia: Jewish Publication Society of America, 1989), p. 321, suggests the followings interpretations: '(i) the second year of the famine, (ii) two years after the arrival of Jacob,
(iii) the second of the remaining five years of famine, (iv) the seventh year of the
famine'. Von Rad, *Genesis*, p. 410, argues that this section presupposes a famine of
two years only instead of seven years. See also, Westermann, *Genesis 37–50*, p.
175; Herbert C. Leupold, *Exposition of Genesis 20–50*, II (Grand Rapids: Baker
Book House, 22nd edn, 1987), p. 1135.

Joseph's Claim of Divine Providence

Joseph simply accepts the offer by the despairing Egyptians. The narrator reveals to us neither his feelings about their plight nor his thoughts about their offer to become slaves to avoid death. In contrast, Joseph pours himself out in responding to Judah's passionate plea. Joseph speaks of his past, of what the brothers have done and of what God has really done. Joseph's interpretation[74] of his own story, or better God's story in his past, has always been seen as the final authoritative explanation of the whole narrative. Its universal acceptance can be best illustrated by von Rad's declaration:

> Here in the scene of recognition the narrator indicates clearly for the first time what is of paramount importance to him in the entire Joseph story: God's hand which directs all the confusion of human guilt ultimately toward a gracious goal.[75]

Joseph's speech involves two main parts: It was God, not his brothers, who sent him into Egypt to preserve life (vv. 4-8a); and God has made him lord over all Egypt to avoid the starvation of his family (vv. 8b-11):

> [4]So Joseph said to his brothers, 'Come near to me, I pray you.' And they came near. And he said, 'I am your brother, Joseph, whom you *sold* into Egypt. [5]And now do not be distressed, or angry with yourselves, because you *sold* me here; for God *sent* me before you to preserve life...
>
> [7]And God *sent* me before you to preserve for you a remnant on earth, and to keep alive for you many survivors. [8] So it was not you who *sent* me here, but God; and *he has made me* a father to Pharaoh, and lord of all his house and ruler over all the land of Egypt. [9]Make haste and go up to my father and say to him, "Thus says your son Joseph, *God has made me* lord of all Egypt...
>
> [11]and there I will provide for you, for there are yet five years of famine to come; lest you and your household, and all that you have, come to poverty" ' (45.4-11).

---

74. Miscall, 'The Jacob and Joseph Stories as Analogies', p. 31, insists on using the word 'interpretation' to describe Joseph's speech. In contrast, it has been variously named a 'disclosure', 'revelation', 'declaration' and 'acknowledgment'. One easily senses what authority his interpretation entails. Cf. Brueggemann, *Genesis*, pp. 343, 345; Humphreys, *Joseph and his Family*, p. 116; Seybold, 'Paradox and Symmetry', p. 72.

75. Von Rad, *Genesis*, p. 398. For similar statements, see Wenham, *Genesis 16–50*, p. 432; Brueggemann, *Genesis*, pp. 343-48.

This speech of Joseph's also gives the reader, though very subtly,[76] a glimpse of his thoughts on the subject (i.e. the choice between death and slavery) about which I have been inquiring all along. Joseph twice at the beginning identifies himself as the one whom his brothers 'sold' (vv. 4, 5) into Egypt. To calm their distress, he softens his wording from 'you *sold*' to 'it was not you *sent* me here, but God' (v. 5). He then abandons the word '*sold*' and repeatedly uses the word '*sent*' instead (vv. 7, 8). A crime of selling a brother becomes an instrument of God's plan. The emphasis here at first is of course on the relationship between Joseph and his brothers. He speaks in a certain way to soothe their shock and fear at their sudden recognition of the victim of their crime years ago. On the other level, Joseph is at pains to come to terms with his own past.[77] What is the purpose of those long years of suffering in the pit of slavery? He once tried hard to erase this hardship from his memory. In naming his first son 'Manasseh', he wished that God had made him forget it all. The encounter with his brothers forces him to confront them and his own past. Now he realizes it was God who sent him into Egypt. Three times he reiterates his own relation with God: 'God sent *me*' (v. 5), 'God sent *me*' (v. 7), and 'not you who sent *me* but God' (v. 8). 'God sent me into Egypt' is a mild wording for the hard reality of his long slavery in this land of his affliction (cf. 41.52). But now he understands that his suffering is for the good of others. God sent him to preserve life (v. 5), to preserve for him a remnant on earth and to keep alive for him many survivors (v. 7).

Joseph's realization that his suffering as a slave was in order to save the lives of others may be triggered by Judah's example. Ackerman remarks that Judah's speech gives Joseph 'the key for interpreting the mystery of his *own* life':

---

76. Von Rad, *Genesis*, p. 397, remarks that 'the text of this wonderful scene scarcely requires the interpretative help of an expositor'. I agree that the disclosure of what God has done by Joseph is plain, but the way and the words he chooses to describe the supposed plan of God are highly subtle.

77. His struggle is evident in many ways: his phenomenal successes in the three houses in Egypt cannot help him to forget the land of his affliction, of his slavery; he weeps many times in his long confrontation with his brothers; his displaced attack on the Egyptians may be a form of rejection of his own slavery and a suppression of anger towards such a painful experience (this point will be discussed more fully later).

> Joseph must learn from Judah: the risking / offering up / suffering /
> descent of a brother can mean life for the family of Israel... Judah did
> not realise that, in offering to remain enslaved so that Benjamin could
> return, he was helping this strange Egyptian understand the meaning of
> his own life.[78]

Consciously or not, Joseph's test (ch. 44) forces a reversal of Judah's
role from a victimizer to a victim of his earlier choice for slavery to
avoid death (ch. 37). Paradoxically, the reversal serves simultaneously
as both a condemnation and recommendation of such a choice. Judah's
willingness to accept slavery makes him a sacrificial victim. Lowenthal
calls this a vicarious enslavement.[79] Westermann considers Judah's
sacrifice to be necessary in order to show his repentance and to make
the reconciliation possible:

> [Judah] prefers to take the punishment upon himself rather than cause his
> father distress yet again. It is indeed vicarious suffering...the healing of
> a breach is possible only when there is one who is ready to take the suf-
> fering upon oneself.[80]

The necessity of Judah's accepting slavery as a sign of repentance
leads to Joseph's acceptance of the painful experience of his downfall
into slavery as necessary for the well-being of others. Joseph's claim
that God sent him into Egypt to preserve life is then a subtle repetition
of the alternative of death or slavery. Instead of death, Joseph speaks of
the opposite: 'life', 'remnant', 'alive', 'survivors'. Instead of his brothers' selling him into slavery, he prefers to think that it is God who sends
him into Egypt. This transformation of his perception from his 'slavery'
to his 'mission', from 'death' to 'life', may help to console both his
brothers' fear and his own bitter memory of the past.

How consciously Joseph is imitating Judah's 'example' is unknown,
if there is any imitation at all, but the rationale behind their actions is
the same: slavery is preferable to death. Yet there are crucial differences between them. Joseph's sacrificial suffering is real and long,
while Judah suffers only for the short duration of his interrogation.
Joseph turns the implication of Judah's action of sacrificial choice into

78. Ackerman, 'Joseph, Judah, and Jacob', pp. 94, 106 (his italics).
79. Lowenthal, *The Joseph Narrative in Genesis*, p. 96. See also Derek Kidner,
Genesis: An Introduction and Commentary (TOTC; London: Tyndale Press, 1967),
p. 206.
80. Westermann, *Genesis 37–50*, p. 138.

an explicit divine claim: *God sent* him to save others' lives just as Judah chooses slavery to avoid the death of another (i.e. his father). And the magnitude of the salvation effected by Joseph clearly outweighs Judah's avoidance of a single death. On the other hand, Judah is willing to offer himself as a slave (ch. 44), while Joseph is forced into slavery without a choice and he accepts his 'mission' only in retrospect. Is Judah then a more willing sacrificial victim? For Joseph, Judah may be only a victimizer deserving a threat of enslavement as a retribution. Joseph himself is a real victim. He still considers the brothers' decision to sell him into slavery as evil (50.20). The choice of slavery to save lives is an act of sacrifice from the mouth of a real victim; it becomes an act of aggression if it is spoken by a victimizer.

If the distinction between victimizer and victim plays an important role in one's perception of the choice between death and slavery, what is its implication for Joseph's enslavement of the Egyptians? Why does Joseph, the past victim, repeat the role of victimizer to decide for slavery instead of death for the Egyptians?[81] Why does he duplicate what his test has just reversed? To be sure, Joseph's decision to enslave others is not exactly analogous to Judah's earlier situation. Joseph does not actively force the Egyptians to choose between death and slavery. Joseph is not a victimizer like Judah. Nonetheless, he is the enslaver and the Egyptians are victims forced to decide between death and slavery because of a disastrous famine and Joseph's relief policy. What is the relationship between Joseph and the Egyptians? Why does he treat his brothers (who deserve real punishment) rather differently from the Egyptians? The second part of Joseph's claim of a divine plan will give the reader some clues to these questions.

Joseph speaks of his position in Egypt with an impressive list of titles: God has made me 'father to Pharaoh', 'lord of all his house,' and 'ruler over all the land of Egypt' (v. 8b). 'God has made me lord of all Egypt' is repeated as a direct speech to Jacob through the brothers as messenger (v. 9; cf. v. 26). The purpose of God's plan to make Joseph lord over Egypt is the same as Joseph's previous words of salvation. It

---

81. Aaron Wildavsky, *Assimilation versus Separation: Joseph the Administrator and the Politics of Religion in Biblical Israel* (London: Transaction, 1993), p. 9, points out this duel roles played by Joseph as 'victim and victimizer' in his rise from 'the pit of misfortune' to 'the moral equivocality, even destructiveness, of his behavior as chief administrator for Pharaoh'.

is to avoid his father's household coming to poverty (v. 11). But the contrast between these two parts of Joseph's claim of salvation is sharp. He is sent as a *slave* by God to save lives and now he is made *lord* over Egypt to effect the salvation. God's sending somehow overrides the human evil of selling in the first part, while he is seen as more directly involved in making Joseph lord over Egypt in the second part. Joseph is either a *slave* or a *lord*, God is either indirectly or directly involved, and the purpose is the same: to save lives.

Lord/Slave and Life/Death

The problem of the choice between death and slavery is one of the major themes of the Joseph story. The underlying oppositions of this choice are lord/slave and life/death. Comparing two parts of Joseph's claim, these two pairs of opposition are detectable. Two of the terms are not present, but they are prominent in the background. The brothers sold him and God sent him. The threat of 'death' looms large in his repeated reminder of preserving a remnant, and of keeping alive many survivors. The word 'slave' is not in Joseph's speech, but he is explaining to his brothers and to himself why he has been a slave. 'Death' and 'slave', both words are uttered loud and clear in the despairing pleading by Judah (and are later echoed by the Egyptians). To a reader with deconstruction in mind, the conspicuous absence of these two terms is not an accident.

In the end, it is the striking presence of the privileged terms of the two oppositions that betrays Joseph's way of thinking. His claim of 'divine providence' centres on these two privileged terms: he has been sold by his brothers but ultimately God has made him *lord* over Egypt to save *life*. Referring to his own slavery, Joseph prefers the wording 'life' and its associated terms, 'remnant', and 'survivors' (45.5, 7). The word 'death' in the choice between slavery and death is now replaced by the word 'life'. Joseph also speaks of God making him lord over Egypt in order to prevent his family coming to poverty (vv. 8-11). Now the idea of death is implicit in the mentioning of the word 'poverty' (v. 11).

The repetition of the choice between slavery (sell) and death (slay) is clear and straightforward in the speeches of Judah and the Egyptians. Its repetition in Joseph's speech is more subtle. His explanation that God sent him into Egypt (via selling into enslavement by his brothers) to save life can still be recognized as a repetition of the same theme:

slavery is a way to avoid death. The structure is the same. Joseph only prefers the privileged term of the opposition of life/death. In Joseph's claim, life is paramount. But it is the same for Judah and the Egyptians. They all want to avoid death. Because of Joseph's understanding of the past—he has gone through a detour from slavery to present lordship—it seems to him that slavery is a way to avoid death, a mission designed by God to enable him to save life. It is a vicarious enslavement.

The second part of Joseph's claim is a victorious lordship, also designed by God to enable him to preserve many lives. It is in this second part of his claim that the mutation of the same theme (i.e. the choice between death and slavery) occurs. It is difficult to detect the iteration. The best way to discover the exact nature of Joseph's claim is to lay bare the opposition underlying the key words or themes. The choice between death and slavery will then give us these two pairs of opposition: life/death and lord/slave. Lordship is simply the other side of slavery. Or to be more precise, lordship is the privileged side of the hierarchical opposition of lord/slave.

Taking Joseph's claim as a whole, he is not merely trying to calm the fear of his brothers when he reveals himself. It can also be seen as an explanation of his own dreams. Why do the brothers have to bow down before him and be lorded over by him? Joseph's revelation of the divine plan to save their lives is a confrontation of the brothers' attempt to destroy the master-dreamer (cf. 37.19). The first part of Joseph's claim concerns the 'divine providence' that overrides their evil attempt and makes Joseph's rise to power as a lord over Egypt possible. The second part of his claim deals directly with the fundamental problem of the conflict, that is, Joseph's dreams which provoke the crime of enslavement. In responding to the hostile questioning of his lordship over them (cf. 37.8), Joseph now replies that his lordship is for their well-being, their salvation from famine.

With the hierarchical oppositions of lord/slave and life/death in mind, Joseph's claim about God's plan to make him lord over Egypt in order to save life is in fact a repetition of the same theme, the choice between death and slavery. The difference is that he chooses the more privileged, positive and acceptable terms to express the same idea. The ugly and offensive terms are suppressed. If he is made lord, someone somewhere has to be subservient to him. His brothers have to bow down before him and have to serve him.

Privileged Terms Preferred

Joseph's claim is quite questionable, but there are several reasons why
it is difficult to detect that fact. First of all, the way he speaks of the
'divine plan' is subtle. The words 'death' and 'slave' are excluded.
Only the privileged terms 'lord' and 'life' occur in his speech, and he
also repeats them with variant forms, 'father', 'ruler', 'remnant' and
'survivors'. Therefore, it is not easy to be aware of the similarity
between the claim that lordship is the way to salvation and the claim
that slavery is the way to avoid death. Joseph focuses on his experience
as a slave first. His rise to power as lord over others seems to be more
acceptable after a descent.

When the narrator presents to us the ironic reversal of Judah's role
from victimizer to victim within his own imposed choice between death
and slavery, Joseph is ignorant of this reversal. He is a victim of this
choice, and his test somehow makes the retribution possible. Ironically,
the victim (i.e. Judah) of this retribution gives Joseph an example of
sacrificial suffering. This prompts Joseph to reveal his identity and to
interpret his past suffering in the light of Judah's example. Unfortunately, Joseph seems to accept slavery as the way to salvation. On the
one hand, he interprets his own slavery as a mission sent by God to
save life. On the other, his claim to lordship over Egypt as destined by
God only affirms the same hierarchical opposition of lord/slave. Duplicating the crime which his test has just reversed and condemned,
Joseph unwittingly demonstrates to us the danger of a simple reversal
of a hierarchical opposition without questioning its validity. Any simple
reversal or exchange of roles (lord/slave, victimizer/victim, enslaver/
enslaved) will only perpetuate the crime which one attempts to undo.

Joseph transforms or inverts Judah's claim, but it retains the same
hierarchical structure. Nothing changes except the roles being ex-
changed. From the way the narrator presents this story, Joseph's claim
at the end may well be an ironic ending. Therefore, Joseph's claim to be
destined by God to save life should not be accepted without reservation.
One should be more careful to avoid the glorification of his lordship
than some authors are, for example:

> It is a dream...led to a vocation for this one *born to rule*, it is a dream
> come true.[82]

---

82. Brueggemann, *Genesis*, p. 293.

The fulfilment of his childhood dreams, which foretold all his brothers bowing down to him, also showed that God had been in control of his career.[83]

God who sent him to and empowered him in Egypt.[84]

You Meant Evil but God Meant it for Good

When Joseph softens the wording 'sold' (45.4, 5) to 'sent' (45.8) to describe his selling into slavery by his brothers, he does not excuse their crime and clearly condemns it as evil (50.20). Even though Judah suggests selling Joseph into slavery to avoid Joseph's death, Judah cannot be credited with a good intention. Slavery is not a lesser evil because the choice between death and slavery is an imposition by the victimizer. The brothers' enslavement of Joseph leads to Joseph's rise to power to save many lives, but it does not diminish their evil. Evil is evil and it cannot be turned to good. There should be no abolishment of the distinction between good and evil.

But what is divine good in Joseph's claim has a similar nature to the human evil committed by his brothers. In Joseph's claim, God has made him lord over Egypt to save many lives, that is, the lordship over others becomes the way to salvation. It is not only a description of a past or present social situation. Rather it is a divine intention foretold in Joseph's dreams, and God will bring it to fruition either with or in spite of human intentions. If the reader accepts Joseph's claim, then one inevitably deconstructs the oppositions of good/evil and divine intention/ human intention. In the context of this story, the human evil that Joseph condemns is not simply slavery, it is rather a slavery entered upon in order to avoid death; on the other hand, the divine good that Joseph claims is not simply the saving of life, it is rather the saving of life through lordship.

The so-called divine good is of the same nature as human evil. Joseph's description of the divine intention is inspired by and modelled upon human intention. So, the 'divine good' claimed by Joseph cannot override the 'human evil' because this 'divine good' is not high above its opposite, 'human evil'. This 'divine good' is contaminated by its opposite at the very heart of its structure.

83. Wenham, *Genesis 16–50*, p. 432.
84. Humphreys, *Joseph and his Family*, p. 115.

Brothers/Foreigners

The opposition of brother/foreigner is prominent in the Joseph story. Judah appeals to his brothers not to kill Joseph because he is 'our brother' (stressed twice, 37.26, 27), 'our own flesh'. The brothers later feel guilty about what they have done to 'our brother' (42.21). Joseph's test is to punish their breaking of the bond of brotherhood. The brothers have to be taught to repent of their evil act towards one of their own. But the mass murder of the Shechemites has not gained much attention as compared with their attempted murder of a brother.[85] The horror of the mass enslavement of the women of the Shechem and their little ones (34.29) is also seldom mentioned. Even so, the enslavement of a single small Canaanite city pales into insignificance compared with Joseph's enslavement of the whole nation of Egypt. Foreigners seem to be expendable. There is a clear line between brothers and foreigners.

However, the borderline between brother and foreigner is not as clear as it appears. The twelve sons of Jacob are supposed to form the identity of an Israelite brotherhood. They are to be separated from foreigners, both Canaanites and Egyptians. Intermarriage with foreigners is undesirable (if not forbidden).[86] Abraham and Isaac both avoid intermarriage of their sons with foreign wives (24.3; 28.2). The genealogy of Jacob in 46.8-27 can be examined to see whether the attempt to avoid intermarriage is successful or not. The genealogy records Jacob's family of 70 who move to Egypt and form the beginning of the Israelite people. At first glance, it lists only three members as children from intermarriage. They are Shaul, Manasseh and Ephraim. Shaul is the son of Simeon by a Canaanite woman (46.10).[87] The other two are the sons

---

85. The mention of Shechem (37.12-15) in this narrative makes the comparison between the attempted murder of a brother and the mass murder of foreigners in ch. 34 unavoidable. In Jacob's blessing, Simeon and Levi are said to be punished for their violence (49.5-7).

86. Wenham, *Genesis 16–50*, p. 319, considers Simeon and Levi to be heroes and he states, 'Undoubtedly, the heroes of this story, though they are the villains of the Joseph story, are Dinah's brothers, particularly Simeon and Levi. Here they are portrayed as fiercely opposing intermarriage with the Canaanites of the land and taking up the sword to avenge sexual misconduct... Gen. 34 traces this concern for purity of line back to Simeon and Levi, forefather of the Israelite priestly tribe.'

87. Calvin, *Genesis*, II, p. 392, condemns Simeon's intermarriage: 'When Moses declares that Shaul, one of the sons of Simeon, was born of a Canaanite woman, while he does not even mention the mothers of the other sons, his intention, I doubt not, is to fix a mark of dishonour on his race. For the holy Fathers were on

of Joseph by an Egyptian wife. But only one of the five sons of Simeon is recorded as being born of a foreign woman. Joseph is sold into Egypt and is forced to take a foreign wife. Jacob later adopts Joseph's two sons as his own and that seems to remedy the situation. The avoidance of intermarriage seems to be successful. The cases of Simeon and Joseph can be seen as an exception, a minor corruption of the Israelite people by foreigners.

However, the text also includes Judah's three sons (Er, Onan and Shelah), but it fails to mention that their mother is a Canaanite woman (38.2). Judah also has two sons by his daughter-in-law, Tamar, whose origin is not certain. The extent of corruption by foreigners is still relatively minor with 3 foreign daughters-in-law and only 6 foreign grandchildren,[88] resulting from intermarriage among Jacob's family of 70. But Jacob's two concubines, Zilpah and Bilhah, are probably foreigners in the light of their status as maids (שׁפחה)[89] given to his wives by Laban. If this is indeed the case, then Jacob himself has 2 foreign wives with 4 sons resulting from intermarriage and has 19 grandchildren from them.[90] There are, then, 25 grandchildren from intermarriage among Jacob's house of 70. Three out of Jacob's 12 sons marry foreign wives and 4 of the sons were born out of Jacob's own intermarriage. Therefore, only five of Jacob's sons can be considered pure. The problem of the 'corruption' of Israel's identity by the foreigner cannot be seen as minor. Earlier attempts to avoid impurity in the lineage by the special arrangement of marriages (Abraham and Isaac) fail miserably in Jacob's family.

It is significant that the identity of the Israelite nation depends not so much on Abraham and Isaac, for they both have 'foreign' descendants (Ishmaelites and Edomites). The identity of the Israelite nation derives from Jacob. If Jacob's concubines are indeed foreign slave-girls, the purity of Israelite identity is corrupted at the very beginning. Even if they are not, the problem of 'corruption' remains. Judah and Joseph, the

---

their guard, not to mix in marriage with that nation, from which they were separated by the decree of heaven.'

88. They are Shaul, Er, Onan, Shelah, Manasseh and Ephraim. Er and Onan already died in Canaan (46.10; 38.2-5; 41.51-52).

89. Hagar is an Egyptian maid (שׁפחה) (16.1 NRSV translates it as 'slave-girl') and she may well be one of the maids given to Abram by Pharaoh (12.16).

90. The sons are Gad, Asher from Zilpah; and Dan and Naphtali from Bilhah. There are 14 grandchildren from Zilpah (46.18) and 5 more from Bilhah (46.25).

most prominent sons of Jacob, both marry foreign woman. The 'corruption' is then not just quantitative but qualitative. They are the protagonists of the whole narrative and the rest of the sons are only minor characters. Almost half of the text in Jacob's blessing concerns the future of these two sons. 1 Chronicles 5.1-2 speaks of the birthright given to Joseph and of a ruler coming from Judah. They are the cornerstones of the future identity of the Israelite nation (both southern and northern kingdoms). The contamination of these two sons will invade the heart of Israelite identity. In short, the situation of intermarriage in Jacob's family makes a rigid distinction between brother and foreigner problematic. It is especially acute in the light of Joseph's situation. On the one hand, he marries an Egyptian (and thus his two sons are half Egyptians by blood). He is a father to Pharaoh (45.8), and he has once desired to forget his own father (41.51). On the other hand, his ten brothers are not his full brothers. Joseph's test (or the brothers' crime) drives Jacob to a point where he speaks of only having two sons (42.38; 44.27), thereby delegitimizing[91] his relationship with the other ten sons and in turn destroying the remaining bond of brotherhood. To Joseph, the Egyptians are no longer total foreigners, and the brothers are still not full brothers even after he reveals himself to them.

It is on the basis of the distinction between brother and foreigner that Judah and Reuben make their appeal not to kill Joseph, their own brother. It is also on this basis that they are condemned for their crime of selling their own brother into slavery. Joseph's test rests on whether they will abandon another brother into slavery or not. Joseph's final rejection of his brothers' offer to be his slaves is also placed in sharp contrast to his acceptance of the enslavement of the Egyptians. All of these try to keep a strict separation between one's own and the other. The problem becomes more evident in the next generation. For Manasseh and Ephraim, the Egyptians are part of their own. How can they as Egyptian-Israelites justify the enslavement of one side of their 'own' people and the free provision of the other side by their father? Fewell and Gunn also explain to us the problem of the distinction between brother and foreigner in Jacob's family:

> One of the surface messages of the story of Dinah's rape is the disdain of intermarriage with the Canaanites. This disdain, however, is revealed to be somewhat pretentious in light of the circumstances that pertain to

91. Wenham, *Genesis 16–50*, p. 427.

Jacob's family. Who, after all, are his children going to marry? They can no longer go back to Paddanaram for suitable mates, because that part of the family has become foreign. As each son takes a bride from among the daughters of Canaan and Egypt, the 'purity' of the family of origin is further diluted, blurring the boundaries between family and foreigner, between 'us' and 'them,' and forever problematizing the exclusive promise of nationhood and the holy war rhetoric of Moses, Joshua, and YHWH.[92]

Summary

I hope that I have succeeded in detailing the frequent repetitions of a choice between death and slavery in this story. My strategy in the above study is to engage my reader in looking at what Joseph really means by his profound theological claims in 45.4-11 and 50.19-20. The idea of 'death or slavery' is not simply an opposition to the idea of 'life and lordship' proclaimed by Joseph as the divine design. The latter pair appear more pleasant, attractive and acceptable, but in reality they are only the privileged terms of the identical structure of the former idea. The idea of providence and of the opposition of good and evil should be put into question after this initial probing.

The scrutiny of the problematic nature of the hierarchical oppositions inherent in Joseph's claim of divine providence provides us a base to challenge Joseph's justification of his divine domination by exposing Joseph's strategy and its fallacy. This will be the aim of the next chapter.

---

92. Danna N. Fewell and David M. Gunn, *Gender, Power, and Promise* (Nashville: Abingdon Press, 1993), p. 86.

Chapter 2

A CHALLENGE TO JOSEPH'S CLAIM OF DIVINE DOMINATION

The basic premise of Joseph's claim of divine domination is simple and clear: the hierarchy of domination and subordination is necessary to secure survival.[1] In other words, Joseph is advocating the idea of sub-servience for survival, or salvation at a price. This sounds unacceptable to modern readers. Some may leave the ideology of the text alone and concentrate on what the story meant in its historical setting without any attempt to judge its message from a modern perspective. This view assumes that the text presents the ideology in a simple and unambiguous way. I will try to demonstrate that the text yields a more complex picture than appears at first. First of all, I should emphasize that I do not intend to question the ideology of divine domination itself. My challenge is rather to *Joseph's claim* of divine domination. I will try to scrutinize the way Joseph presents his claim in order to expose its persuasive strategy as well as its incoherence and fallacy.

Sending his brothers to bring his father down to Egypt, Joseph tells them to report to him that that God has made him lord over all Egypt. 'Make haste and go up to my father and say to him, Thus says your son Joseph, God has made me lord of all Egypt; come down to me, do not tarry' (45.9).

Joseph of course knows that it was Pharaoh who made him lord: 'you shall be over my house, and all my people shall order themselves as you command' (41.40). I suppose that Joseph does not mean to disre-

---

1.   Claus Westermann, *Joseph: Studies of the Joseph Stories in Genesis* (trans. Omar Kaste; Edinburgh: T. & T. Clark, 1996), p. ix, points out that Joseph's dreams are about political authority and its justification: 'the recurrent preoccupation with the problem of political authority and, more specifically, the fundamental problem of royal authority: How is it that a man can lord it over his own brothers?' Sailhamer, *Pentateuch as Narrative*, p. 207, also sees the motif of 'bowing down' as 'an acknowledgment of royalty and kingship'.

gard human involvement in historical events. It is fair to interpret him as saying that God is working behind and beyond human activities.[2] It is difficult to object to his claim that God has made him lord over all Egypt. After all, his dreams announce his rise to power. And it is a chain of events, most of which are outside his control, that leads him to this position of power.[3] It could only be seen as a miraculous work of God. Even Pharaoh acknowledges the Spirit of God within Joseph (41.38). From the perspective of the story itself, anyone who tries to put into question his claim of God's sanctioned domination is bound to face a formidable, if not impossible, task. However, Aaron Wildavsky, a scholar who specializes in political analysis, questions Joseph's claims of God's will in his book on Joseph:

> Joseph keeps saying (to Pharaoh, to his brothers) that everything that happens is due to God's will. But he does not pray nor does God appear to him nor does he eat or dress or (often) behave as if he were a religious person. Moses does.[4]

Wildavsky is suspicious of the truthfulness of Joseph's persistent claims of God's will, but his arguments do not confront Joseph's claims directly. Instead, he targets his criticisms towards Joseph's behaviour. Wildavsky's main arguments are that Joseph's deeds do not substantiate his words, and his religious behaviour is compared unfavourably with that of Moses. Wildavsky is not alone in targeting criticisms towards Joseph's behaviour rather than towards his claims. This is one of the strategies used by many readers to avoid confronting Joseph's claims. I will detail these strategies in Chapter 4. The difficulty in questioning Joseph's claim of divinely inspired domination is partially due to Joseph's clever use of Judah's pit to justify his dreams. I will try to expose its fallacy in order to put his claim into question.

---

2.   Brueggemann, *Genesis*, p. 293, 'The theme of the Joseph narrative concerns God's hidden and decisive power which works in and through but also against human forms of power.'

3.   Kidner, *Genesis*, p. 180, thus comments, 'The account of the dreams, coming at the outset, makes God, not Joseph, the "hero" of the story: it is not a tale of human success but of divine sovereignty.'

4.   Wildavsky, *Assimilation versus Separation*, p. 3. Among the critics of Joseph, Wildavsky is one of the few who have expressed doubts over Joseph's frequent claims of knowing God's will.

*Strategic Use of Judah's Pit to Justify
his Claim of Divine Domination*

Structural Similarities between Judah's Pit and Joseph's Dreams
There are some intriguing tactics in Joseph's disclosure speech that
help him to justify his claim of divine domination. This speech (45.4-
11) is well recognized by many as the 'key'[5] to the understanding of the
meaning of this story, so it deserves a detailed examination. The nature
of Joseph's understanding of his past suffering and the purpose of his
dreams in 45.4-11 serves to explain the significance of the past rather
than to predict the future as he has done in his dream interpretation.[6]
The first thing he mentions when he discloses his identity is his past
enslavement experience (45.4-8a). While Reuben allows Joseph to be
thrown into a pit in the wilderness, it is Judah who suggests selling him
into slavery which can be represented symbolically by the pit. For the
sake of the comparison I intend to make between the motif of pit and
the motif of dreams in this chapter, I designate Joseph's bondage experience in the pit and in Egypt as 'Judah's pit' and its opposite as
'Joseph's dreams'[7] of ruling over others. The ordeal of the pit of slavery surely haunts him. It is certainly his desire to come to terms with it.[8]
For whatever motive, he subjects his brothers to a long test. He first im-
prisons them by way of a punishment of pit for pit. Then demanding
and retaining Benjamin, he plots the re-enactment and trial of their past
crime.[9] This strategy apparently works and they respond with confession

---

5. Wenham, *Genesis 16–50*, p. 432, 'The statements about God's overruling of
human affairs are undoubtedly the key to understanding the whole Joseph story.'
6. Miscall, 'The Jacob and Joseph Stories as Analogies', p. 38, remarks on
'Joseph's speech, an interpretation of the past which also reveals a definite attitude
towards the past'.
7. All dreams (Joseph, the butler and the baker, and Pharaoh) in the Joseph
story come in pairs. Joseph explains the doublet in Pharaoh's case as a sign of the
certainty of fulfilment (41.32). I therefore refer to Joseph's dreams in the plural as
opposed to the pit in the singular. Turner, *Announcements of Plot in Genesis*,
p. 147, discusses Joseph's futile attempt to fulfil the dreams and he bases his argument on the clear distinction between his two dreams.
8. Cf. Alter, *Art of Biblical Narrative*, p. 167.
9. Alter, *Art of Biblical Narrative*, pp. 155-77, gives a concise description of
this process of enactment. See also Ackerman, 'Joseph, Judah, and Jacob', pp. 88-
90; Sternberg, *The Poetics of Biblical Narrative*, pp. 293-94.

of their guilt. Joseph then discloses his identity and reveals to them the workings of God for them.

Joseph's insight into the purpose of his suffering in the pit may derive from Judah's passionate plea in ch. 44.[10] It is through Joseph's test of the brothers that Judah is finally prompted to offer himself as a slave instead of Benjamin in order to avoid the possible death of his father. From Judah's sacrificial example, Joseph seems to come to the understanding that his past suffering is averting the possible death of many others. If the pit is somehow necessary for the survival of many, then what is the reason for his dreams of dominating his brothers and family? Joseph immediately ascribes the same purpose of salvation to his dreams of domination in the second part of his speech (45.8b-11). It is not clear how Joseph comes to this conclusion and whether it is justified. His disclosure speech presents these two necessities in sequence: the need of the pit for survival and the need of the dreams for salvation.

These two claims, the pit of slavery (45.4-8a) and the dreams of lordship (45.8b-11), form an integrated whole for Joseph to explain the meaning of his past experience. In his understanding of God's overall plan, there are two opposite roles for him. First as a slave, then as a lord to carry out God's mission. Despite their obvious divergence, the pit of slavery and the dreams of lordship share some common characteristics. Both his descent and his ascent are allegedly destined by God who works providentially to secure survival for many. They share the same purpose of salvation, but there is a 'price'[11] to be paid on the part of the human characters. Joseph acknowledges this price in his role of being 'sent' into slavery in the first part of his speech (45.4-8a).[12] When Reuben allows Joseph to be thrown into a pit, it becomes paradoxically simultaneously a place of slavery and survival for Joseph. In a strange twist of destiny, Joseph's words take his past suffering in the pit to be a 'necessary' step to enable him to rise to power for the survival of

10. Cf. Ackerman, 'Joseph, Judah, and Jacob', p. 106; Brueggemann, *Genesis*, p. 343.

11. Turner, *Announcement of Plot in Genesis*, p. 172, remarks on the price paid by the Egyptians for their survival, 'Through his agricultural policy Joseph does save the lives of the Egyptians, but does so at a price—their enslavement (47.13ff.).'

12. Cf. Ackerman, 'Joseph, Judah, and Jacob', p. 107, who comments that 'the favored one must descend / be offered up / be risked so that "Israel" (referring both to the father and to the clan) might not perish'.

Victim and Victimizer

many.[13] His speech retrospectively turns this ambiguous situation into
the idea of the necessity of subservience for survival. However, in the
second part of his speech about the fulfilment of his dreams, he stresses
only his rise to power over Egypt and diplomatically avoids mentioning
the price and the necessity of his brothers' 'bowing down' as envisaged
in his dreams.

Nevertheless, Joseph's whole speech gives the impression that the
price of subservience seems to be unavoidable if the benefit of salvation
in the pit and the dreams is to materialize. Joseph has to suffer as a
slave first in order to be able to save others later, and his brothers have
to accept their subservience in order to be saved. Willingly or unwill-
ingly, a price has to be paid. Joseph seems to accept it retrospectively,[14]
though not without considerable struggle and pain. As for the brothers,
they oppose their subservience to Joseph fiercely at the beginning of the
narrative, but at the end their choice is limited. They have to accept
their fate. Therefore, in Joseph's understanding the pit of slavery and
the dreams of domination share an important common structure: the
necessity of subservience for survival. And they build on a hierarchical
opposition of lord and slave. While Joseph's brothers have engineered
his enslavement and later have to submit to his domination, it is Joseph
who alone figures at both ends of this hierarchy as lord and slave.

Judah's pit and Joseph's dreams share a similar hierarchical structure
and purpose of salvation, but there is a subtle but important difference.
In hindsight, the pit of slavery inflicted on Joseph by Judah makes possible the fulfilment of his dreams of achieving salvation. The 'necessity' of subservience for survival in Joseph's case is, however, highly
qualified. Its 'necessity' does not eliminate the brothers' responsibility
for their crime; as Wenham remarks, 'Though Genesis emphatically
states that God uses the sins of Joseph's brothers for good, it nowhere
excuses their sins or pretends they can be forgotten; rather, they needed

13. Wenham, *Genesis 16–50*, p. 493, comments, 'The idea that God overrules
the plans of the wicked to achieve his own purposes of good is of course an
assumption that pervades Scripture (e.g. Prov. 16.9; 19.21). Indeed, it seems to be
suggested that, through the suffering of the righteous Joseph at the hands of his
wicked brothers, life was brought to the world.'

14. Robert L. Cohn, 'Narrative Structure and Canonical Perspective in Genesis',
JSOT 23 (1983), pp. 3-16 (14), 'Only in retrospect does he acknowledge God's
guiding hand.'

to be acknowledged and repented of.'[15] While Joseph forgives their crime of condemning him into slavery, he nevertheless denounces it as evil in unambiguous terms (50.20).[16] In contrast, there is no such quali-fication for the brothers' 'necessary' subservience for survival. No one else is said to be responsible for their fate of being subordinated. When he explains his dreams of lordship in his speech, he refers only to his domination over Egypt without mentioning the brothers' subservience. Does he pretend it can be forgotten?[17]

The motif of divine providence appears in both Judah's pit and Joseph's dreams. First, the divine providence is best expressed by Joseph's understanding of his pit experience. He alters the 'selling' into slavery by his brothers to God's 'sending' him into Egypt to preserve their lives in 45.5-8a. God can override human evil to accomplish his divine good purpose.[18] Secondly, Joseph's dreams of domination provi-dentially come to fruition despite all human opposition.[19] The brothers have tried to get rid of the dreamer in order to obliterate his dreams. The false accusation by Potiphar's wife and the neglect of Joseph's fate by the butler also present an obstacle to their fulfilment. However, as

15. Wenham, *Genesis 16–50*, p. 433. It is fair to see the brothers' pit of slavery inflicted on Joseph as a *crime* and Joseph's own dreams of domination over them as a *price* for salvation, even though they share the same structure and purpose.

16. Miscall, 'The Jacob and Joseph Story as Analogies', p. 38, remarks, 'Joseph sees God bringing good from evil, but not thereby forgiving sin.'

17. The idea that God destines the brothers to bow down in order to be saved does not go unnoticed, but Joseph simply avoids it in his speech. Calum M. Car-michael, 'The Law of the Forgotten Sheaf', in K.R. Richards (ed.), *Society of Bib-lical Literature 1981 Seminar Papers* (SBLSP, 20; Chico, CA: Scholars Press, 1981), pp. 35-37 (36), comments, 'The unfolding of the dream in reality occurs when Joseph's brothers come to Egypt in order to obtain grain to keep them alive. In doing so, they have to acknowledge Joseph's supremacy over them. The relief of their distress is dependent upon this subordination.' See also Brueggemann, *Genesis*, p. 335.

18. Allen P. Ross, *Creation and Blessing* (Grand Rapids: Baker Book House, 1988), p. 716, 'The sovereign plan of God, designed to save many people, in some way incorporated the evil of the brothers and used it as the means of bringing about the good.' See also Wenham, *Genesis 16–50*, p. 493.

19. Brueggemann, *Genesis*, p. 301, 'all sorts of enemies of the dream try to resist: the brothers, the woman (chap. 39), the famine (chap. 41), all resist the dream and fail'. Quoting Brueggemann's comment here, Turner, *Announcements of Plot in Genesis*, p. 166, further remarks, 'It is true that the active opposition of these foes is overcome.'

Turner asserts, 'attempts to thwart God's purpose merely speed its triumph'.[20] The similarity between Judah's pit and Joseph's dreams in terms of divine providence again displays a subtle difference: the pit is evil and it will be overridden; the dreams are however treated as positive and they will overcome all oppositions.

Joseph's speech implies that the pit's necessity is highly qualified, while his dreams are without similar qualification and his domination over his brothers is seen as absolutely necessary for the survival of all. Some readers concur with Joseph's viewpoint and unreservedly accept the dreams as coming from God.[21] Any defence for the necessity of his domination is bound to repeat Joseph's declaration of divine purpose of salvation[22] without realizing the similarity of the necessity of sub-servience for survival in both the pit and the dreams. There may be times in this imperfect world when the situation of subservience for survival is unavoidable.[23] Therefore, it is not easy to dismiss such a notion. However, it is the double standards exercised by Joseph's understanding towards Judah's pit and his dreams that should be con-fronted. If both the pit and the dreams are founded structurally on the same idea of subservience for survival, it does not seem to warrant their different emphases in terms of the nature of their necessity and of the extent of divine involvement.

My attempt in this work is to expose the similarities and differences between Judah's pit and Joseph' dreams instead of determining whether they are indeed necessary or providential in nature. It is not my inten-tion to prove objectively whether the idea of subservience for survival itself is justifiable. My aim is rather to see if any single judgment on the

20. Turner, *Announcements of Plot in Genesis*, p. 169. Ackerman, 'Joseph, Judah, and Jacob', pp. 86-87, also asserts the power of 'God's control of history' and comments, 'the story…showing how human beings cannot thwart the divine purpose'. See also Harold G. Stigers, *A Commentary on Genesis* (Grand Rapids: Zondervan, 1976), p. 274.

21. Brueggemann, *Genesis*, p. 346, remarks, 'Joseph was dreamed to be a ruler. Now he is a "ruler-lord-father", not just over the family, but over the empire. And it is the work of God. No one could stop it.'

22. Benjamin Goodnick, 'The Character of Joseph: Reconsidered', *Journal of Psychology and Judaism* 12 (1988), pp. 215-29 (227), comments, 'Realizing their confusion and inability to reply, Joseph attempted to ease their hearts and minds: they were only instruments; the course of his life had been predestined. His present status had been ordained in order to save the whole family for a higher purpose.'

23. Cf. Stigers, *A Commentary on Genesis*, p. 320.

pit and the dreams is fairly applied. It seems that there is a consistent disparity of judgment by Joseph and many readers: the pit is accepted with qualification as necessary but evil,[24] while the dreams are considered unequivocally as absolutely necessary and a divine good.[25] There are reasons for the acceptance of Joseph's claims by some readers despite the above disparities. The following discussion will detail Joseph's strategy to support his claims.

The Dreams are Justified through the Pit

Joseph's justification of his dreams of divine domination is mediated through the necessity of the pit and its correlated idea of divine providence. In the overall development of narrative plot, his gradual acceptance of his pit of suffering is embedded between his remembering of the dreams at the beginning of his test (42.9) and his disclosure of the divine purpose of his dreams (45.8b-11). Everything reported in between seems to be concerned with the chastisement due to the brothers who are responsible for his plight. It climaxes at his disclosure of the divine purpose of his suffering. During this long segment of narrative, his dreams are relegated to the background.

As for the brothers, it is the moment for them to come to terms with their guilt for inflicting the pit of slavery on Joseph. Their crime naturally deserves attention when they come to face their victim. There is also a need for Joseph to deal with the agony he has just expressed in 41.51-52 before the encounter with his brothers, where he attempts to forget the past affliction together with all his father's house. He even attributes the attempt to forget to divine action. During the prolonged confrontation with his brothers (chs. 42–44), he is clearly struggling to come to terms with his past pit of suffering as indicated by his frequent weeping.[26] The pit comes back to haunt him and he cannot forget as he once wished.[27] An explanation has to be provided for his past ordeal. There are three aspects of this trauma of the pit that need to be

---

24. Janzen, *Genesis 12–50*, p. 175, does not excuse the guilt of the brothers but considers that Joseph finally can accept the suffering in the pit 'as part of the fabric of his life at God's hands'.

25. Brueggemann, *Genesis*, p. 335, comments, 'Joseph's dominant role in Egypt is necessary and presumed.'

26. Cf. 42.24; 43.30; 45.2; 50.17.

27. Sternberg, *The Poetics of Biblical Narrative*, p. 287, 'now that the past has forced itself on him'.

accounted for: the evil act of his brothers, Joseph's suffering and, above all, the intention of God.

Joseph's anguish towards his past is at first suppressed, but it resurfaces when he encounters his brothers. His words here are another attempt to come to terms with the pit and its pain. Again it is done by appealing to God's action. Rather than negatively forgetting it, he now actively sees the positive side of the pit, as a way for salvation. This helps him to reconcile himself both with his own pit and with his brothers. Since God has not made him forget his family, he has to find a new reason to explain the past.

In the first half of his disclosure speech (45.4-8a), Joseph finally finds all the answers to his satisfaction. His understanding is that it is God who has permitted the brothers to sell him into slavery in order to save many lives.[28] Joseph's pit of suffering is endorsed with the providential nature of the divine good intention in overriding human evil. This allows for the freedom of human agency and the divine will at the same time.[29] In the second half of the speech (45.8b-11), he explains the purpose of his dreams as a divine destiny to fulfil God's plan for salvation. The divine providence serves to stress the power of God to anticipate human actions. And God can use them in due course for the purpose of salvation. However, the salvation is of a particular kind, accomplished in a providential way, namely through the evil of the brothers as understood retrospectively by Joseph and also through the ruling over them foretold by his dreams. Sharing the same purpose of salvation, the pit and the dreams become a sequence to achieve this good end.

The sequence from the pit to the dreams. The idea of salvation in the pit of providence is extremely convincing to many readers.[30] Since Joseph presents the pit and the dreams in such an intertwined sequence in his disclosure speech, the pit of providence will become an obstacle to anyone who attempts to disagree with his dreams of domination. The reason is that the fulfilment of the dreams is essential in order for the ideal of the pit of providence to be realized. The following is a detailed explanation of Joseph's strategy.

28. Cf. Janzen, *Genesis 12–50*, p. 175.
29. Skinner, *Genesis*, p. 487; see also Ross, *Creation and Blessing*, p. 673.
30. Cf. Kidner, *Genesis*, p. 207; von Rad, *Genesis*, p. 432; Wenham, *Genesis 16–50*, p. 493.

Joseph ascribes a salvific purpose to his dreams, but he does not argue explicitly for the idea that salvation will be gained at the price of subservience. The reader can deduce it from his words, but it is not the way he presents it. It is rather the order of presentation in his disclosure speech that may prove to be more vital in his strategy to justify his dreams of domination than outright argument. When Joseph's speech integrates the pit and the dreams in an overall divine plan of salvation, they become inextricably intertwined. It looks as if neither of them can stand alone anymore. On the one hand, the pit of providence (45.4-8a) cannot stand alone without the fulfilment of his dreams of domination (45.8b-11). The pit presupposes the dreams. Without the dreams, the pit is useless. It requires the dreams to complete the salvation it aims at. On the other hand, the pit is a stepping stone in Joseph's rise to power. However, while the pit presupposes the dreams, the reverse is not true. The dreams do not presuppose and require the pit. By the traditional understanding of divine providence, the dreams can in principle be realized without the brothers' evil of throwing Joseph into the pit of slavery.[31] The irony of this story is that the pit makes possible the fulfilment of the dreams.[32]

The pit presupposes the necessity of Joseph's dreams in order for its providential nature as understood by Joseph to be realized. In other words, the dreams make it possible for the pit to accomplish its providential purpose to save in spite of human evil. Without the dreams, Joseph's pit of slavery will not enable him to save anyone. The divine providence (associated with the pit) by itself cannot be adequate for the

31. Ross, *Creation and Blessing*, p. 673, thus comments that if 'the brothers obeyed and followed God's plan, they would have enjoyed his blessings to the full and spared themselves and their family the pain'.

32. Fritsch, 'God Was with Him', p. 31, 'His brethren, who had acted in blind ignorance when they sold him into Egypt, were actually helping to bring about God's will "to save much people".' Sailhamer, *Pentateuch as Narrative*, p. 207, also comments, 'Little did they suspect that the very plans which they were then scheming were to lead to the fulfillment of those dreams. In every detail of the narrative the writer's purpose shows through, that is, to demonstrate the truthfulness of Joseph's final words to his brothers: "you meant it for evil, but God meant it for good" (50.20).' Hugh C. White, 'The Joseph Story: A Narrative which "Consumes" Its Content', *Semeia* 31 (1985), pp. 46-69 (61), remarks, 'The supreme irony of this strategy is that by inciting the brothers to take action against the "dreamer" and his dreams, the familial system of jealous hatred is made to serve the very end of Joseph's ascendancy which it seeks to defeat.'

salvific purpose; it builds on the subsequent dreams for its complete success. Therefore, if one accepts the pit as providential, then the subsequent dreams of domination are hard to refute. Rejecting the latter will require one to retract the acceptance of the former. It is a clever strategy by Joseph to present both in this intricate sequence. Once the pit is accepted, the dreams are virtually inevitable by Joseph's account, but is this so? If one has to suffer for others in the pit, it does not automatically justify the need to dominate others in order to save them. But Joseph's presentation is so structured that if one accepts his explanation of the necessity of his suffering in the pit, his dreams of domination are then inevitable. It is useless for him to be sold into the pit without a subsequent rise to power. He will not be able to save others without the fulfilment of the dreams.[33] So these two are intricately intertwined and they become inseparable. When Bush comments that Joseph 'must pass through a deep scene of affliction' before he obtains his destined 'glory', it demonstrates that Joseph succeeds in making them inseparable.[34]

The pit helps the course and cause of the dreams. This 'pit-dreams' sequence is effective because the pit provides a strategic device for Joseph to justify his dreams which, if standing alone, would certainly meet stronger resistance. The brothers' throwing Joseph into the pit of slavery helps his dreams of domination in two ways. It makes possible the realization of the dreams which they seek to destroy.[35] More importantly, their revolt provides grounds for the vindication of Joseph's domination over them. Attention to the cause of the family conflict, that is, Joseph's dreams, is diverted away to the crime committed by the brothers. Throughout the long passage from chs. 42 to 45, Joseph consistently insists on focusing on the problem of his brothers, prompting many readers to direct their attention to the motives behind his testing

---

33. Longacre, *Joseph*, p. 43, recognizes that Joseph's rise to power through providential measures is essential in enabling him to save others from starvation.

34. George Bush, *Notes on Genesis* (Minneapolis: James Family Christian Publishers, 1979), p. 234. Similarly Walter Russell Bowie, *Genesis* (IB, 1; Nashville: Abingdon Press, 1952), p. 810, remarks that in God's providence the story of Joseph's life had to enter into a 'dark chapter' (slavery and exile) before 'his possibilities' (power and honour) could be fulfilled.

35. Ross, *Creation and Blessing*, p. 673, remarks, 'In spite of their attempts to change the divine plan, eventually they found out that God's plan would triumph.'

and harsh treatment of them.[36] The awkward question of the justification of the dreams is effectively dropped, at least temporarily. Only after he gives a definite sense of meaning to his suffering in the pit in his disclosure speech does he explain indirectly the purpose of his dreams, which triggered his testing in the first place. The justification is indirect because he mentions lordship only over foreigners rather than over his brothers.

Judging from the response of his brothers, Joseph's strategy of hiding the justification of his dreams behind his suffering in the pit is successful. They have no objection to what he says about God's intentions behind their crime and his rise to power. At the end of the story, the narrator returns to the motif of dreams when they bow down again before Joseph in fear of his revenge (50.18). They bring our attention back to the pit when they ask for forgiveness (50.15-17). Joseph says nothing about his dreams but reaffirms the good providential purpose of his suffering in the pit (50.20). His attitude is forgiving, but Holbert rightly points out that, as in his disclosure speech, Joseph still emphasizes their sin against him here.[37]

Ostensibly, his speech is an earnest consolation to ease their guilty conscience and not a defence of the legitimacy of his superiority and their necessary subservience.[38] In reality, his words excuse the pit of slavery and his dreams of domination at the same time. Admittedly, his consolation cannot be described as devious because he himself has to come to terms with the past affliction, which he now genuinely believes to have been necessary and providential in God's plan for the good of others. The brothers are criticized for repaying evil for good. First,

36. The following readers are drawn to examine the motives and nature of Joseph's test in a large part of their discussion on this story: Alter, *Art of Biblical Narrative*, pp. 155-77; Sternberg, *The Poetics of Biblical Narrative*, pp. 285-308; John Holbert, 'Joseph and the Surprising Choice of God', *P(ST)J* 38 (1985), pp. 33-42; Ackerman, 'Joseph, Judah, and Jacob', pp. 85-113. See also Sol Schimmel, 'Joseph and his Brothers: A Paradigm for Repentance', *Judaism: A Quarterly Journal of Jewish Life and Thought* 37 (1988), pp. 60-65; Miscall, 'The Jacob and Joseph Stories as Analogies', pp. 28-40; Gabriel Josipovici, 'Joseph and Revelation', in *idem, The Book of God: A Response to the Bible* (New Haven: Yale University Press, 1988), pp. 75-89; Turner, *Announcements of Plot in Genesis*, pp. 154-61.

37. John Holbert, *The Storyteller's Companion to the Bible*, p. 195.

38. Westermann, *Genesis 37–50*, p. 143, describes Joseph as doing anything he could to calm them and remove their fear.

Joseph's good intention to look after their well-being meets with an evil response. Secondly, they attempt to destroy the dreams that are designed to save them. In contrast, Joseph repays good for evil. Therefore, they deserve far more severe retribution, real slavery rather than simply 'bowing down'. Their subservience is more symbolic than real and cannot be compared to Joseph's long years of suffering as a slave in a foreign land. His innocence in each downward turn of his fortune no doubt makes one easily 'identify with him and sympathize with him'.[39] It becomes a helpful step towards the acceptance of his subsequent rise to power. [40] Fritsch thus comments on his fall and rise, 'Our hearts go out for Joseph [*sic*] as he languishes in prison for a crime he never committed, and we are glad when he is elevated to his high position in the court of Pharaoh.'[41] The emotional hurdle Joseph suffers takes on the appearance of a smart pre-emptive move to divert attention from the dreams of domination to the pit of providence.

The contrast between Joseph's righteousness and the treacherousness of his brothers is great. As a result, it should not surprise us if there is no strong objection to his domination over the far less respectable brothers.[42] They are certainly evil. Any uneasiness about lording it over them could be easily submerged in an outpouring of righteous rage against their murderous attack on their defenceless brother who comes to look after their well-being. Nevertheless, Joseph has to offer a reason to justify his domination. Indeed, he provides one—his domination is for the purpose of salvation of many lives. Understandably, his brothers, who are affected the most by his dreams, could not be in a position to question him after their crime and his forgiveness. However, readers

39. Josipovici, 'Joseph and Revelation', p. 84.

40. Ackerman, 'Joseph, Judah, and Jacob', p. 94, argues that Joseph's 'ascendancy to power would be an important part of the divine plan to keep alive the family of Israel' and that there is a 'relationship between his past suffering and his present power' of which Joseph has to come to a new understanding; Westermann, *Genesis 37–50*, p. 249, also notes that the 'ascendancy recurs after a fall'.

41. Fritsch, 'God Was with Him', p. 22. Joseph's rise to power is thus seen as a 'well-earned reward' after long years of trial and tribulation (p. 27). Ackerman, 'Joseph, Judah, and Jacob', p. 86, also remarks, 'The reader notes with satisfaction that Joseph's rise to power in Egypt results from a combination of pious behavior, divine help, and his wise advice at court.'

42. Carmichael, 'The Law of the Forgotten Sheaf', p. 36, suggests that the subservience of the brothers to Joseph is 'the consequence of their tyrannical act of selling him into slavery'.

can evaluate objectively his justification, especially as the excuse of saving lives looks remarkably similar to Judah's previous rationalization. Unfortunately, many readers are trapped by the focus set by Joseph. His strategic use of the pit of providence succeeds in diverting attention away from the problem of dreams of domination. For example, Westermann has raised the question of the justification of Joseph's domination over his brothers at the beginning of his book, but it is soon overshadowed by his discussions about the brothers' crime, Joseph's effort to bring them to come to terms with their guilt, and finally their reconciliation.[43] If his dreams are discussed, the focus is usually on the glory of the dreamer rather than the subservience which the brothers have to accept.

At the beginning of the story, Joseph's dreams of domination face fierce opposition from the brothers and doubt and rebuke from his father. Some readers treat the idea of salvation at a price of subservience in his ideology with suspicion at worst or guarded approval at best. However, they do not hesitate to embrace Joseph's claim of the pit of providence.[44] With the pit first presented and accepted, one is no longer able to reject the dreams without risking retraction of the acceptance of the former. At first sight, the case for the pit of divine providence looks convincing, but once it is exposed as founded on the premise that the dreams are also necessary, then it may be seen as merely a clever tactic rather than a valid argument. The emphasis on the pit of providence might on the surface seem useful to Joseph's justification of the dreams. It provides an opportunity to divert attention to the need for a proper examination of the justification of the dreams. But it also exposes the dubious necessary link between the pit and the dreams. The dreams have to be judged according to their own merit.

Unfortunately, many readers fail to relate the pit sufficiently with the dreams. Joseph, however, puts them side by side in his revelation of their purposes in 45.4-11. They have been individually scrutinized, but their relationship is seldom analysed in a systematic way. The aim of

43. Westermann, *Joseph*, pp. 10, 61-99.

44. E.g. Bowie, *Genesis*, p. 802, suggests that Joseph's ideology is a belief in autocracy which occurred in the earlier history of Israelite nation, but is later replaced by the teaching of the great prophets who proclaim the rights of common people to justice. However, in God's providence Joseph's life is transformed from a 'vain self-seeker' to a 'servant' who no longer sees his dreams as concerned with 'his supposed pre-eminence' but about 'the fate of a nation'.

the above discussion is to put into question the seemingly smooth transition from the necessity of the pit to the necessity of the dreams in Joseph's disclosure speech. He paints his suffering in the pit and dreams of domination in the best possible light. He suffers as a slave for others and he also lords it over others for their benefit. But this attention on the pit may also be used to undermine his justification of his dreams. First, the pit is placed in dangerously close proximity to the dreams (45.5-11). This helps to compare their similarity in the idea of subservience for survival. Secondly, Joseph's reassertion of the pit, despite its usefulness, as evil (50.20) may solicit a similar response to its counter-part, his dreams, once their similarities are identified.

Joseph's Claim of Domination over Egypt

Egyptian Enslavement is a Faithful Application of a Divine Principle

In order to evaluate Joseph's justification of his claim of domination (45.8b-11), it is imperative to relate it to his subsequent policy of mass enslavement (47.13-26). Since they are intimately connected, I would argue that his policy of mass enslavement is not accidental but derives from his belief in divine domination. If the link can be reasonably established (through the following survey of the same rationale held by almost all the characters involved in this story), it will pose a challenge to Joseph's claims of divine domination. This is because if the real nature of his domination is meant to be enslavement for those under him, it would be difficult for him to justify God's involvement.

The enslavement of the Egyptians has never been seen as an ideal situation; some readers attempt to defend Joseph's policy as a pragmatic approach to the dire situation the people face.[45] For example, Stigers admits that there is a problem in Joseph's action, 'food is secured while the victim and his children become slaves'. He remarks that the cuneiform documents of 'the Middle East are full of examples of those come to poverty who sold themselves into slavery for sustenance'. Therefore, instead of criticizing Joseph's measures, he asks, 'How else could the problem have been solved within the experience and institutions available to them?'[46] He acknowledges the Egyptian

---

45. Leupold, *Exposition*, pp. 1134, 1138, argues that 'extreme emergencies' call for 'stern measures' and Joseph's action is 'apparently unavoidable under the circumstances'.

46. Stigers, *A Commentary on Genesis*, p. 320. Morris, *The Genesis Record*,

enslavement (ch. 47) as less than ideal, but he finds no problem with Joseph's claim (ch. 45) of ruling over others.[47]

While the pragmatic approach usually sees no connection between Joseph's disclosure speech and his enslavement policy, some other readers criticize his treatment of the Egyptians as a deviation from his divine mission. According to Watt, Joseph has been transformed from 'egocentric centrality' to maturity when he comes to realize that he is 'chosen by God's providence to go ahead and prepare for the salvation of his family, giving them the nurturing and protection that they did not give him'. But, on the exchange of food with the Egyptians for their lands and freedom, Joseph is criticized for becoming 'a tyrant wielding power as a corrupt form of leadership'.[48]

Lerner contrasts Joseph's revelation of God's plan and his relief policy. Joseph is criticized for 'ruthlessly pursuing a course of coercive economical centralization'. He argues that 'Joseph's tyrannical stance was not part of the original divine plan' and that it 'deviates' from God's intention on several points:

> The original plan does not mention selling the grain back to Egyptians, but states simply that the 'food shall be for store in the land'. The purpose of the plan was not to increase Pharaoh's power, but to guarantee that 'the land perish not through the famine'. Also, the original plan did not call for uprooting the people from the land and concentrating the population in the cities.[49]

The three policies that Joseph administers in his relief effort (i.e. the 'selling the grain', the increase of 'Pharaoh's power' and the 'uprooting of the people') are indeed not explicitly stated in Joseph's interpretation. Lerner attempts to use them to prove that the Torah 'dissociates his behaviour from the original Divine purpose'.[50] However, the divine plan of salvation interpreted by Joseph does include the means to achieve it, that is, he is made a lord by God to rule over the people (45.8b-11). To what extent his domination is sanctioned by God is uncertain. Whether the above policies are within God's authorized power is a matter of contention. If Lerner accepts Joseph's claim of a

p. 640, recognizes that Joseph's measures 'certainly left something to be desired in terms of human freedom' but they are preferable to mass starvation.

47. Stigers, *A Commentary on Genesis*, pp. 271, 274.
48. Watt, 'Joseph's Dreams', pp. 68, 69.
49. Lerner, 'Joseph the Unrighteous', pp. 278-79.
50. Lerner, 'Joseph the Unrighteous', p. 281.

divine plan, it will be difficult for him to reject Joseph's dreams and his claim of domination over Egypt in his disclosure speech. However, he considers that Joseph 'is depicted as having somewhat narrow social horizons' by the Torah for relating to the brothers 'his dreams of dominion over the whole family'. And his action 'presages his moral failure as ruler of Egypt'.[51] Lerner accepts Joseph's explanation of the divine plan, but his attitude to his rise to power is rather ambiguous.[52]

Joseph's 'harsh' treatment of the Egyptians gives an impression that the good purpose he claimed previously in his disclosure speech is tainted by his subsequent action. In the following discussion, I will argue that it is an incorrect impression and suggest that there is a firm causal connection between Joseph's ideology expressed in his claim of divine domination and his later policy of mass enslavement.

Against the Pit but not its Underlying Rationale
The connection between what Joseph believes about divine domination and how he behaves in his policy of mass enslavement should be properly investigated. I would argue that his behaviour merely exemplifies the ideas already embodied in his belief in divine domination. First of all, one may observe the recurring rationale of 'subservience for survival' in this story, in order to discover the interrelationship between Judah's pit of slavery inflicted on Joseph and Joseph's dreams of domination over his brothers and the Egyptians. The contrast of Judah's pit and Joseph's dreams in 45.4-11 can be further analysed with other instances of a similar idea of subservience for survival.

There are four instances of pits and two instances of the dreams that involve the idea of subservience for survival in this story. The first pit explicitly named as such is found in Reuben's attempt to save Joseph's life by allowing the brothers to throw him into a pit. Then another brother, Judah, in objecting to a direct murder, suggests selling Joseph

---

51. Lerner, 'Joseph the Unrighteous', p. 279.

52. Similarly, G. Charles Aalders, *Genesis*, II (trans. William Heynen; Bible Student's Commentary; Grand Rapids: Zondervan, 1981), pp. 256-57, 297, acknowledges that 'Joseph's regulatory measures can hardly be considered as ideal.' He considers the tax of one-fifth yield from their efforts is not excessive. But he questions the 'whole procedure' of requisitioning the grain from the people and later selling it back at the cost of all their possessions and their freedom. Joseph's actions, in his view, 'cannot be ethically and morally justified'. Nevertheless, he also accepts Joseph's explanation of his mission from God.

into slavery, which I refer to as a kind of symbolic pit for Joseph. These two are unfortunate incidents for Joseph, yet he remains alive despite the threat of death. The third pit is inflicted upon Judah who once suggested selling Joseph into slavery. Now their fate is reversed, Joseph forces Judah to opt for slavery to avoid the threat of death. The difference this time is that the life of the father rather than the victim himself is under threat. Judah willingly accepts slavery on behalf of Benjamin to avoid the death threat to Jacob. This sacrifice may be the stimulus that helps Joseph to understand his past pit as having a similar purpose to save lives. This is then the fourth pit which one can locate in this story. It is a reinterpretation of the second pit, the one Judah inflicts on Joseph.

The two occasions of subservience for survival as expressed by the dreams motif are found at 45.8b-11 and 47.13-26. Joseph's words in 45.8b-11 are implicitly an explanation of the purpose of the dreams he had at the beginning of the story (37.5-11). But the subservience in his disclosure speech refers not to his brothers but to the Egyptians whose subservience in the form of slavery is reported in 47.13-26 in detail. The following is a brief survey of these six instances of 'subservience for survival', focusing especially on the characters' attitudes towards the situation that one needs to exchange subservience for survival.

Tactical use by Reuben (37.21-22). The motif of the pit first appears when Reuben allows his brothers to throw Joseph into a pit. It is originally meant to be a grave for Joseph, then as a temporary refuge by Reuben's rescuing effort, and finally it becomes the place signifying a long period of subservience. The ambiguity of the pit symbolized as death or subservience could be recast from a slightly more positive perspective as subservience for survival if one treasures survival above all else.[53] This idea of the pit as subservience for survival is probably what Reuben tactically employs in order to rescue Joseph from his brothers. For Joseph himself, being thrown into a pit is only a first step into the downward turn—from temporary loss of freedom in a pit, to permanent loss of freedom through slavery in Potiphar's house, and finally to the most hopeless situation as a slave in a prison house. Therefore, the pit

---

53. Hugh C. White, 'Reuben and Judah: Duplicates or Complements?', in James T. Butler, Edgar W. Conrad and Ben C. Ollenburger (eds.), *Understanding the Word* (JSOTSup, 37; Sheffield: JSOT Press, 1985), p. 91, regards the throwing of Joseph into the cistern as a 'realistic' alternative proposal.

for Joseph symbolizes the pain of subservience in various degrees of affliction that he would be desperate to forget, but his eldest brother's measure nevertheless succeeds in saving his life. Later in the narrative, a series of dilemmas confronts the characters and causes them to opt for subservience in order to survive. They are captured, graphically and symbolically, in Reuben's tactical use of the pit as a sanctuary for Joseph from the threat of death.

Opportunistic use by Judah (37.26-27). Seizing the opportunity of the Ishmaelites who are passing by, Judah seems to give a verbal articulation of Reuben's secret intention to use the pit of subservience to save Joseph by his suggestion to sell him into permanent slavery instead of killing him.[54] Joseph is saved out of the pit in the wilderness but only in exchange for being sold into the pit of slavery in Egypt. While Reuben's pit symbolizes the ambiguity of grave and refuge, Judah here articulates explicitly the alternative of death (to kill) or slavery (to sell).[55] To be sure, the emphasis of Judah's words is still on the avoidance of killing rather than as an explicit attempt to justify the idea of subservience for survival.

Vicarious use by Judah (44.33-34). This desire to avoid death is reinforced by Joseph's later test of his brothers, which hinges on the threat of death to their father. The fragility of their father is the cornerstone of Judah's passionate plea to Joseph to release Benjamin. And Judah's sacrificial move to offer himself in exchange of Benjamin to avoid the death of his father is unquestionably exemplary. While the prospect of being enslaved may be awful to Judah, what he fears most is the prospect of bringing down the grey hairs of his father with sorrow to Sheol (44.31). Again, Judah's emphasis is on the avoidance of the death of his father. The notion of subservience for survival does not figure explicitly in his plea to Joseph. On the other hand, he probably would not resist it. On both occasions, it is his own initiative to opt for slavery in order to make possible the survival of Joseph and Jacob. Therefore, one can say

54.   Janzen, *Genesis 12–50*, p. 150, suggests that Judah's intention is to '"kill two birds with one stone"—get rid of Joseph and make a windfall profit'. However, Judah's suggestion of profit may be just an attempt to persuade the brothers to listen to him.

55.   Bush, *Notes on Genesis*, p. 234, comments, 'we imagine his [Judah] drift is mainly to intimate that it would be *better* to sell him than to slay him' (his italics).

that there is no change[56] in Judah's attitude towards the idea of the necessity of subservience for survival. He does not hesitate to apply it whenever a situation arises to demand it. Ironically, it is Judah who acts as an exemplar for the idea of subservience for survival in its vicious as well as vicarious manifestations.

Providential use interpreted by Joseph (45.4-8a). Judah's vicarious example is instrumental in Joseph's sudden discovery of the divinely providential nature of his past experience in the pit. It helps Joseph to reinterpret his past suffering as a similar sacrifice. His painful experience becomes meaningful to him. Reflecting on Judah's act of sacrifice, he concludes that God providentially has allowed him to be sold (or 'sent' in his new understanding) into slavery in order to save many lives. However, a subtle but significant change of emphasis occurs in Joseph's appropriation of Judah's example. Judah articulates and acts upon the alternative of death or slavery, while Reuben first hints at it when he allows the brothers to throw Joseph into a pit. It is in Joseph's repeated emphasis on survival, in terms of 'preserv[ing] life', 'a remnant on earth', 'keep[ing] alive for you many survivors' (45.5, 7), that the idea of subservience for survival appears explicitly for the first time. The shift occurs not only in terms of vocabulary; more significantly, the imposition of the awful choice of death or slavery is transformed by Joseph into the explicit justification of subservience for survival. The subservience, even in the form of slavery (as Joseph reflects on his own past), is accepted and tolerated in order to achieve survival. The difference between Judah's alternative of death or slavery and Joseph's justification of subservience for survival is small. They are in essence identical except in words. The change into positive terms is, however, not insignificant. Repeatedly emphasizing salvation and survival is one of the factors that help Joseph to win his audience's acceptance of his later claim of divine domination.

---

56. However, the brothers have changed in other aspects. Terence E. Fretheim, *Genesis* (The New Interpreter's Bible, 1; Nashville: Abingdon Press, 1994), p. 641, commends Judah's self-sacrifice: 'it stands in the narrative as a sign of the great change that has come over the brothers'; Sternberg, *The Poetics of Biblical Narrative*, p. 296, praises them for undergoing 'a surprising change for the better...the change of heart from fraternal enmity and vindictiveness to solidarity'; Ross, *Creation and Blessing*, p. 657, notes the 'changes in the brothers' which explains why 'the favoritism of Benjamin did not seem to pose a problem' for them.

Divine principle proclaimed by Joseph (45.8b-11). Once Joseph is inspired by Judah's vicarious example to understand his past pit of subservience as essential to the welfare of others, he eagerly proclaims the purpose of his dreams of domination by means of the similar rationale of enabling salvation for many. He transforms the notion of subservience for survival into the divine principle of domination for salvation and proclaims it as the ideal solution destined by God to overcome the famine. There is clearly a shift of emphasis from subservience to domination, from death to salvation, and from human device to divine decree, thus apparently altering the characteristics of subservience for survival. However, by tracing its development in this story, one has to acknowledge that Joseph's dreams of domination for salvation (as well as Judah's pit of death or slavery) are only mutations of the rationalization of 'subservience for survival'.

Pragmatic practice interpreted by some readers (47.13-26). The final concrete and full realization of the principle of subservience for survival could be none other than an unprecedented mass enslavement of the Egyptians in return for their extraordinary salvation. Joseph's relief policy provides a clear demonstration of the firm conviction of his new-found insight. Where else could one find such a succinct articulation of the notion of subservience for survival than in the gratitude of the Egyptians offered to Joseph: 'And they said, "You have saved our lives; may it please my lord, we will be slaves to Pharaoh"' (47.25).

However, one should not forget that it is also the desperate begging of the Egyptians to Joseph that best illustrates graphically the struggle between death and slavery:

> Why should we die before your eyes, both we and our land? Buy us and
> our land for food, and we with our land will be slaves to Pharaoh; and
> give us seed, that we may live, and not die, and that the land may not be
> desolate (47.19).

The Egyptians are clearly forced to give up their belongings one by one (money, herds, land and finally their bodies). They accept enslavement in the end but it is not without a struggle to hold on to their bodies and land as far as possible. They finally give in because they want to avoid imminent death and the desolation of their land. Therefore, the Egyptians want to avoid being enslaved as far as possible, but they never reject the notion of subservience for survival. Indeed, it is their own initiative to offer themselves as slaves to secure survival. Joseph gladly accepts it because it is wholly compatible with his belief. Therefore, he also could not be said to reject the hierarchical relationship and its underlying rationale, in principle in ch. 45 and in practice in ch. 47. Both his claim and his policy are based solidly on the principle of sub-servience for survival. The development of the idea of subservience for survival gains credence only in its faithful application in Joseph's policy of mass enslavement of the Egyptians.

Final submission of Joseph's brothers (50.15-18) and his reassertion of the rationale (50.20-21). Are the brothers convinced by Joseph's asser-tion of domination for salvation? Years ago, they plotted to annihilate the dreamer and his dreams (37.20). Will they finally acquiesce in Joseph's justification of his dreams? There is no immediate response from the brothers to Joseph's speech. Only after their father's death does the text provide a hint of their attitude towards Joseph's dreams of domination.

> When Joseph's brothers saw that their father was dead, they said, 'It may be that Joseph will hate us and pay us back for all the evil which we did to him.' So they sent a message to Joseph, saying, 'Your father gave this command before he died, "Say to Joseph, Forgive, I pray you, the trans-gression of your brothers and their sin, because they did evil to you." And now, we pray you, forgive the transgression of the servants of the God of your father.' Joseph wept when they spoke to him. His brothers also came and fell down before him, and said, 'Behold, we are your ser-vants [slaves]'[57] (50.15-18).

57. The semantic range of the Hebrew word עבדים includes the meaning of both 'servants' and 'slaves' in English. The word has been used by the brothers to address themselves as servants to the Egyptian vizier in a deferential manner (42.10, 11, 13). The two meanings of the same word occur together when Judah offers himself as a slave to the Egyptian vizier: 'Now therefore, let your servant (עבד), I pray you, remain instead of the lad as a slave (עבד) to my lord' (44.33; cf. 44.9, 16). Cf. Robert Alter, *Genesis: Translation and Commentary* (New York: W.W. Norton, 1996), p. 261. Surprisingly, RSV translates עבדים as 'servants' in 50.18, just as KJV does. In contrast, when the brothers and the Egyptians previously offer themselves as עבדים to Joseph, RSV always deviates from the rendering of 'servants' (normally in KJV) and translates it as 'slaves': 'And Judah said, "What shall we say to my lord? What shall we speak? Or how can we clear ourselves? God has found out the guilt of your servants [KJV 'servants']; behold, we are my lord's *slaves* [KJV 'servants'], both we and he also in whose hand the cup has been found." But he said, "Far be it from me that I should do so! Only the man in whose hand the cup was found shall be my *slave* [KJV 'servant']; but as for you, go up in

Offering themselves as slaves to Joseph is a complete reversal from
their original revolt against his dreams. One may then infer that it is a
sign of their change of attitude from initial resistance to final acquiescence in Joseph's domination. However, it is possible that the brothers'
earlier furious rejection of Joseph's dreams is not directed towards the
hierarchy of domination and subordination itself. They are rather
against Joseph's usurpation of the privilege of power normally
accorded to the eldest son.[58] The role of the patriarch, and in turn his
firstborn successor, who holds the responsibility to protect and save his
family together with the privilege to dominate it, is never questioned
but repeatedly demonstrated in this story.[59] For example, Jacob has
absolute power over his family. Without his permission, no one in the
family can take away his favourite son Benjamin even if it will endan-
ger the lives of all his family (43.8). Reuben the eldest son twice
attempts to assume the responsibility to protect the family members
without much success (37.21-22; 42.37).[60] However weak he is, at least

peace to your father' (44.16-17). "Why should we die before your eyes, both we
and our land? Buy us and our land for food, and we with our land will be *slaves*
[KJV 'servants'] to Pharaoh; and give us seed, that we may live, and not die, and
that the land may not be desolate." And they said, "You have saved our lives; may
it please my lord, we will be *slaves* [KJV 'servants'] to Pharaoh" ' (47.19, 25).

   Incidentally, KJV opts for the MT reading in 47.21 to describe Joseph's treatment
of the Egyptians as mass relocation ('As for the people, he removed them to cities
from one end of the borders of Egypt to the other end thereof'). RSV follows LXX
and the Samaritan text for mass enslavement ('and as for the people, he made slaves
of them from one end of Egypt to the other'). Kidner, *Genesis*, p. 211, suggests that
the reading of mass enslavement 'makes better sense in view of the people's own
declaration in vv. 19, 25 ("we will be slaves")'.

   58. While recognizing the brothers are incensed at the prospect that 'their little
brother' should rule over them, Westermann, *Joseph*, pp. 9-10, asserts that they, as
'nomads' at 'a time of patriarchs', question the very idea that brothers should lord it
over one another. However, he also recognizes the hierarchical structure in the
family, 'In the patriarchal period when groups of parts of the family were away
from the father, the eldest present took over the role of the father when it was necessary; he bore responsibility for this limited time. When the group returned home,
he had to answer the father's questions' (cf. *Genesis 37–50*, p. 41).

   59. Watt, 'Joseph's Dreams', pp. 63-64, suggests that, by sending Joseph out
'unprotected and defenseless' to face his hostile brothers, Jacob 'had broken the
rule on which patriarchal families are founded, namely, that the head of the family,
the father, secures safety and protection for all other members of the family'.

   60. Morris, *The Genesis Record*, p. 541, describes Judah's effort to rescue

he claims to have authority over the life or death of his own two sons
(42.37).[61] As for Judah and Joseph, it is obvious that in this story they
are competing with each other to replace Reuben as successor to Jacob
as patriarchal head of the family. It is significant that the text describes
how they both act or promise to provide for the 'little ones' in this family (43.8; 50.21).

The privilege of domination with the obligation of provision is com-
monplace in patriarchal society. Therefore, it is Joseph's usurpation of
the firstborn privilege of domination in the family,[62] rather than the
hierarchical structure or the rationale of subservience for survival
behind it, that provokes the brothers' opposition. His claim of domination for salvation is only a reassertion of a prevalent ideology already
shared by his brothers.[63] What is new in his dreams of domination is

Joseph from the brothers: '[he] tried henceforth as best he could under the circumstances to exercise the moral leadership which his firstborn position in the family
should have elicited'.

61. Instead of taking Reuben's appeal as 'a mere index of recklessness', Sternberg, *The Poetics of Biblical Narrative*, p. 299, considers his effort as an 'indirect
father-to-father approach: "My two sons thou mayest kill if I do not bring him to
thee." '

62. Lerner, 'Joseph the Unrighteous', p. 279, suggests a similar reason: 'Isaac
and Jacob before him had been selected as the sole inheritors over their brothers and
Joseph's brothers must have suspected that he was preparing to follow suit by
usurping their collective succession of Jacob.' Greenspahn, *When Brothers Dwell
Together*, discusses the surprising preference for younger siblings in biblical stories. He argues that 'primogeniture may not be as ancient or as universal a human
practice as is commonly supposed'. And he concludes that, in Israelite practice,
'property was typically divided among a decedent's heirs, most often his sons.
Although one child may have been treated preferentially, that choice was left
largely in the hands of the incumbent, whose decision need not have been based on
age. Royal succession proceeded similarly, with no evidence of any rigidly automatic system' (p. 82).

63. Similarly, the brothers may already vaguely share the idea of the hand of
God behind and through human events well before Joseph's disclosure. They
acknowledge God's actions when they discover the silver in their sack (42.28), and
when they are confronted with the theft of the silver cup (43.16). Comparing the
Joseph-narrative with the earlier parts of Genesis, Skinner, *Genesis*, p. 487,
remarks, 'The profoundly religious conviction which recognises the hand of God,
not merely in miraculous interventions, but in the working out the divine ends
through human agency and what we call secondary causes, is characteristic of the
Joseph-narrative amongst the legends of Genesis.' Joseph's speech of divine providence, however, articulates this conviction explicitly. Joseph also asserts that God

that the younger son not only rules over his elder brothers, but that the patriarch should bow down before him too (37.10).

After Jacob's death, the brothers fear for their lives.[64] To avert possible retaliation from Joseph, they again accept subordination (in the form of slavery) to their younger brother (50.18). Evidently, there is no change of attitude towards the imposition of death or slavery. Their final act of opting for slavery only reiterates the same rationale underlying their original crime of selling Joseph into slavery: to avoid death at all cost. The retribution is complete at the end of the story. The victimizers become the victims of their imposition of death or slavery. The ironic reversal, once imposed on Judah (44.33-34) alone, now repeats itself on the brothers as a whole.

Fretheim, having detected the brothers' consistent belief in the hierarchical relationship, comments, 'the brothers still fear Joseph; they still stand in a lord/servant relationship with Joseph, in fact, they seek to perpetuate it [in 50.15-18]'.[65] He has an opposite assessment of Joseph's attitude towards hierarchical relationship. He admits that Joseph 'appears paternalistic' in ch. 45 because, initially, he 'calls himself a brother (v. 4), but father/lord/ruler language finally predominates (vv. 8-9, 13; cf. v. 26)' in his speech.[66] Based on Joseph's rejection of Judah's offer to be his slave, he concludes that Joseph rejects 'any hierarchical relationship among the brothers':

> There [in 50.15-21] Joseph will reject the ruler/slave image. The dream
> of 37.7 was earlier realized, without the brothers' knowledge (do they

overrules human evil to bring about his good purpose. This is probably an aspect of divine providence that is novel to the brothers who consistently perceive God's hand mainly in chasing their past crime.

64. A similar threat of fratricide occurs when Esau plans to avenge his brother's wrong after their father's death (27.41). Or the revenge they fear is simply slavery in a foreign land as they once imposed on Joseph. Such an ending is as good as death; Alter, *Art of Biblical Narrative*, p. 165, delineates the brothers' thought quite reasonably: 'having sent Joseph southward to a distant slave-market, the brothers might properly think him gone forever, as good as dead, or perhaps after all these years of grinding servitude, dead in fact'. Furthermore, Judah finally declares Joseph's death (44.20) after the repeated references to Joseph's absence as 'no more' (42.13, 32, 36), a possible euphemism for death in Alter's opinion.

65. Fretheim, *Genesis*, p. 643.

66. Fretheim, *Genesis*, p. 643, also notes that Joseph's 'directives to the brothers abound'.

now realize it?), but the images of that dream must not be allowed to shape their ongoing life together.[67]

To interpret Joseph's refusal to retaliate as a blank rejection of the hierarchical relationship is a dubious inference.[68] It is not in harmony with the excitement Joseph expresses in the realization of his dreams of becoming father, lord and ruler. More importantly, if Joseph really rejects 'the ruler/slave image' of his dreams, it is difficult to explain why he would help to turn the Egyptian society into such a steep hierarchical order.[69] In apparent inconsistency, Fretheim later acknowledges that Joseph's 'policy [on the Egyptians] results in a concentration of property and power in the crown'. He even faults Joseph 'for having insufficient vision, especially in making his emergency measures

67. Fretheim, *Genesis*, pp. 641, 643.

68. Fretheim, *Genesis*, pp. 671-72, takes Joseph's 'rebuke and reassurance: "[Fear not!] Am I in the place of God?"' as having 'a double reference—to their request for forgiveness and to their offer to become slaves'. 'Joseph is not God... He remains subject to God as the brothers are; they stand together under the authority of a divine other.' Thus Fretheim explains Joseph's intention to leave everything 'up to God' to avoid any hierarchical relationship among the brothers. Following Hugh C. White's suggestion that a confession of sin would establish spiritual inferiority in the forgiven (*Narration and Discourse*, p. 267), Fretheim considers that a word of forgiveness in this context will run the risk to 'initiate or maintain a hierarchical relationship' and will destroy the status of 'moral equals' among all parties in this dispute (p. 673 n. 227). In contrast, Wildavsky, *Assimilation versus Separation*, p. 156, asserts, 'Joseph rejects the offer to make him formally the master of his brothers without necessarily rejecting the substance of mastery.' His argument is that Joseph uses the formula 'fear not' (50.19, 21), a phrase used by God to reassure the patriarchs Abram, Isaac and Jacob (cf. 15.1; 26.24; 46.3), in addressing his brothers. Even Joseph's assertion—'I will sustain you' (50.21)—is seen as a sign that 'his drive for power is as strong as ever'. Holbert, *The Storyteller's Companion to the Bible*, p. 195, criticizes Joseph's reassurance from the brothers' perspective: 'as far as they have seen, Joseph's power and manipulation of their lives has been nearly god-like. And, they might ask, how can we not be afraid in the face of this still mysterious brother?'

69. Wildavsky, *Assimilation versus Separation*, p. 145, comments on Joseph's social restructuring, 'From an inclusive hierarchy in which landowning peasants were part of a system of reciprocal obligations, Egyptian society became an exclusive hierarchy in which only a few were deemed worthy and the rest were subjugated.'

permanent "to this day" (v. 26)'.[70] But he defends Joseph's 'harsh measures' on the basis of emergency:

> The people of God who are here engaged in seeking to alleviate the devastating effects of the famine on people who stand outside of their own community, by working in and through a variety of governmental structures. Their methods may not be a model of perfection, but taking the opinions of the hurting people themselves into account, they enter into the fray on behalf of life rather than death.[71]

Joseph's policy on the Egyptians is further excused because it is a case of the people of God seeking the benefit of those who stand outside of their own community. While recognizing the ironic parallel[72] between Joseph's enslavement of the Egyptians with the Israelites later bondage in Egypt, Fretheim insists that 'the imperfect structures' can be tolerated:

> There may be some irony in that, as Joseph makes 'slaves' of the Egyptians (though not to himself), so the later pharaohs—who do not have the wisdom and commitments of Joseph—will make 'slaves' of his family. While we cannot be certain, this reversal raises the question whether later pharaohs extend Joseph's economic policy to include the Israelites. Any governmental policy can be twisted in such a way as to become demonic. Yet, that must not be allowed to immobilize people in their efforts to work for life in and through imperfect structures.[73]

Joseph's economic policy is an 'imperfect structure', but Fretheim seems to suggest that it becomes 'demonic' only when it includes the Israelites. Now it becomes clear to the reader that Joseph does not reject

---

70. Fretheim, *Genesis*, p. 654. Hurowitz, 'Joseph's Enslavement of the Egyptians (Genesis 47.13-26) in Light of Famine Texts From Mesopotamia', p. 360, also considers that 'the biblical story portrays the enslavement as permanent'. However, Wenham, *Genesis 16–50*, p. 452, blames Pharaoh rather than Joseph for retaining 'the land and people as his serfs in perpetuity' and compares it unfavourably to the Israelite law of returning to the destitute their land or freedom in the year of Jubilee.

71. Fretheim, *Genesis*, p. 655.

72. Quoting Ginzberg's accusation to Joseph's brothers: 'Because ye have sold Joseph to be a slave, therefore ye say year after year, slaves were we unto Pharaoh in Egypt' (*The Legends of the Jews*, p. 17), Wildavsky, *Assimilation versus Separation*, p. 15 n. 28, directs the parallel against Joseph instead, 'May we not ask, however, with equal conviction, when we know better the story of Joseph the administrator, whether the Egyptians were better able to enslave the Hebrews because Joseph helped so mightily to enslave the Egyptians to Pharaoh?'

73. Fretheim, *Genesis*, p. 655.

'any hierarchical relationship' in Fretheim's view. It is the hierarchical relationship 'among the brothers'[74] that is rejected. Furthermore, since 'to work for life' is of paramount importance, he argues strongly for rather than against Joseph's rationale behind the mass enslavement. Fretheim's position is vulnerable and he has to face the criticism of a double standard, like the following one from Wildavsky: 'Are serfdom and forced deportations morally acceptable because they involve foreigners?'[75] Wildavsky has no hesitation in condemning both Joseph's measures and their rationale: 'Joseph should not have done to the Egyptians what Israelites ought not to do to one another [i.e. enslavement and forced deportation]'; 'these measures raise the question of whether the moral law may be violated in the name of survival'.[76] However, he also admits the equivocality of the moral law:

> In biblical times, Israelites were both strangers (in other countries) and natives (in their own). They ruled other peoples in their own land while being ruled by others abroad. They were also masters who held slaves (usually but not always foreigners) and slaves of foreigners who took them into captivity. The Joseph stories are set in Egypt where, in Moses' time, the Hebrew people became slaves to Pharaoh. It would not be so easy, therefore, for Israelites to write unequivocal rules about how natives and strangers, slaves and masters, should be treated. While the Torah forbids Israelites to make slaves of their own people (Lev. 25.39-40), it does permit them to own foreigners as slaves and, under conditions of dire poverty, to sell themselves into slavery to their own people.[77]

If the rules are unequivocal, how can Wildavsky's condemnation of Joseph be so forceful? Indeed, it is not clear which aspect of the moral law Wildavsky thinks Joseph has violated. The moral law, which he refers to, just happens to allow the Israelites to do to strangers what Israelites ought not to do to one another (i.e. 'to own foreigners as slaves'), even without the conditions of dire poverty! To be accurate, Joseph himself does not own any foreigners as slaves. He only permits them to sell themselves into slavery, 'in the name of survival', to their

74. Fretheim, *Genesis*, p. 641.
75. Wildavsky, *Assimilation versus Separation*, p. 7.
76. Wildavsky, *Assimilation versus Separation*, p. 144.
77. Wildavsky, *Assimilation versus Separation*, p. 216. He immediately mentions the stipulation of setting free the slaves after a certain time, but does not use it as a reason against Joseph as Fretheim does.

own ruler Pharaoh. Strictly speaking, Joseph can lawfully own his brothers as slaves, not in retaliation but due to dire poverty.[78] The moral law, which Wildavsky quotes, clearly sanctions both Joseph's enslavement of the Egyptians and the rationale behind it.

Joseph refrains from enslaving his brothers but he does not reject the subordination symbolized by their repeated 'bowing down' before him. Furthermore, he clearly appeals to divine authority to justify his dreams of domination over his brothers in order to secure their survival. This contradicts Fretheim's assertion that Joseph rejects 'any hierarchical relationship among the brothers' because Joseph and the brothers 'all stand together under the authority of a divine other'.[79] As far as Joseph's claim of domination is concerned, it is more reasonable to infer that divine authority sustains rather than suspends the hierarchical relationship.

Pragmatic Attitude Towards the Rationale of Subservience for Survival
As shown in the above survey, the brothers, Joseph and the Egyptians, all initially resist strongly the prospect of subservience (or slavery). One way or the other, they acquiesce in the necessity of the pit (or the dreams). The story hides nothing about the bowing down of the brothers, the enslavement of the Egyptians and their accompanying painful struggle. The misfortune of Joseph as a slave and his lingering agony about his past are dramatically detailed in this story. In spite of his tolerable condition under his benevolent masters, his incredible success does not lessen his pain.

Despite all the pain involved, the characters always opt for subservience for survival. It is repeatedly manifested in various guises: Reuben employs it as a strategic means for saving Joseph; Judah applies it to Joseph and to himself; Joseph discovers its providential nature in his pit and his dreams; and the Egyptians initiate the offer of slavery for survival. Joseph's response to the offers of subservience is twofold: in the case of Judah's petition, he formally adopts the idea to explain the divine purpose of his own pit and his own dreams; to the begging of the Egyptians, he simply puts into practice what he seems to

78. Similarly, if Joseph already adopted Egypt as his home country, the moral law still permits him to carry out the same policy to his 'fellow countrymen' under conditions of dire poverty.

79. Fretheim, *Genesis*, pp. 641, 671-72.

believe to be a justified principle without any sign of hesitation. Finally, at the end of the story, the brothers collectively bow down before Joseph to acquiesce in the necessity of their subservience and in response Joseph reaffirms his provision for their survival. Therefore, all the characters are forced into subservience one way or another, but the notion of subservience itself is never repudiated by any of the characters. In fact, it is never contested either in principle or in practice. The characters oppose only the pits and the dreams, but not the rationale behind them. They consistently exhibit a pragmatic attitude to the idea of subservience for survival. There is no change of attitude towards it during the course of the whole story. The characters never find their subservience amiable, but they certainly reckon it admissible as a better alternative than death. Therefore, the story demonstrates that it is possible for one to abhor the pit while endorsing the ideology behind it. Rejecting the pit but not the rationale behind it, the characters in this story are, unfortunately, blind to the cause of their predicament.

Joseph's Declaration of Domination over Egypt
All characters in the story may indeed see the subservience for survival proposition as pragmatic, yet Joseph sees it as ideal, not only in the pit of providence but also in more acceptable terms in his declaration of his dreams of domination over Egypt:

> So it was not you who sent me here, but God; and he has made me a father to Pharaoh, and lord of all his house and ruler over all the land of Egypt…God has made me lord of all Egypt…and there I will provide for you…lest you and your household, and all that you have, come to poverty (45.8-11).

Since Joseph knows the famine will be long and severe, when he declares that he is destined to rule over Egypt, sooner or later, he as well as the readers know that the exact nature of his domination is the enslavement of the Egyptian people. Events in ch. 47 may follow ch. 45 as a further development of the plot by the narrator to prove that the Egyptian enslavement is a logical consequence of Joseph's claim of divine domination over them. Significantly, it is by Joseph's own confession that the link between his claim of domination and his policy of mass enslavement is established. Therefore, his policy on the Egyptians is a derivation, rather than a deviation, from his claim of domination. One could not really condemn his policy on the Egyptians without also examining the validity of his claim.

It is one thing to accept the subservience for survival pragmatically, it is another matter to promote it wholeheartedly. This is what Joseph does in declaring his dreams as divinely sanctioned domination over Egypt. The consequence of this conviction is enormous: it makes it possible for one to have the will power to carry out enslavement on such a grand scale as making a whole nation into slaves. The juxtaposition of the horror of such a mass enslavement and the painful fate Joseph has suffered as an individual slave is striking. The mass enslavement, executed by this suffering slave, is surely a supreme 'ironic twist' of events of this story, as Sailhamer succinctly remarks:

> The whole story of Joseph and his brothers began with Joseph being sold (37.28) into slavery (39.17) for twenty pieces of silver (37.28). Now, at the conclusion, Joseph sells (47.20) the whole land of Egypt into slavery (vv. 19, 25) and takes 'all the silver in the land' (v. 18).[80]

How is such a shocking ending possible? Is it a classic example of subtle displacement of anger? Joseph could not direct his revenge against his brothers. Is it possible that foreigners somehow became the victims of his past torment?

It is by no means fortuitous that the divine domination proclaimed by Joseph is repeatedly said to be over the Egyptians rather than over his brothers as originally envisaged in his dreams. While he reveals himself to the brothers in a highly emotional state, he remains cautious over announcing his domination by hurriedly ordering all the Egyptian servants out of his court. He certainly does not want the Egyptians to overhear his proud claim of ruling over them. The brothers are no longer the subjects of his claim of domination and the Egyptians are physically expelled; Joseph's effort to avoid expressing the emphasis of subservience to them is evident.[81] He carefully avoids mentioning any negative aspects of his dreams to his brothers. He is silent about their subservience pictured as 'bowing down' in his dreams. It is certainly a deliberate move in order not to antagonize them as he has done at the

80. Sailhamer, *Pentateuch as Narrative*, pp. 227-28.

81. Von Rad, *Genesis*, p. 398, gives a different reason for the expulsion: 'Joseph had all strangers leave the room, not primarily because he did not want to show himself before his retinue in such an emotional state, and not primarily so as not to embarrass his brothers before the Egyptians, but rather because something had to be done which concerned only him and his brothers for which they had to be quite alone.'

beginning of the story.[82] Instead, he repeatedly emphasizes the glory of being made a lord, not over them but over Egypt. Lowenthal notices this subtle avoidance:

> It seems that by calling himself 'ruler over all Egypt' Joseph intimates with a smile that his dream did not mean what *they* had thought, to wit, that he wanted to become *their* 'ruler' (cf. 37.8), but that God would make him *Egypt's* ruler.[83]

It seems to be more acceptable to dominate other people than his own brothers. However, the narrator's description of the Egyptians' expulsion and Joseph's manoeuvre to avoid any reference to his brothers' subservient role in his domination can only heighten our awareness of the fate of their subservience.

Instead of focusing on the 'bowing down' of the brothers, Joseph directs their attention (as well as the readers') to his domination over the Egyptians. This is a precarious manoeuvre. It prompts one to ask again, 'Are Joseph's dreams of his brothers bowing down before him qualitatively different from Judah's pit of slavery inflicted on Joseph?' Admittedly, the motif of 'bowing down' by no means equals slavery. Joseph does not make the brothers slaves in the end (50.18). Their 'bowing down' apparently symbolizes a kind of subservience less severe than real slavery.[84] From this perspective, Joseph's dreams and Judah's pit are in no way the same, but the question may be rephrased

82. Some readers condemn his reporting of his dreams to his brothers as unwise and presumptuous. See Chapter 4, footnote 17.

83. Lowenthal, *The Joseph Narrative in Genesis*, pp. 104-105 (his italics). In contrast, Brueggemann, *Genesis*, p. 346, has a slightly different emphasis on Joseph's word of lording it over Egypt, and comments, 'Now he is a "ruler-lord-father", not *just* over the family, but over the empire' (my italics).

84. There are differences in the severity of subservience between the brothers' bowing down, the Egyptians' slavery in their own land, and Joseph's slavery in a foreign land. But on a closer look at Joseph's own experience as a slave, one cannot be sure that the nature of severity of subservience is the primary issue. Joseph's extraordinary experiences as a favoured slave both in Potiphar's house and the prison are far better than most ordinary slaves'. Schimmel, 'Joseph and his Brothers', p. 65, comments on Joseph's slavery experience: 'objectively speaking, it is true that Joseph's experiences in Egypt, though having their bad moments, are, according to the tone of the Biblical text, not excessively unpleasant or degrading, even during the period of his slavery and captivity'. However, this does not prevent him declaring unambiguously that his past slavery is evil.

more precisely by stating explicitly the purpose of salvation and the means to achieve it in both the dreams and the pit, 'Are Joseph's dreams of domination for salvation qualitatively different from Judah's pit of slavery for survival?' This question then reveals the same rationale behind the dreams and the pit.

More importantly, Joseph's avoidance of mentioning the brothers' subservience in his speech displaces his domination over the Egyptians. Even to the Egyptians, Joseph's declaration of domination also suppresses the motif of bowing down. Only later in ch. 47 does this motif of subservience appear, even in the form of slavery. If one treats the motif of 'bowing down' as referring only to subservience as a servant (a less harsh degree of subservience), one cannot dismiss the real enslavement of the Egyptians, no matter how benevolently it is carried out. In addition, he contrasts his present domination with his past slavery in his speech. It is then reasonable to see that Joseph's domination points beyond subservience to servitude. Judah's imposition of death or slavery on Joseph is no longer opposed to Joseph's dreams of domination over his brothers. It is rather opposed to his dreams of domination over the Egyptians. The similarities between them are striking. Both suffer real slavery in order to avoid the threat of death. Therefore, it is not unfair to compare the pit of slavery Joseph suffers at the hand of his brothers and his dreams of domination when he delights over the Egyptians. Joseph's attempt to avoid offending his brothers becomes an indictment of his domination, because it reveals its true meaning, that is, slavery.

Joseph's Ignorance of the Ironic Reversal of Judah's Role

How does one challenge Joseph's claim of domination for survival in his disclosure speech? To relate it to his later policy on Egyptian enslavement is one way to caution readers to think harder whether his claim is to be treated as acceptable. It is also important to examine the circumstance in which he learns the idea of subservience for survival from Judah's example. It will reveal that he is actually mistaking an inexcusable rationale for a profound truth.

It is not by chance that it is Judah who comes forward to plead for Benjamin before Joseph. He was the one who was responsible for suggesting enslavement for Joseph. The evil of the brothers is best represented by his role, which is set up at the beginning of the conflict, and requires confrontation at the end of the story.[85] Joseph's test is designed to confront their past treachery. Judah, acting for the brothers, now acknowledges their guilt and offers them to be slaves to Joseph (44.16). Instead of accepting their offer, Joseph presents them with the ultimate test by setting free all of them except Benjamin 'in whose hand the cup was found' (44.17). Ackerman suggests that Joseph 'places the brothers in a position of having to choose whether or not to repeat their crime of Genesis 37'. He comments, 'Will yet another favored brother be sacrificed, escalating the danger to the life of Jacob?'[86] Facing the prospect of the enslavement of Benjamin and the certain death of his father, Judah responds by offering to take the place of Benjamin to avoid the death of his father:

> Now therefore, let your servant, I pray you, remain instead of the lad as a slave to my lord and let the lad go back with his brothers. 34 For how can I go back to my father if the lad is not with me? I fear to see the evil that would come upon my father (44.33-34).

He who once suggested slavery for his brother (37.26-27) now proposes slavery for himself. The ironic reversal is well recognized by many readers.[87] It is also important to note that Judah's vicarious virtue

85. John H. Sailhamer, *Genesis* (The Expositor's Bible Commentary, 2; Grand Rapids: Zondervan, 1990), p. 245, points out that the plot of this narrative 'was woven around the interplay between Joseph and Judah'. Significantly, he contrasts Joseph's role in creating 'the conflict and tension [i.e. through his dreams and test] throughout the narrative' with that of Judah 'who resolved the conflict' in the end.

86. Ackerman, 'Joseph, Judah, and Jacob', p. 98.

87. Cf. Sternberg, *The Poetics of Biblical Narrative*, p. 308, who remarks, 'the initiator of the sale of the first favorite into slavery should enslave himself to set the second free'; Ackerman, 'Joseph, Judah, and Jacob', p. 89, comments, 'While in prison, the brothers must decide which one will return to tell Jacob that nine more of his sons have been taken and that Benjamin must also come down to Egypt; they realize that Jacob will hold back. Desolately, the brothers in the prison/pit contemplate the prospect of death or slavery—just as Joseph had earlier sat in their pit awaiting death. He is meting out, measure for measure, what he had suffered in the past. The outburst of "measure for measure" activity soon ends.' For similar remarks on this ironic reversal, see also Ernest Neufeld, 'The Anatomy of the Joseph Cycle', *Jewish Bible Quarterly* 22 (1994), pp. 38-46 (44); Alter, *Art of Biblical Narrative*, p. 175; Lois Feuer, 'Happy Families: Repentance and Restoration in *The Tempest* and the Joseph Narrative', *Philological Quarterly* 76.3 (1997), pp. 271-87 (275).

in giving himself up for the well-being of his brother and father results from the same act that chastises his past vicious crime.[88]

Is it Joseph's intention to turn Judah from a victimizer to a victim of his own rationalization? Is he ever aware of such a reversal? His test at first sight seems to serve not only as a confrontation of Judah's crime but also as a condemnation of its underlying rationalization to choose slavery rather than death. However, this postulation of Joseph's intention becomes suspect, especially in the light of what he is going to do to the Egyptians. There are a number of reasons to suggest that Joseph never intends to question Judah's rationalization. First, Joseph does not know what has been discussed among the brothers. He is certainly ignorant of Reuben's speech and his secret intention to rescue him when he is still afar off from them (v. 18). He is already in the pit when Judah speaks to the brothers, so he is unable to know of Judah's suggestion and its rationalization of exchanging slavery for death. Later we are told that Joseph had pleaded with them in vain (42.21), but we do not know whether they tell him anything about their intention. Joseph in the pit may not be certain of what his brothers are going to do with him. Is he aware of their intention to kill him? If he is, indeed, stolen by the Midianites,[89] he may not even be aware of their intention to sell him. Whatever happens at that moment, the fact that he ends up being carried away into slavery is certain to him. He will surely hold them responsible for his plight.

Secondly, Joseph's test in detaining Benjamin may entail both his enslavement *and* Jacob's death. It is not exactly the dreadful choice, of death *or* slavery, which Judah has inflicted on Joseph. Judah repeatedly stresses that Benjamin cannot leave Jacob (44.22, 29) and Jacob's life is bound up in the lad's life (v. 30). Their fate becomes inseparable and the enslavement of Benjamin 'would most certainly mean the death of Jacob'.[90] The test is thus not structured on the alternative of slavery or

88. At the same time, the concern for their father forces the brothers to accept the paternal favouritism upon Benjamin and Joseph. Redford, *Biblical Story of Joseph*, p. 73, thus comments, 'Joseph effects a situation which parallels his own abduction: Benjamin is to be left alone in his elder brothers' power for a considerable time. Like Joseph, Benjamin is his father's favorite, and the brothers have as much reason to envy him as Joseph. How will they treat him?'

89. See footnote 109.

90. Maurice Samuel, 'The True Character of the Biblical Joseph', *BR* 2.1 (1986), pp. 38-51, 68 (50). Ackerman, 'Joseph, Judah, and Jacob', p. 106, suggests

2. *Joseph's Claim of Divine Domination* 91

death. However, once Judah comes forward to offer to be enslaved to avoid the death of his father, the awful alternative he has imposed on Joseph reappears. The reversal of Judah's role as a victimizer to becoming a victim of his own rationalization becomes evident.

Thirdly, it could not be possible for Joseph to anticipate (or manipulate) Judah's response in this precise way. Therefore, it is unlikely that he devises his test to solicit a reversal to condemn Judah's rationalization. His motive may be a revenge, an attempt to help the brothers to face up to their past crime, or a mixture of these. The test is then devised to condemn the crime of enslavement but not the rationale behind it. Even though Joseph never means to condemn Judah's rationalization, the result is the same. His test does create a reversal of Judah's role from a victimizer to becoming a victim of his own device. The poetic justice, which the narrator presents to us, does not necessarily require awareness of it by the characters involved. It is probably a manoeuvre intended by the narrator to condemn Judah's rationalization behind his crime.

Therefore, the ironic reversal is the result rather than the aim of Joseph's test. He does not consciously participate in the narrator's plot to denounce the false imposition of the alternative of death or slavery. Ironically, drawing insights from such a false alternative, Joseph interprets his past suffering in the pit as well his dreams. Accepting Judah's response as a sign of repentance (44.33-34), he reveals himself and immediately explains that his past slavery has been sent by God to save his family (45.5-8a). It is reasonable to infer that Judah's sacrificial model of trading one's own freedom for that of others helps Joseph to unlock the mystery of his suffering.[91] Since Judah's response is beyond Joseph's control, it is this element of unexpectedness that creates a sense of genuine recognition, on Joseph's part, of the necessity of his suffering for others too.[92] His journey of bondage, starting at the pit, suddenly becomes meaningful and useful. The pit, which functions as slavery and salvation in this narrative, is seen as a paradox.[93] Joseph's

that 'perhaps Joseph did not realize what additional grief to his father his test of the brothers would cause'.

91. Fretheim, *Genesis*, p. 641, suggests that 'Joseph's theological interpretation of events builds upon Judah's confession.'

92. Miscall, 'The Jacob and Joseph Stories as Analogies', p. 31, points out that Joseph genuinely believes in his claims.

93. Seybold, 'Paradox and Symmetry', p. 72.

subsequent explanation of his mission to rule over others (45.8b-11) is inspired by his new understanding of the paradox of his misery in God's plan. The paradox of the pit is accepted as necessary for survival; Joseph immediately asserts the necessity of his dreams of domination for the same reason. Both the pit and the dreams share the same idea of subservience for survival but with a critical difference: the pit is paradoxical that human evil crime is overridden for divine purpose, while the dreams assume a different characterization as divine good destiny[94] for Joseph who is the agent in God's plan. Thus there is a shift from a paradox of the pit of slavery to a paradigm of the dreams of lordship in Joseph's disclosure speech (45.5-11).

Joseph offers the purpose of salvation as the reason for his dreams of domination. However, the emphasis on the purpose of salvation is not good enough because Judah once used the same rationale to spare Joseph's life by selling him into slavery. What he finds a wonderful idea (of subservience for survival) is in fact depicted by the narrator in the very beginning of this story as nothing but a reprehensible excuse by Judah (37.26-27). It once eased the brothers' conscience over committing the hideous crime of selling their own brother into slavery by pretending that they wanted to avoid fratricide. Now the same excuse is again used by Joseph to ease the brothers' conscience for the same crime in the name of survival of the whole family. As a result, the victim of Judah's vicious action becomes the permanent captive of the victimizer's ideology through adopting on his vicarious action as a model (44.33-34) without knowing his previous excuse. The consequence of this delusion is twofold: Judah's rationale becomes the foundation for Joseph to interpret God's intentions for his suffering in the pit and dreams of domination; the subsequent enslavement of the Egyptians seems to be inevitable once Judah's rationale is sanctioned rather than condemned. In the light of this, there is neither contradiction in Joseph's belief nor inconsistency between his belief and his behaviour. He is convinced that God has sent him into slavery in order to save lives. He also truly believes in the necessity of lording it over others to save their lives.

It is apparently harmless for Joseph to consider his suffering in the pit as a self-sacrifice that ultimately brings salvation for others. However, Fretheim suggests that there is a potential danger in the act of self-

---

94. Cf. Alter, *Art of Biblical Narrative*, p. 139; Turner, *Announcements of Plot in Genesis*, p. 166; Ackerman, 'Joseph, Judah, and Jacob', pp. 98-99.

sacrifice. Commenting on Joseph's rejection of Judah's offer to take Benjamin's place, he remarks, 'Joseph recognizes that self-sacrifice is not necessarily a good thing, not least because it can be used in abusive ways to promote the elevation of one person over another.'[95] It is true that Joseph declines the offer, but it is incorrect to infer that he rejects the spirit of the self-sacrifice. In retrospect, Joseph actually accepts his past suffering as a sacrifice destined by God to a good purpose (45.5-8a). But Fretheim accurately points out that the idea of self-sacrifice may lead to promoting hierarchical power, and it is indeed fully realized in Joseph's subsequent claim (and administration) of domination over Egypt (45.8b-11; 47.13-26). There is a sudden shift of emphasis from a paradox of his suffering in the pit to a paradigm of domination in Joseph's disclosure speech. But the shift is not simply a case of mistaking a paradox for a paradigm. Neither is it simply a situation in which Joseph exploits his self-sacrifice in abusive ways to promote his domination. As noted at the beginning of this chapter, Joseph presents the pit and the dreams in a way that the paradox of self-sacrifice already harbours the necessity of the subsequent domination. Without his rise to power, his suffering in the pit is pointless because it will not help him to save lives. There will be nothing paradoxical about it. Therefore, the shift from paradox to paradigm is inevitable if one ever accepts Joseph's explanation of the good purpose of his suffering. Since it is difficult to be critical of Joseph's past suffering, any appreciation of its nature as good, providential, or paradoxical, is already trapped into accepting the 'pit-dreams' sequence which Joseph presents so skilfully.

Joseph's strategy is extremely effective in persuading many of his audience to accept the purpose of salvation of his misery (45.5-8a) and mission (45.8b-11). Is he aware of his own strategy? He is probably not because he even convinces himself of the necessity of subservience for survival, and acts accordingly—as seen in his policy of the enslavement of the Egyptians. The story comes to an ironic reversal when Joseph's test forces Judah to exchange his subservience for the survival of his father. It repeats the identical false alternative that Judah has inflicted on his brother. The effect of the test as a condemnation of Judah's excuse is clear. However, Joseph is not aware of it and his ignorance leads to his perpetration of Judah's excuse with tragic consequence—the enslavement of a whole nation.[96]

95. Fretheim, *Genesis*, p. 641.
96. Redford, *Biblical Story of Joseph*, pp. 73-74, notices another error Joseph

Desperate Compromise versus Deliberate Positive Move

Comparing Reuben's action with Joseph's portrait of God is another effective way to bring into doubt Joseph's justification of domination. In this story, Redford identifies two versions of a 'good brother' who attempts to save Joseph. He suggests that the Judah version is an 'expansion' of a pre-existent Reuben version.[97] Coats accepts Redford's observation that Reuben's role is morally superior to Judah's, but rejects the assumption that a good story could not have two 'good' brothers. He considers that the two roles add to the tension of the plot by their contrast.[98] Some readers are highly critical of Reuben's behaviour too. Their criticisms are twofold: he is criticized for lacking the moral courage to confront the brothers' evil;[99] and his futile attempt to restore Joseph to his father is thwarted by Judah's suggestion.[100] Thus he is judged morally weak and strategically ineffective.[101] His

perpetrates in his test, 'The end result of Joseph's contrived situation is to be identical with his own experience: Benjamin is to be enslaved, and in order to bring this about Joseph has his cup "planted" in the boy's sack. By thus falsifying evidence Joseph has committed the same violation as that perpetrated by his brothers with his coat!'

97. Redford, *Biblical Story of Joseph*, pp. 139-48. For a detailed discussion of this complex problem, see also White, 'Reuben and Judah', pp. 73-97; Edward L. Greenstein, 'An Equivocal Reading of the Sale of Joseph', in Gros Louis and Ackerman (eds.), *Literary Interpretations of Biblical Narratives*, pp. 114-25; Coats, *From Canaan to Egypt*, pp. 60-74; von Rad, *Genesis*, p. 353; Wenham, *Genesis 16–50*, pp. 354-55.

98. Coats, *From Canaan to Egypt*, p. 69.

99. Cf. Morris, *The Genesis Record*, p. 542, who criticizes Reuben for failing to exercise, in his position as the eldest son, 'overt moral leadership' to prevent the brothers from harming Joseph; Brueggemann, *Genesis*, p. 304, calls him 'a responsible coward'.

100. If Joseph is stolen by the Midianite traders from the pit to be sold to the Ishmaelites without the presence of the brothers, then Judah's plan to sell Joseph for money is as unsuccessful as that of Reuben (37.28).

101. Cf. Alter, *Art of Biblical Narrative*, p. 170, who calls him 'the man of impulse who violated his father's concubine and who has made a blundering attempt to save Joseph'; Sternberg, *The Poetics of Biblical Narrative*, p. 296, labels Reuben as a 'well-meaning but ineffective leader and spokesman'; Ackerman, 'Joseph, Judah, and Jacob', p. 101, details Reuben's goodness as ineffective in chs. 37 and 42.

intention to save Joseph may not arise from a truly altruistic motive.[102] Judging from his response to Joseph's disappearance, he seems more concerned about his own difficulty in reporting to his father than about Joseph's fate.[103] Nevertheless, Joseph apparently exonerates him by opting to detain the second-born brother (Simeon), instead of the eldest, after overhearing that Reuben has tried to discourage their assault (42.22-24).[104]

There is an important difference between Reuben's attempt and that of Judah that casts the latter as a truly sinister character. The narrator in this story is usually reticent and seldom informs us of the motives of the characters. But here he specifically reveals Reuben's secret intention to allow Joseph be thrown into a pit 'that he might *rescue* him out of their hands, to *restore* him to his father' (37.22).[105] Commenting on Reuben's action, Leupold considers it as a complete failure:

102. Morris, *The Genesis Record*, p. 541, argues that 'Reuben, of all the brothers, would seem to have the most cause to resent Joseph, since Jacob obviously intended to give Joseph the birthright instead of him' and his defence of Joseph is, therefore, 'the more commendable.' White, 'Reuben and Judah', pp. 91-92, also finds Reuben 'a hero' the reader can identify because he contrasts him with Judah whose motivation to save Joseph is 'primarily self-serving'. However, Wenham, *Genesis 16–50*, p. 354, questions Reuben's motive too and sees it as an attempt 'to atone for his misbehavior with Bilhah' (cf. 35.22; 49.4); Similarly, Holbert, *The Storyteller's Companion to the Bible*, p. 170, comments, 'Thus out of his desire to save Joseph or because of his responsibility as firstborn, he sees Joseph as his meal ticket back into the favor of his father.' As for Judah's motive, Ackerman, 'Joseph, Judah, and Jacob', pp. 100-101, suggests that since the second- and third-born sons (Levi and Simeon) have also fallen out of Jacob's favour (cf. 34.30; 49.5-7), Judah as the fourth-born would stands to gain the most by getting rid of the remaining rival (Joseph) for special status among his brothers. For similar suggestion, see also Judah Goldin, 'Youngest Son or Where Does Genesis 38 Belong?', *JBL* 96 (1977), pp. 27-44 (42).

103. Cf. Goldin, 'Youngest Son', p. 40, who comments, 'the father might well blame him for the disaster: You are the oldest, why did you not stop them?'; Zornberg, *Genesis*, p. 269, suggests that Reuben's plea for Joseph is 'more concerned about the direct "hands-on" involvement in blood than about Joseph's fate'; White, 'Reuben and Judah', p. 93, criticizes his 'self-pitying bathos ("The lad is not, and I, where shall I go?")'; Janzen, *Genesis 12–50*, p. 151, 'Reuben's cry is for himself.'

104. Sternberg, *The Poetics of Biblical Narrative*, p. 291, suggests that 'Simeon, as Leah's second son, makes the perfect hostage for Benjamin, Rachel's second.'

105. Neufeld, 'The Anatomy of the Joseph Cycle', p. 45, remarks, 'Reuben's suggestion to put Joseph in the pit is intended to be the means of saving him from death, since Reuben expects to pull him out later. But the rest of the brothers see the

> The good objective of Reuben is in part cancelled by the fact that he
> sought to meet evil with cunning craft. This craft failed of its purpose.
> More resolute opposition to the evil plans of the brothers should have
> been interposed.[106]

Reuben's tactic certainly left something to be desired in terms of moral
integrity, but it contains an important element that opposes his action
with that of Judah and God. In Reuben's scheme, the pit for Joseph is a
temporary one.[107] His intention is not only to *rescue* Joseph's life but
also to *restore* his freedom later. In contrast, Judah suggests permanent
slavery for his brother in a foreign land. Similarly, the divine domination for salvation in Joseph's perception of God's plan is a permanent
feature. It is not an interim measure but an indispensable means to a
good end. Later, the enslavement of the Egyptians by Joseph is not
described as a temporary measure either. Reuben's intention is rescue
as well as restoration. It indeed fails miserably. The intentions of Judah
and God prevail brilliantly, but they are rescues without emancipation.
A pit of temporary shelter in Reuben's plan contrasts sharply with
Joseph's claim of a principle of permanent servitude in exchange for
salvation. God is now seen as being as pitiless as Judah is in securing a
no less brutal fate for those who are rescued.

The attempt to compare the impotent Reuben with the powerful God
is at first sight an unusual move. The powerful God is obviously more
successful in planning and executing his plan to save lives than the
impotent Reuben. This contrast however can not hide the fact that they
resort to the same measure. Furthermore, if Reuben is forced into a
compromise over his brothers' crime, Joseph does not present God's
scheme as an unavoidable concession. The contrast between Reuben's
tactical use of the pit and God's paradigmatic use of domination and
subordination is striking. However, God's means of leading to a good
end is remarkably similar to that of Reuben's attempt. But it is portrayed by Joseph as nothing less than the ideal way of handling the
human predicament.

God's recycling of the idea of subservience for survival identified in
Reuben's pit is a surprise move. A comparison between them will soon

pit as the means to Joseph's death without actually shedding his blood.'
  106. Leupold, *Exposition*, p. 967.
  107. Holbert, 'Joseph and the Surprising Choice of God', p. 35, remarks,
'Reuben wants to buy time, so that he can later return, rescue Joseph, and bring him
back to Jacob.'

lead to another observation that it is not that God who later accommodates himself by human manoeuvre. Joseph's dreams already suggest this idea if his interpretation is to be believed. Therefore, Joseph's dreams set the model that the characters later adopt in various situations. Even the Midianite traders and Potiphar reiterate the similar motif of subservience for survival.[108] From Joseph's viewpoint, it is not surprising that he shows no gratitude towards the Midianites or Potiphar for saving or sparing his life at the cost of slavery or imprisonment. The Midianite traders lift Joseph from the pit and sell him to the Ishmaelites. They might be credited for saving Joseph's life from a possible death in a pit in the wilderness.

> Then Midianite traders passed by; and they drew Joseph up and lifted him out of the pit, and sold him to the Ishmaelites for twenty shekels of silver; and they took Joseph to Egypt (37.28).[109]

The pit is said to be empty and there is no water in it (37.24), so Joseph does not face the immediate danger of drowning. But being trapped in a pit in the wilderness without water is life-threatening. The brothers can simply walk away and it would not be long before Joseph would perish without rescue.[110] The Midianite traders 'drew (מֹשֵׁךְ) Joseph up' and 'lifted (עלה) him out of the pit (בוֹר)'; these two Hebrew verbs sound rather like a rescuing effort. When Jeremiah is also rescued out of a pit (בוֹר), they again appear together.[111] 'Then they drew (מֹשֵׁךְ)

---

108. Seybold, 'Paradox and Symmetry', p. 70, observes, 'Joseph's brothers and his captors have always opted for the alternative that allowed Joseph to live.'

109. For the ambiguity of this transaction (who sells Joseph and brings him into Egypt?), see Redford, *Biblical Story of Joseph*, pp. 145-46. For the purpose of comparison, I adopt the explanation that it is Midianites (not the brothers) who draw Joseph out after finding him in a pit.

110. Reuben intends to come back to rescue him because he may assume the brothers would simply walk away leaving Joseph to perish in the wilderness without killing him with their own hand (37.21-22). White, 'The Joseph Story', p. 63, therefore comments, 'cast him into an open pit, the unspoken assumption being that he would be left there to die'. Stigers, *A Commentary on Genesis*, p. 275, remarks, 'The reference to no water emphasizes that time would ensure his demise through death by thirst.' See also Morris, *The Genesis Record*, p. 541.

111. Bush, *Notes on Genesis*, p. 231, refers to Jeremiah's imprisonment in a pit, 'It was into a vault of this kind that the prophet Jeremiah was thrust, at the instigation of his enemies, Jer. 38.6. And such, doubtless, was the "pit" or "cistern" into which Joseph was now put by his brethren. From such receptacles figuratively con-

Jeremiah up with ropes and lifted (עלה) him out of the cistern (בור)'
(Jer. 38.13).

A similar phrase 'He drew (עלה) me up from the pit (בור)' in Ps.
40.2(3) has also been used by the psalmist to describe a rescue by the
Lord. Joseph later in the prison begs the butler, 'But remember me,
when it is well with you, and do me the kindness, I pray you, to make
mention of me to Pharaoh, and so get me out (יצא) of this house (בית)'
(40.14). And the narrator describes his final release, 'Then Pharaoh sent
and called Joseph, and they brought him hastily out (רוץ) of the dun-
geon (בור)' (41.14).

It seems that the Midianites happen to go by and find Joseph in a pit
and lift him out and sell him to the Ishmaelites. This probably matches
Joseph's version of the event. Later he refers to this incident as a theft
(40.15) rather than a 'rescue', however. He obviously has no wish to
feel thankful for their action even though it might have prevented his
death. However, it is still fair to say that Joseph owes his life to the
Midianites. They are not responsible for Joseph's falling into the pit.
Unfortunately their 'rescue' is only from one pit to another. They trade
Joseph's freedom for his life. In a sense, it is a fair exchange, survival
at a price. It is the same spirit behind Joseph's justification of his domination for salvation. Like the Midianite traders, God could not be held
responsible for those who became victims in a pit or in a natural
famine. But if any rescuing action has a price of subservience attached
to it, then God is portrayed as no better than the Midianite traders.[112]

In Potiphar's case, Joseph is imprisoned because of the false accusation of Potiphar's wife. But he is not sentenced to death[113] and it might

sidered, does the Lord deliver his people. Zech. 9.11, "I have sent forth thy prisoners out of the pit wherein is no water".'

112. I have to admit that the two Hebrew verbs עלה קשׁך ('drawing up' and 'lifting up') in describing the Midianites' actions do not by themselves point to a
rescuing effort. However, I just want to highlight the possible problematic nature of
the idea of subservience for survival through their actions. Whether the narrator intends such a parallel or not is secondary to my purpose.

113. Goodnick, 'Character of Joseph', pp. 221-22, comments, 'A crime of this
stature—an attempted rape by a foreign slave against the wife of a high official—
would undoubtedly be punishable by death.' And he further notes the ambiguity of
Potiphar's fury, 'The text states his master 'was furious (39.19). We may ask
against whom his fury was directed.' Westermann, *Genesis 37–50*, p. 67, also observes the ambiguity of Pharaoh's anger and interprets that 'he is not convinced of
Joseph's guilt' due to the relatively light punishment. When Potiphar's wife

be a sign of Potiphar's disbelief of her accusation. Sparing his life, slavery in prison is imposed on him instead. The motives of both the Midianites and Potiphar are unlikely to be sympathetic towards Joseph. Nevertheless, their actions of lifting him out of the pit or of putting him into the prison make possible his survival. It is a rather extraordinary exercise to compare them with God's saving action as described by Joseph. However, these two incidents exemplify the bare structure of the idea of subservience for survival, irrespective of the motives of those who execute it. Juxtaposed with Reuben's pit, Judah's pit of slavery, Joseph's understanding of God's intention in his pit of suffering and his dreams of domination, and finally the policy of Egyptian mass enslavement, they serve to dramatize the incongruity between these four elements while exposing their underlying similarity.

Summary

The way Joseph presents his claim of domination is clever. The emphasis of his suffering in the pit for the benefit of others greatly helps him to justify his subsequent claim of domination. Joseph is carefully to avoid offending his brothers in his disclosure speech, but it is his own words of dominating over Egypt that make an obvious link between his claim of domination and his subsequent policy of mass enslavement. It is one thing to accept pragmatically the exchange of subservience for survival; it is another matter to declare such choice as ideal and divinely sanctioned, in such a way as Joseph interprets his dreams. Because of his ignorance of Judah's excuse and its ironic reversal effected by his test, his solicitation of the purpose of salvation becomes rather a liability to his justification. It exposes the fact that the measure (and the ideology behind it) taken by the characters (Reuben, Judah and God as portrayed by Joseph) are remarkably similar. They all share the same 'good' intention to save life and also the same choice of a pit, as a means to avoid death.

The comparison between them also reveals a disturbing difference. The weak eldest brother is forced by the circumstances to make a

complains to the servants (vv. 14-15) and to her husband (vv. 17-18), she accuses him of bringing Joseph into their house as much as she complains of Joseph's alleged sexual assault. This explains the ambiguity of Potiphar's response to her criticism. To see the seriousness of offending one's master's wife, Haman's death penalty in Est. 7.8-10 is a good comparison.

compromise and allow his brother to be thrown into a pit in the hope of
rescuing him later. In contrast, Joseph claims that the all-powerful God
succeeds in his plan to subjugate the people whom he intends to save.
What exactly can one criticize Reuben for if he adopts the same tactic
of subservience for survival? The same question can be asked concerning Judah's similar excuse to avoid his brother's death by selling him
into slavery. To argue that God does not act wrongly as the human
characters do, it seems that the means (to achieve salvation through
subservience) cannot be a determining factor. First of all, it is easy to
recognize that Judah's attempt to save Joseph is stained by his complicity with the murder in the first place. Reuben could not be criticized
for his complicity with the murder plot,[114] but he could be reproached
for not being strong enough to defend his brother. Joseph's claim of a
divine plan to save lives in a providential way overriding human evil
intention (45.5-8a) pictures God more favourably than Reuben. However, his repeated claims that God is going to bring about the famine
(45.25, 28, 32) parallel God with Judah in a rescue from a situation
which the rescuer has created in the first place. This problem leads us to
examine the reliability of Joseph's words and the narrator's stance
towards them in the next chapter.

114. Leupold, *Exposition*, p. 965, recognizes that 'Reuben has had no hand in
formulating the plans for evil.'

Chapter 3

IS JOSEPH THE NARRATOR'S MOUTHPIECE?

Joseph ascribes many events in the story to God's initiative. Has God 'sent' him into slavery? Has he destined Joseph to rise to power to save many lives? The answers to these questions for many readers are undoubtedly in the affirmative. Joseph is taken as 'God's spokesman'[1] and his claims about God's intentions encounter little resistance. Since God, as a character in this story, does not appear and speak explicitly as much as he did in the previous patriarchal stories,[2] the knowledge of his intentions can be gained only through the narrator's portrayal. Therefore, instead of inquiring directly whether Joseph is God's spokesman or not, I prefer to reformulate the questions into the following: Does the narrator agree with Joseph's claims to knowing God's intentions? Is he the mouthpiece of the narrator?

Some readers find Joseph's claim of divine domination for survival justifiable, but others regard it as an outdated ideology. Nevertheless, both sides assume the coalescence of the narrator's perspective with

1. Cf. Ross, *Creation and Blessing*, p. 636; Fretheim, *Genesis*, p. 621, also comments that 'God speaks through Joseph'; Longacre, *Joseph*, p. 48, remarks that 'Joseph considers himself to be a spokesman for God... Pharaoh himself is convinced that a supernatural power has spoken through Joseph.'

2. Cf. Brueggemann, *Genesis*, p. 290; Westermann, *Genesis 37–50*, pp. 251-52. Nahum M. Sarna, *Understanding Genesis* (New York: Schocken Books, 1970), pp. 212-13, notices a different nature of dreams in terms of their clarity between the Joseph story and the previous patriarchal stories: 'Throughout the biblical world, dreams were recognized as vehicles of divine communication. Several instances of this have already been encountered. God revealed His will in dreams to Abimelech, King of Gerar (20.3), to Jacob (28.12ff.; 31.11) and to Laban (31.24). In each experience the theophany is straightforward and the message perfectly clear. This is not the case with Joseph's dreams, nor with those of the butler and the baker and Pharaoh. Here, the symbol, not the words, is the language of intelligence, and the dream is therefore enigmatic.'

that of Joseph. For example, Niehoff asserts that 'Joseph's consciousness of God's omnipresence is further developed in Gen. 45.5-8 where
he makes a more comprehensive statement which provides the overall
theme of the narrative. It emerges from this concurrence of the story's
theme and Joseph's personal convictions that the narrator in fact uses
this figure to express his own ideas.'[3] Brueggemann also confidently
assumes the coalescence of the narrator with Joseph's viewpoint:

> It is clear that the disclosure statements of 45.4-8 and 50.19-20 are the
> major theological statements which interpret the entire narrative. Only in
> these two places does the narrator make obvious the programmatic claim
> that God's leadership, though hidden, is the real subject of the narrative.[4]

However, since the narrator is reticent and seldom expresses overt
comments, his view should not be taken for granted without careful
investigation. This chapter questions the certainty of this assumption by
looking into the interrelation of Joseph's various claims. My aim is
modest. I will not attempt to determine beyond doubt the narrator's
definite standpoint on Joseph's claims. However, if Joseph's words can
be exposed as fairly incoherent, then the possibility of the narrator's
disagreement with the protagonist can be established.

Discrepancies between Joseph's Disclosure Speech and his Two Previous Claims

Miscall reminds us of the fact that in this story the major characters frequently ascribe events to divine intervention[5] and their assertions have
to be verified individually by the text. Concerning Joseph's claims,
Miscall makes two important narrative observations: 'Joseph's speech
tells much of his character and his development in theological awareness, but it does not necessarily say that God did actually intervene in
past events'; 'The narrator does not affirm Joseph's interpretation nor

3.   Niehoff, *The Figure of Joseph*, pp. 35-36.
4.   Brueggemann, *Genesis*, p. 290. For a similar conviction, see also Westermann, *Genesis 37–50*, p. 251; Longacre, *Joseph*, pp. 42-43; von Rad, *Genesis*,
p. 438; Wenham, *Genesis 16–50*, p. 432.
5.   Miscall, 'The Jacob and Joseph Stories as Analogies', p. 33. Humphreys,
Joseph and his Family, p. 119, 'With the exception of chapter 39… and the notice
of the night vision (46.1-4), the narrator makes no direct mention of the deity. The
few references to God are all spoken by some figure in the novella.'

does God himself appear in the narrative to confirm it.'[6] Therefore, Miscall carefully accentuates Joseph's role in his interpretation:

> Rather, *he interprets* the past as having been turned to good by God. The intervention is present and future oriented as *Joseph believes* that God has used him to ensure a remnant for the family... *Joseph sees* God bring good from evil but not thereby forgiving sin (my emphasis).[7]

Miscall attempts to insert a gap between Joseph's perspective and that of the narrator. It is not because he has any objection to Joseph's interpretation. Instead, he is only critical of his test of his brothers and considers it a 'purely human activity with no relation to any divine plan'. However, Joseph never declares that his test is part of God's plan. Objection to the test neither invalidates Joseph's claims, nor calls into doubt the narrator's acceptance of it. Since Miscall accepts that 'the endings [of the story] are in accordance with the divine plan and promises',[8] he in effect equates Joseph's perspective with that of the narrator.

The story seems to end favourably for Joseph and his interpretation. It is difficult to distance the narrator's perspective from that of Joseph, even though the reader is well aware that in principle they do not neces-

---

6.   Miscall, 'The Jacob and Joseph Stories as Analogies', p. 31. These remarks involve two narrative principles: a character's speech characterizes the speaker rather than those he or she speaks about; and the narrator's overt comment is required to verify the truthfulness of the character's viewpoint. Cf. Rimmon-Kenan, *Narrative Fiction*, pp. 60-65; Alter, *Art of Biblical Narrative*, pp. 116-17.

7.   Miscall, 'The Jacob and Joseph Stories as Analogies', p. 38.

8.   Miscall, 'The Jacob and Joseph Stories as Analogies', p. 34. O'Brien, 'Contribution of Judah's Speech', p. 447, observes that the text maintains its reticence to Joseph's speech of God's care and preservation of the family in 45.5. He does not question whether 'God has been at work'. He rather asserts that 'there is no claim to know precisely how God has been at work'. Since Joseph has already declared that God sent him into slavery and made him lord for the preservation of the family, it seems to be sufficiently concrete for readers to evaluate his claim about how God has been at work. Concerning the 'divine providential design' expressed by Joseph, Humphreys, *Joseph and his Family*, pp. 124-25, also comments that 'it is important to note once more that the words are uttered by Joseph; they are not a statement addressed directly to us by the narrator'. However, he has no doubt about their validity and proceeds to conclude, 'finally the brothers come to know what Joseph and the reader know, and all come to know through Joseph's recognition that the tug and pull of this family's story must be comprehended within a larger divine design, and the design is one that seeks to preserve life'.

sarily coincide. However, Joseph's final verdict on the past series of events at the end of his test (45.4-11) and at the end of the whole story (50.20) may be subjected to an ironic treatment by the narrator.[9] To assess the possibility of this view, it is imperative first to examine the coherence of his claims in order to determine the narrator's view on them. Joseph's claims have been individually placed under critical scrutiny by many readers.[10] Unfortunately, no systematic analysis of their interrelation has been carried out. This misses the opportunity to reach an overall picture of what he really ascribes to God. If one puts all his claims together, their contradictions may surface more easily. Since they are embedded in their own contexts in this relatively complex story, their problems are easily overlooked.

In the previous chapter, I have exposed Joseph's strategies in his disclosure speech (45.4-11). Now I focus on the relationship of this declaration of God-planned salvation with his two previous claims of divine actions: God-sent famine (41.25, 28, 32) and God-made forgetfulness of his father's house (41.51). The examination of their interrelation will reveal serious discrepancies between his claims. It will cast a shadow on the truthfulness of his words and, in turn, will damage his credibility as the mouthpiece of the narrator.

Joseph's Claim of Divine Help to Forget his Father's House (41.51)
When Joseph is finally out of the pit and appointed by Pharaoh to rule over all the land of Egypt, the hardship and affliction he has endured in the experience of the pit still affect him. His wish to blot out the memory of his past suffering is ambiguous when he names his two new-born sons:

9. Josipovici, 'Joseph and Revelation', p. 85, offers one such ironic ending. Against Joseph's claim of being chosen by God over his brothers, he suggests that 'the narrative delivers its final irony' because 'it will be Judah's seed which will inherit and not Joseph's'.

10. E.g., on divine providence, see Redford, *Biblical Story of Joseph*, p. 74; von Rad, 'The Joseph Narrative and Ancient Wisdom', pp. 297-98; On divine domination, see Wildavsky, *Assimilation versus Separation*, p. 142; Josipovici, 'Joseph and Revelation', p. 85; On forgetting his father's house, see Calvin, *Genesis*, II, p. 332; Wildavsky, *Assimilation versus Separation*, pp. 122-23; On the God-sent famine, see Westermann, *Genesis 37–50*, p. 92, who detects a glaring contradiction between the 'message of woe' in Pharaoh's dreams and Joseph's announcement of 'prosperity for the Pharaoh'.

Joseph called the name of the first-born Manasseh, 'For', he said, 'God has made me forget all my hardship and all my father's house.' The name of the second he called Ephraim, 'For God has made me fruitful in the land of my affliction' (41.51-52).

Why does Joseph want to forget it all? Is it because it matters no more? Or is it because it hurts? It is hard to find out his exact intention behind his desire to forget the past, but it is interesting to note that his intention would most probably fail. Each time when Joseph calls his son, Manasseh ('to forget'), it will certainly remind him of the past suffering rather than forgetting it. Naming in the Bible serves as a reminder. How can people forget something if they keep on reminding themselves? Some readers tend to take Joseph's word at its face value. For example, Ackerman remarks, 'We have just been told how Joseph, in naming his Egyptian-born sons, had put the past behind him.'[11] Joseph's word only expresses his wish and perspective; one cannot take his word for granted however sincerely it is uttered. His speech-act actually undermines his intention. To remember to forget is contradictory. He is trapped by his past rather than letting it go.

Does Joseph really forget the past or not? And more importantly, has God made him forget, as he claims, or not? If God has indeed made Joseph forget all his past suffering, Joseph's way of commemorating this divine help would only undo what God has achieved. Joseph's choice of his sons' names indeed expresses 'Joseph's thankfulness to God' and 'his faith that God has been with him and blessed him', as Wenham comments.[12] But if God has been with Joseph in the past, he is certainly not with Joseph at this time and cannot be seen to be involved in Joseph's ambivalent attempt to forget the past suffering. It is not the first time Joseph ascribes events to God. Readers who usually believe in Joseph's word would contradict him this time, especially about the forgetting of his father's house. John Calvin warns that the 'sin of Joseph', the oblivion of his father's house, cannot be excused:

> Behold Joseph, although he purely worships God, is yet so captivated by the sweetness of honour, and has his mind so clouded, that he becomes indifferent to his father's house, and pleases himself in Egypt. But this was almost to wander from the fold of God.[13]

11. Ackerman, 'Joseph, Judah, and Jacob', p. 87.
12. Wenham, *Genesis 16–50*, p. 398.
13. Calvin, *Genesis*, II, p. 332. Wildavsky, *Assimilation versus Separation*,

Wenham, on the other hand, feels that 'the very mention of his "father's house" shows that he has not really forgotten his extended family whom, unbeknown to him, he will shortly meet again'.[14] Although he does not say so explicitly, Wenham in effect casts doubt on Joseph's claim. Von Rad also considers that the narrator is at odds with Joseph's claim when his brothers soon come to bow down before him. However, he thinks that 'forget' does not, in the strict sense of the word, mean here 'not remember' but rather 'to have something no longer'. Joseph's claim is thus seen as referring 'more to an objective external fact rather than to a subjective, psychological process' of forgetting 'with an overtone of bitterness'.[15] Given the emotional turmoil later in his encounter with his family, it is hard to accept that Joseph's attitude to the past can be as detached as von Rad suggests.

Lowenthal seems, on the one hand, to be unable to accept Joseph's intention to forget his family, and, on the other hand, he does not want to object to Joseph's claim. So he comes up with a different understanding of his word and 'God has caused me to forget' now comes to mean 'God wants me to act as if I have forgotten.'[16] He suggests that God wants Joseph to do nothing about communicating with his family until his dreams of his brothers bowing down are fulfilled. It is another attempt to avoid confronting Joseph's apparently unreliable claim about God's action. Aalders is surprised at Joseph's claim and explains,

> Certainly Joseph is not priding himself on having forgotten his family in Canaan. It means, rather, that Joseph recognised that God had been so good to him in Egypt that all his grief endured at the hands of his brothers could now be forgotten.[17]

Instead of forgetting his brothers (his father's house), Joseph is said to forget all the grief caused by them. There are clearly two items in Joseph's list of forgetting: 'all my hardship and all my father's house' (41.51).[18] Aalders simply reiterates the first and drops the second from

pp. 122-23, criticizes Joseph's naming of his two sons as a step towards Egyptianization.

14. Wenham, *Genesis 16–50*, p. 398.
15. Von Rad, *Genesis*, p. 379; cf. Humphreys, *Joseph and his Family*, pp. 88-89, recognizes that the naming interlude gives us access to Joseph's inner self and his actual feelings.
16. Lowenthal, *The Joseph Narrative in Genesis*, p. 60.
17. Aalders, *Genesis*, p. 217.
18. Sarna, *Genesis*, p. 289, attempts to understand it as 'an instance of hendia-

the list. He is not alone in this evading tactic. Other readers try to identify the hardship as 'loneliness and misery',[19] 'old life of persecution',[20]
and 'slavery in Canaan and Egypt'[21] without even mentioning his
father's house at all.[22]

Ostensibly, the first name 'Manasseh' serves as a determination to
forget the past suffering in Canaan and the second name 'Ephraim' is a
celebration of present fruitfulness in Egypt. It is seen as a simple cross-
ing over from past to present, from suffering to fruitfulness, and from
Canaan to Egypt. But his act of commemorating the forgetting betrays
his troublesome feelings and self-contradictory state of mind towards
the past and the present. And whatever spectacular success he enjoys in
the three houses (Potiphar's house, the prison house, Pharaoh's house),
Egypt remains to him forever the land of affliction as recalled in the
name 'Ephraim'.[23] Joseph becomes stuck at a threshold, neither able to
escape totally from the past, nor really at peace with the present. Both
Canaan and Egypt are pits to Joseph. Symbolically, Joseph is still in the
pit and has not emancipated himself from the trauma which his brothers
put him through.

Joseph's claim to God's intervention has troubled many readers
because not only his past suffering but also all his father's house are to
be forgotten. This directly contradicts his subsequent important claim to
God's intervention:

dys', i.e. 'my suffering in my parental home'. See also Janzen, *Genesis 12–50*,
p. 165. Since Joseph makes no effort to contact his family after his rise to power, it
is more probable that he really wants to forget his father's house in Canaan.

19. Ronald F. Youngblood, *The Book of Genesis* (Grand Rapids: Baker Book
House, 2nd edn, 1991), p. 257.

20. Brueggemann, *Genesis*, p. 329.

21. Fretheim, *Genesis*, p. 622.

22. There are many other attempts to explain away this seemingly unethical
behaviour of Joseph, with or without grammatical and lexical help. E.g., Stigers, *A
Commentary on Genesis*, p. 293, tries to explain that to forget his parents means 'to
renounce any dependence on them for deliverance or hope from adverse predi-
caments'; Westermann, *Genesis 37–50*, p. 97, translates the clause in 41.51
ואת כל־בית אבי as 'I am far from my father's house'; Alter, *Genesis*, p. 242, con-
ceives that it is 'somewhat odd that Joseph should celebrate God for having made
him forget his father's house'. He regards נשה as נשה I 'to hold in debt' rather than
נשה II 'to forget'. In its piel conjugation, the translation in this context will be: 'God
has released me from all the debt of my hardship, and of all my father's house.'

23. Lowenthal, *The Joseph Narrative in Genesis*, p. 60, notes, 'Egypt will
always remain his "affliction", i.e. "exile" from his Fathers' land.'

> And God sent me before you to preserve for you a remnant on earth, and
> to keep alive for you many survivors... Make haste and go up to my
> father and say to him, 'Thus says your son Joseph, God has made me
> lord of all Egypt; come down to me, do not tarry; you shall dwell in the
> land of Goshen, and you shall be near me, you and your children and
> your children's children, and your flocks, your herds, and all that you
> have' (45.7-10a).

If God has made him forget his father's house as he claims, how could
he later lay claim to the opposite idea that God has used him to keep
alive his father's house? If he errs in the first claim, how can one be
sure that his second claim is correct? One has to remember that these
two claims to God's intervention concern the same object, his father's
house, but with totally opposite consequences: its obliteration or salvation. Undoubtedly, Joseph is a great interpreter of dreams, but we
should not be quick to accept his understanding of his past and his
claims of God's involvement in it without proper examination of their
coherence.

Thus, the first obvious sign of discrepancy occurs when, in the middle of his praise to God, Joseph makes a striking remark alleging that
God has made him forget his father's house. In view of subsequent
events, this claim of God's action is quite awkward. It contradicts the
intention he ascribes to God in 45.4-11 that he is sent to save his family.
However, this contradiction can be resolved by seeing Joseph as simply
misunderstanding God's intention at first. He wants to get rid of the
past, but events catch up with him that make him come to a truer
knowledge of God's intention.[24] His initial ignorance could strengthen
rather than weaken his credibility as a spokesman of God, whose real
intention is hidden even from the protagonist at the outset.[25] Joseph's
final disclosure can then be seen as an authentic revelation.

Joseph's naming of his two sons is an act that attempts to bury the
past and begin a new life after his rise to power in ch. 41. Through this
incident the narrator reveals Joseph's feelings and his state of mind
regarding the past. It also serves as a starting point for his journey of

24. Longacre, *Joseph*, p. 49, comments, 'the next wave of divine providence
will catch him somewhat by surprise, if not off-balance'. For Longacre, Joseph's
ignorance of his mission before his encounter with his brothers heightens the effect
of divine providence. See also Baldwin, *Genesis 12–50*, p. 177.

25. Alter, *Art of Biblical Narrative*, p. 159, stresses that Joseph, as a great interpreter, also has to learn the true meaning of his own destiny.

'discovery' through the long trial of his brothers until he finally gives us another definite view of his shared past with his brothers in chapter 45.4-11. He moves from his claim of divine help to forget his family to his claim of a divine plan to save it. His initial claim should be given sufficient attention in order to appreciate the dramatic transformation of his understanding of the past.

Joseph's Claim of the God-sent Famine (41.25, 28, 32)
Joseph's claim to God's help in forgetting his family is far more inconsequential than his claim that the famine is God-sent. His attempt to forget the past affliction and his father is understandable. Nevertheless, it has troubled many readers and they devote much effort to explaining this anomaly, either condemning it or defending it. Joseph's word about God-sent famine clearly contradicts his later claim that God also has planned to save lives from this famine. But this incongruity escapes the notice of many readers and it deserves the following detailed discussion in order to examine its implication for the reliability of Joseph's words.

In enslaving the Egyptians, Joseph may be unwittingly repeating the crime which his test has reversed and condemned. To be fair, he is an enslaver but not a victimizer in the same way as Judah. Judah's pit of slavery imposed on Joseph is a hideous crime while Joseph's enslavement is a relief programme from a horrible famine. He does not force the Egyptians to choose slavery for survival. He only accepts their proposal.[26] The Egyptians are victims only of a disaster. Therefore, it seems unfair to compare Judah's pit of slavery with Joseph's dreams of domination even though they share the same idea of subservience for survival. Yet the famine is not simply a natural disaster. In interpreting Pharaoh's dreams, Joseph makes a firm connection between the deity and the dreams.[27] He ascribes their interpretation to God (40.8) and

26. Since 'the peasants initiate the idea of their own enslavement (v. 19)', Sarna, *Genesis*, p. 323, concludes that there is a 'shifting [of] the onus of responsibility for the fate of the peasants from Joseph to the Egyptians themselves' in the narrative. For similar comments, see Skinner, *Genesis*, p. 500; Leupold, *Exposition*, p. 1135.

27. Cf. Humphreys, *Joseph and his Family*, pp. 121-22; but Coats, *From Canaan to Egypt*, p. 27, disagrees with such claims of divine origin and remarks, 'Joseph's interpretation and counsel derive basically from his own skill rather than from divine intervention. To be sure, he attributes his interpretation to God. But there is no direct divine intervention in the process of interpretation (contrast Dan. 2.19).'

reaffirms this divine source to Pharaoh, specifically denying any human involvement in interpretation: 'It is not in me; God will give Pharaoh a favourable answer' (41.16). Joseph not only links both the dreams and their interpretation to God, he also tells Pharaoh three times in quick succession that the thing (דבר) in his dreams is fixed by God and is what God is about to do (עשׂה) shortly:

> Then Joseph said to Pharaoh, 'The dreams of Pharaoh is one; God has *revealed* (נגד) to Pharaoh what he is about to *do* (עשׂה)' (41.25).

> It is as I told Pharaoh, God has shown (ראה) to Pharaoh what he is about to *do* (עשׂה) (41.28).

> And the doubling of Pharaoh's dreams means that the thing (דבר) is fixed by God, and God will shortly bring it to *pass* (עשׂה) [God will shortly *do* it] (41.32).

Joseph makes it extremely clear to Pharaoh that God is going to bring about the seven years of plenty and the seven years of famine. The images of the swallowing up of the fat cows by the gaunt (רע) and thin cows, of the good ears by the thin ears, certainly depict Pharaoh's dreams as an ominous message.[28] This explains why Pharaoh is deeply troubled by his dreams (41.8). Joseph prefaces his interpretation with a clear statement about the nature of the dreams. His dreams are revelation by God of 'what he is about to *do*' (v. 25). He reiterates it in the middle of his interpretation (v. 28). This is a clear declaration that the seven-year famine revealed in Pharaoh's dreams is not simply a natural disaster. To make sure that no one will miss or misunderstand this important message, Joseph declares one more time in his conclusion

---

28. Westermann, *Genesis 37–50*, p. 91, remarks, 'an announcement which throws the whole weight on to the announcement of a misfortune. Only one sentence is given to the years of plenty (v. 29), whereas five are given to the famine (vv. 30-31). This announcement of misfortune recalls unmistakably both in form and content the prophetic proclamation of woe'; The emphasis on the famine, according to Wenham, *Genesis 16–50*, p. 393, 'clearly fits in with the Pharaoh's own recognition that his dream threatened disaster'; Sailhamer, *Pentateuch as Narrative*, p. 214, notices the repetition of the adjective רע for the cows (41.3, 4, 19, 20, 27) and comments, 'It seems to stress the "evil" (רע) appearance of the cows in contrast with the good of the first group.' But quoting from Deut. 30.15, he implies that the 'good' is a provision from God while God warns against the 'evil' (רע). It clearly contradicts Joseph's repeated assertions that both 'good' and 'evil' cows are brought about by God.

that what God has fixed in his dreams, he 'will shortly bring it to *pass*' (v. 32).

Joseph's interpretation of Pharaoh's dreams contains two assertions. The first is about God's revelation of the future event. Joseph employs two different Hebrew words (נגד, ראה, vv. 25, 28) to describe this act of revelation by God while Pharaoh uses another Hebrew word (ידע, v. 39) in response. Moreover, it is not only a revelation; it is also a declaration of 'what God is about to do'. In contrast, Joseph employs the same Hebrew word (עשה, vv. 25, 28, 32) three times to describe the future action of God.[29] He alleges that God is going to cause seven years of plenty and seven years of famine. Significantly, the same word עשה reappears in the most famous claim of Joseph in 50.20: 'As for you, you meant evil against me; but God meant it for good, to *bring* (עשה) it about that many people should be kept alive, as they are today.'[30] God is then said to bring salvation.

There are seven years of plenty and seven years of famine in Pharaoh's dreams. The latter will swallow the former, clearly indicating that the dreams signify a catastrophe. But Joseph does not interpret it simply as a natural disaster. In unequivocal terms, he declares that the catastrophe is the result of divine action: 'what God is about to do', and 'the thing (דבר) is fixed by God'. Thus, God is not simply predicting or revealing a famine but is going to bring it to pass. Bush accurately presents the emphasis of these two assertions of Joseph:

> Joseph again tells Pharaoh that God was both the revealer and the doer of those things that were pre-signified by the dreams. We need often to be put in mind that God is both the speaker of his word and the doer of his works.[31]

---

29. Morris, *The Genesis Record*, p. 581, includes v. 16 to describe God's actions, 'it is noteworthy that Joseph insisted, not less than four times, that all of this had come from God (verses 16, 25, 28, 32). God had sent the dream, God had given the interpretation, and God would bring it all to pass.'

30. Sarna, *Genesis*, p. 285, also notices the same Hebrew verb in Joseph's advice to Pharaoh: 'Let Pharaoh do (עשה) *this*, and let him appoint officers over the land' (KJV 41.34). And he comments, 'Joseph deliberately uses the same verbal stem he has used three times before in connection with the impending divine action (vv. 25, 38, 32), as though to imply that Pharaoh is the human counterpart of God.'

31. Bush, *Notes on Genesis*, p. 279. Howard F. Vos, *Genesis* (Chicago: Moody Press, 1982), p. 144, also recognizes that 'Joseph did not merely report what would happen, but what God was about to do (see vv. 25, 28, 32), God was in control of natural forces.'

Joseph's interpretation will inevitably yield this obvious problem: on the one hand God is making a destructive famine, on the other hand he is planning a deliverance by making Joseph a lord over Egypt to prepare for the famine. How can Joseph justify his claim that God saves the people from the famine which God has delivered in the first place? According to Joseph, Pharaoh's dreams do not merely 'come from the deity as indication of what is to come', as Humphreys would like to describe it.[32] The years of plenty and famine are not only predicted and revealed by God, they are also fixed by God and they are what God is about to do.[33] According to Joseph's claim, it is God who has planned the famine, has revealed the dreams to Pharaoh, has helped Joseph to interpret them, and has made him lord over Egypt.[34] And the purpose of this sequence of events is to save many lives (45.5, 7; 50.20). The contradiction is clear. Joseph claims that God plans a famine in order to save lives. Has God also planned the enslavement of the Egyptians? If the answer is negative, the Egyptians are then victims of Joseph's relief policy.[35] If the answer is positive, Joseph is claiming that the Egyptians are the victims of God's plan.

32. Humphreys, *Joseph and his Family*, p. 121.

33. In contrast to Joseph's assertion of God's active role in the famine, Redford, *Biblical Story of Joseph*, p. 98, suggests an opposite role in the cultural background: 'Such world-wide famines, often of seven years' duration, are rooted in old fertility myths. Through the death of a god or demon, through divine neglect, or through sheer inability on a god's part to prevent it.'

34. After his interpretation, Joseph advises Pharaoh to set a wise man over Egypt to prepare for the trouble ahead. Pharaoh responds by appointing Joseph himself: 'You shall be over my house... I have set you over all the land of Egypt (41.40, 41). The narrator immediately reiterates Pharaoh's appointment (41.43) without referring to God's intention. But it is typical of Joseph's tendency to identify divine action behind human action. He tells his brothers that it is God who has made him lord over Egypt (45.8-9). While the psalmist agrees with Joseph that '[God] had *sent* a man ahead of them' (Ps. 105.17; cf. Gen. 45.5, 7, 8), he repeats the Genesis narrator's comment that Pharaoh 'made him lord of his house, and ruler of all his possessions' (Ps. 105.21). Stephen in Acts 7.9-10 also refers to Pharaoh as the one who made Joseph governor over Egypt, but he prefixes it with God's presence with Joseph, 'God was with him...gave him favor and wisdom before Pharaoh.'

35. Calvin, *Genesis*, II, p. 410, accuses the Egyptians of neglecting 'the useful admonition of God, at the time when they ought to have made provision for the future'. Stigers, *A Commentary on Genesis*, p. 320, also suggests that the 'bank-

Natural disaster or divine judgment? There are attempts by some read-ers to avoid the contradiction and its implications. The way they tend to do it is to minimize the role of God in the famine.[36] Against Joseph's repeated assertions that God brings about the famine, Fretheim takes it as a 'natural disaster'.[37] 'The heart of Joseph's interpretation,' he com-ments, 'takes the form of announcements about the future (vv. 29-32), though he does not construe them as divine judgment'.[38] If the famine is not a divine judgment, it is probably a natural disaster and not a direct action by God.[39] Kidner suggests that there is a difference between a judgment and a friendly warning: 'To a threat of judgment this will be repentance; to a friendly warning, realistic precautions.' Since there is no repentance but acceptance of Joseph's advice by Pharaoh, he thus understands the famine as only a friendly warning of 'one of life's irregularities'.[40] White also links the famine with other events in the stories as chance circumstances: 'famine, chance encoun-ters with the Ishmaelite caravan, chance sale of Joseph and his rise to a highly placed governmental official'.[41] The role of God as the cause of the famine is suppressed. However, his role in helping Joseph to predict the famine and to plan ahead for it is given plenty of attention. Ross thus comments, 'This revelation was not only the means to get Joseph to power; it was also the means by which God would save Egypt and the world in the time of crisis, causing everyone to know that deliver-

---

rupting of the Egyptians' was because they had made no provision for their own future needs. But it is not a fair judgment because they have contributed one-fifth of their products to prepare for the famine (41.34, 48). In contrast, Joseph's own fam-ily have contributed nothing but are freely provided for.

36. Vos, *Genesis*, p. 142, understands Joseph's claims accurately when he comments that God 'was preparing a crisis' and 'was preparing a leader for the cri-sis'. His emphasis is on the God's role in sending a solution and he neglects to ask why is there a crisis in the first place.

37. Fretheim, *Genesis*, p. 623.

38. Fretheim, *Genesis*, p. 621. Baldwin, *Genesis 12–50*, p. 175, also asserts that the famine 'is not presented as a judgment for wrongdoing, but rather "an act of God", predetermined (v. 32) and now announced in advance so that the kingdom of Egypt can take necessary steps to provide for the famine years'.

39. However, besides direct intervention, God can deliver a judgment through a natural disaster.

40. Kidner, *Genesis*, p. 196. Vos, *Genesis*, p. 144, also sees it as a 'friendly warning'.

41. White, 'The Joseph Story', p. 59.

ance comes from God—if people would believe the Word from God and prepare accordingly.'[42]

Nonetheless, Joseph's repeated assertions of 'what God is about to do' is so explicit that the active role of God in the famine cannot be entirely ignored.[43] An explanation has to be offered to justify God's actions of destruction and deliverance if Joseph's claims are truthful. If this problem could be made parallel with his problem 'to forget and not to forget', then one may simply assume that he commits the same mistake of speaking contradictorily about God's intentions. He seems to be unclear whether God intends 'to destroy or not to destroy'. 'To destroy or not to destroy' is mutually exclusive, but 'to destroy and to deliver' is not mutually exclusive. On a close inspection, the question of whether to destroy or not to destroy is not an accurate description of what Joseph has said. It is rather a matter of 'to destroy and to deliver'. Both actions are not necessarily as mutually exclusive as the case of forgetting his family. If one interprets the famine as a direct intervention from God as a judgment, then it is possible to see God as the source of both destruction and deliverance. Westermann seems to understand the cause of the famine in this way when he compares Joseph's words to Pharaoh with the prophetic message of woe and welfare.[44] He associates Joseph's description of the famine as being 'reminiscent of announcements of disaster in words of the prophets':

> Verse 32b should be compared with Isa. 28.22: 'for I have heard a decree of destruction from the LORD GOD of hosts upon the whole world', and with Isa. 5.19: 'let the plan of the Holy One of Israel hasten to fulfilment'...we have here a very early joining of dream interpretation and prophetic discourse. In both of them the concern was to announce that which God would do.[45]

At first sight, when Westermann identifies Joseph's interpretation of Pharaoh's dreams with God's 'decree of destruction' in the prophetic

---

42. Ross, *Creation and Blessing*, p. 642. Redford, *Biblical Story of Joseph*, p. 70, also stresses the prediction of the famine and its counter-measure: 'Joseph was to rise to greatness through his prediction of a famine and on his ideas on how to alleviate it.' See also Sarna, *Genesis*, p. 285; Fretheim, *Genesis*, p. 623.

43. Commenting on 41.25, 28, 32, Wenham, *Genesis 16–50*, p. 399, stresses the role of God, 'Here the double mention of God emphasizes the divine origin both of the dream and of its interpretation.'

44. Westermann, *Genesis 37–50*, p. 92.

45. Westermann, *Joseph*, p. 49.

discourse, one would assume that he interprets the famine as divine punishment.[46] However, he does not treat Pharaoh's dreams as punishment of any sort. He rather explains them as indicating 'the special relation of the king to the divine'. Pharaoh is privileged with divine dreams to protect the people from starvation. Rather than as the object of punishment, he is seen as 'the distributor of divine blessing'.[47] Significantly, Westermann's description of God's role in the famine undergoes a subtle change:

> Verse 25 states what it is about God that is praised; Joseph makes known to Pharaoh *what God is about to do*. As in chapter 40, the announcement is a statement of *something which is going to come about*. But it has an *extra* meaning, namely, that the announcement of this event makes it possible for many to encounter the *coming event* in such a way that it becomes redemptive for them. Here the dream motif is brought into a solid relationship with the theme (chapter 50.20) which interprets the entire story; *God guided everything* in the Joseph story in such a manner that many people were kept alive by it.[48]

Joseph's disclosure of '*what God is about to do*' suddenly becomes a statement of '*something which is going to come about*'. God as the cause of the event (i.e. famine) is silently dropped and the event itself takes on a self-determined appearance. Furthermore, instead of asking why God brings about the famine, Westermann explains how '*God guided everything*'[49] to keep alive many people in the famine. Two shifts of emphasis can be observed in his interpretation. First, the famine is no longer an event brought about by God. It is increasingly seen as a natural disaster.[50] Secondly, God's role in salvation over-

---

46. Westermann, *Joseph*, p. 49. The context of these two passages in the book of Isaiah contains clear accusation of sin: e.g. 'drunkard' (28.1, 3) and 'lies and falsehood' (28.15; 5.18-20). In contrast, there is total absence of accusation of sin in Pharaoh's dreams and Joseph's interpretation of them.

47. Westermann, *Joseph*, p. 47.

48. Westermann, *Joseph*, p. 45 (my italics).

49. Wenham, *Genesis 16–50*, p. 399, also emphasizes the 'divine control of history and its corollary that inspired men can predict the future'. Thus, God's involvement in making the famine becomes a more indirect role: guiding, controlling and predicting.

50. Westermann, in the preface to his book, *Joseph*, p. vii, states clearly that the famine is a natural disaster: 'By no fault of its own, the family becomes enveloped by the kind of catastrophic famine that is as common in our day as it was in theirs.' Ross, *Creation and Blessing*, pp. 639, 651, also at first explains the dreams as con-

shadows completely his role in bringing about the starvation.

Brueggemann is more forthright in asserting that God is the source of destruction and deliverance. At first, he remarks that the story is about the 'given' problem of famine for which 'no one is responsible'.[51] If no one is responsible, he seems to understand the famine as a natural disaster. But later, when he contrasts Pharaoh's rule with divine sovereignty, the famine is explicitly described as the work of God:

> The power of God is contrasted with feeble power of Pharaoh. The criterion of the true God (cf. Isa. 41.21-29) is that God is the one who can cause a future. In Genesis 41, it is clear that Pharaoh can cause no future. Nor can he resist the future that God will bring... It is God who will give life and bring death, who will cause the Nile to produce or cause famine to come (cf. Deut. 32.29; Isa. 45.7). Such a dream must have seemed nonsense to the Pharaoh... The narrative announces the free, sovereign God is at work in the very center of Egyptian existence.[52]

He identifies the role of God as the one 'who will give life and bring death'.[53] This probably sounds not only 'nonsense' to Pharaoh, but to many readers as well if no good reason is given. He offers the sovereignty of God as the ground for this 'nonsense'. But he also tries to avoid the impression of arbitrariness by constructing the famine as a divine polemic against 'Pharaoh's claim to authority'. According to him, the famine is 'an assault on the Nile', exposing 'the helplessness of the empire' and 'the futility of Egyptian ways of existence'.[54] He then interprets the famine as a divine judgment against Pharaoh and his people. Although no specific sin is identified, Luther declares

cerning 'God's future actions in Egypt (vv. 25, 28)', but later he treats the famine in the dreams as one of the 'unusual and unexpected events', an expression more probably referring to a catastrophic natural disaster than direct divine action.

51. Brueggemann, *Genesis*, p. 295. However, on the next page of his book, he soon qualifies his assertion and adds that the problems are 'not caused by human agent' (p. 296). Therefore, 'no one' does not include the divine being.

52. Brueggemann, *Genesis*, p. 331.

53. Brueggemann, *Genesis*, pp. 323-24, describes the dreams of Pharaoh's two officers in ch. 40 as being '*theonomous*'. It is concerned with 'God's rule' and means that 'only God knows the future and only God decides the future'. In Joseph's words, 'the inscrutable and authoritative way of God brings life and it brings death' (his italics).

54. Brueggemann, *Genesis*, p. 327. Bush, *Notes on Genesis*, p. 280, also considers that the famine is used by God to judge the Egyptians who 'idolized their river'.

unambiguously that 'it was because of God's wrath and punishment for sins that God punished this people with famine.'[55]

However, Vos rightly remarks, 'There is no hint that the famine was viewed as a judgment. There was no condemnation connected with it.'[56] While acknowledging that there is no description of sin about Egypt and Pharaoh, Stigers still considers the famine a judgment on them. He even asserts that 'it would be difficult, and surely it is not necessary, to single out some particular sin or sins of Egypt; the idolatry of Egypt was a continuing thing and such judgment could have come any time'.[57] This interpretation is based purely on assumption without any textual evidence. It also contradicts Joseph's reply to Pharaoh, 'God will give Pharaoh a favourable (שׁלוֹם) answer' (41.16).[58] More importantly, the famine affects not only the Egyptians, but also all the people outside Egypt including Jacob's family (41.57). The judgment would be too indiscriminate if all people have to suffer for the sake of 'the idolatry of Egypt'.

Wenham also suggests that God sent 'two ominous dreams' in order to disturb 'the smug complacency of the Pharaoh' who is guilty of viewing 'himself as divine'.[59] Again, not only is it unjust to bring calamity to all the people on account of a single person's fault, the result also argues against this interpretation. If the purpose of the dreams is against either Pharaoh in particular or the Egyptian Empire as a whole, it fails miserably. Pharaoh, with increasing wealth and power, benefits

---

55. Martin Luther, *Lectures on Genesis: Chapters 45–50* (ed. Jaroslav Pelikan; Luther's Works, 8; Saint Louis: Concordia Publishing House, 1966), p. 124, even suggests that the Egyptians are reduced to slavery on account of their sins and they must bear this 'servitude patiently'.

56. Vos, *Genesis*, p. 144. Cf. Kidner, *Genesis*, p. 195-96.

57. Stigers, *A Commentary on Genesis*, p. 289.

58. Westermann, *Genesis 37–50,* p. 92, observes a seemingly 'glaring contradiction' between the message of woe in Pharaoh's dreams and Joseph's assurance of a divine favourable answer to him. He resolves it by interpreting the dreams as a warning of a forthcoming disaster. Through 'Joseph's astute advice', God's message to Pharaoh in the dreams 'serves the welfare of both him and the land'.

59. Wenham, *Genesis 16–50*, p. 399, explains 'the double mention of God' in 41.32 as an emphasis on 'the divine origin both of the dream and of its interpretation'. However, it will be more accurate if the divine origin of 'the thing', i.e. the famine, is also stressed in his understanding this verse. But by admitting that the two ominous dreams are sent by God to Pharaoh, Wenham is clear in taking the famine as a divine punishment.

the most from this 'judgment'. Egypt alone is given the foreknowledge to prepare for the famine. Its position would definitely be strengthened among those who come from all the earth to buy grain. The result of the 'judgment' does not accord well with its purpose if Pharaoh and Egypt benefit from it greatly at the end. Therefore, the suggestion of the famine as a divine judgment against Pharaoh and Egypt cannot be sustained. A comparison of Pharaoh's dreams with the message of divine judgment in the prophetic discourse is not justified. It lacks the essential ingredients of the prophetic judgment. The condemnation of sin and the calling for repentance are not featured in Pharaoh's dreams or in Joseph's interpretation.[60] Furthermore, it is not clear who is the object of such judgment. Is it Pharaoh, his people, or all the earth?

Removal of Jacob's family to Egypt. Besides taking sin as a reason for God sending a famine as a judgment, some readers offer another reason for the famine. When Barnhouse defends Joseph against the criticism that he makes Egypt 'a nation of slaves', he insists that 'the Egyptians were not slaves' but 'free tenants' who paid a reasonable 20 per cent income tax. He explains that 'a sort of feudal system was instituted' in Egyptian society as a result of Joseph's action.[61] More importantly, he exonerates Joseph by pointing out the cause of the famine that requires the relief policy in the first place:

> Critics have accused Joseph of unethical conduct, but they fail to take into consideration that *God had caused the famine* and had ordered all the details of Joseph's advancement to create these very circumstances. To develop Israel from a family into a nation, God changed the social structure of Egypt.[62]

Recognizing the cause of the famine and its consequential change to the social structure of Egypt, Barnhouse is more attentive to the implications of Joseph's speech than many readers. In his view, God rather than Joseph will be primarily responsible for the plight of the Egyptians and other starving people. To justify God's action, he suggests the need 'to develop Israel from a family into a nation'. He asserts that

60. Ross, *Creation and Blessing*, p. 637, however, credits Pharaoh's acceptance of Joseph's interpretation as a sign of his submission to God, thus 'his lands were spared'.

61. Donald Grey Barnhouse, *Genesis: A Devotional Commentary* (Grand Rapids: Zondervan, 1973), p. 217.

62. Barnhouse, *Genesis*, p. 216 (my italics).

the Lord makes days of fatness and of drought, but He will always provide for His own... plant them in Egypt so that they could become a nation under the most favorable circumstances, and then to bring them back to the land.[63]

Aalders shares the same view that 'God in His sovereign plan brought [the famine] upon that part of the world' in order to resettle Jacob's family to Egypt and to make them a great nation there.[64] To mitigate the seeming unfairness of bringing famine upon Egypt just for the benefit of Jacob's family, Barnhouse has to insist that the Egyptians are saved but not enslaved. Ross, however, accepts the fact that the Egyptians 'were in bondage to Pharaoh'.[65] He also believes that God uses the famine as 'the means of bringing the family to Egypt'. But he avoids blaming God for the Egyptians' suffering by interpreting the famine as a natural disaster.[66]

There is no strong evidence in the text that the famine is a divine judgment. It also does not look justifiable for God to make a famine just in order to resettle Jacob's family and in the process hurt many innocent people.[67] Finally, some readers attempt to resolve the problem by appealing to God's sovereignty to bring destruction and deliverance.[68] However, it is a precarious place to stress God's power to destroy and to deliver when Judah also delivers Joseph from the destruction for which he is also held responsible.

Joseph's Credibility as the Narrator's Mouthpiece

Has God really made the famine? The narrator does not give an explicit answer. It is then better to ask whether the narrator probably agrees

63. Barnhouse, *Genesis*, p. 181.

64. Aalders, *Genesis*, p. 257. Stigers, *A Commentary on Genesis*, p. 289, not only considers the famine as judgment on sinful people, but also as a means used by God 'to secure the removal of Jacob and his clan to Egypt'. He explains the purpose for the resettlement. Jacob's family are to be removed from 'the temptation to intermarry' with the corrupted Canaanites, and this problem will not happen in Egypt 'because of Egyptian dislike of foreigners' (p. 270).

65. Ross, *Creation and Blessing*, p. 687.

66. Ross, *Creation and Blessing*, p. 651.

67. The question why God makes the famine is bound to be asked if he also intends to save lives from it. Joseph declares clearly God's purpose for his dreams is to save lives, but he does not explain the purpose of Pharaoh's dreams.

68. E.g. Brueggemann, *Genesis*, p. 331; Aalders, *Genesis*, p. 257.

with this particular claim by Joseph or not. Before considering the narrator's viewpoint, it is important to ponder first whether Joseph really means what he says about the God-sent famine. It will have significant implications for Joseph's credibility as the narrator's mouthpiece.

Joseph Means What He Says

Joseph may consider the purpose of salvation sufficient for the justification of his domination, but Judah's similar rationalization of rescuing him from death into slavery (37.26-27) renders his excuse rather hollow and questionable. And if Joseph really means that God brings about the famine, then the final obstacle to equating Joseph's dreams with Judah's pit will be removed. It is difficult to differentiate between them because they are so much alike. Judah's rescue is preceded by his involvement in the act of endangering his brother. Thus by repeatedly declaring that God has made the famine (41.25, 28, 32),[69] Joseph is portraying God as acting like Judah as the source of both danger and deliverance. Moreover, he undermines himself further by pronouncing his final verdict on the opposition between Judah's pit and his dreams: 'As for you, you meant evil against me; but God meant it for good, to bring it about that many people should be kept alive, as they are today' (50.20).

In his previous disclosure speech (45.4-11), he stressed the overriding of human action (to sell) by divine action (to send). Now his clear-cut judgment of good and evil establishes his dreams as radically different to Judah's pit. However, his repeated assertions of the God-sent famine force one to concede that remarkable similarities exist between them. Therefore, on the one hand, his assertions create a force pulling his dreams and Judah's pit together, but on the other hand, his judgment also attempts to rupture them. The tension created by his words is undoubtedly dramatic.

Ostensibly, Joseph refers the evil to the pit inflicted on him by his brothers; his condemnation is not directed to Judah's rationale of subservience for survival because he is unaware of it. The ironic reversal of Judah's role as a victimizer (37.26-27) to a victim of his own device (44.33-34) is a clear sign that the narrator is critical of the idea of sub-

---

69. Three times he claims that God has made the famine, and he also claims three times that God has sent him and made him lord to preserve lives from this famine (45.5, 7, 8-11). Unfortunately, the interrelation of these contradictory claims has rarely been noticed in the past.

servience for survival. If the pit of slavery is the only target of condemnation, then a simple punishment of pit for pit, slavery for slavery, is sufficient to denounce Judah's selling his brothers into slavery. However, Joseph's test involves a larger scheme made by the narrator that puts Judah through the agony of facing the threat of the death of his father on the one hand, and the threat of slavery on the other. Judah's lengthy speech of anguish in 44.18-34 best captures this painful struggle. It repeats a situation under which he has to opt for his own subservience in order to secure the survival of his father. Therefore, the condemnation of Judah, through this ironic reversal, reaches beyond his crime to the hideous pretence behind it. As I have argued in the previous chapter, it is unlikely that Joseph would aim at such a reversal.

Joseph is ignorant of Judah's rationalization and its ironic reversal by his test. He also unwittingly repeats its basic idea in his justification of his dreams. To compound his ignorance further, his claim of a God-sent famine parallels Judah's roles as both destroyer and deliverer with that of God. Therefore, it is highly possible that Joseph is the target of the narrator's ironic treatment.[70] The juxtaposition of his claim to domination expressed in his dreams with Judah's rationalization of the pit of slavery puts into the question of the certainty of the coalescence of perspectives of Joseph, the narrator and God.[71] On the other hand, if the narrator intends to use Joseph as a mouthpiece to advocate the ideology of subservience for survival, then allowing Judah to act as an anti-hero and his rationalization as a counterpoint to Joseph's claim will not be a wise strategy.

Joseph Does Not Mean What He Says

The opposite option, that is, that Joseph does not mean to say that God has made the famine, hardly looks any better as far as Joseph's credibility is concerned. There will be a critical difference between Judah's pit and Joseph's dreams if the famine is a natural disaster. It will reduce the similarity between them but at a price of weakening the authority of Joseph's interpretation of dreams. As a result, his role as a reliable spokesman of God becomes questionable.

70. The ironic treatment of Joseph by the narrator has been recognised by some readers in the case of his claim of God's help to forget his father's house. See footnote 24.

71. E.g. Hugh C. White, 'Where Do You Come From?', in *idem, Narration and Discourse*, pp. 269, 270.

Many readers take the famine as a natural disaster without any discussion. It is probably because it makes no sense to them why God
wants to plan salvation from a famine which he has created in the first
place. The assumption that it is a natural disaster will differentiate
Joseph's dreams from Judah's pit. Judah saves life which he endan-
gered in the first place, while Joseph saves lives from a natural disaster.
Judah's crime is then not comparable with Joseph's salvation. However,
the posing of the distinction of crime and natural disaster, if used as an
attempt to defend Joseph, will open a Pandora's box revealing all kinds
of difficulty for his credibility.

First of all, Joseph's accurate interpretation of Pharaoh's dreams is
crucial to establish his authority in interpretation and it makes possible
the fulfilment of his own dreams. It is difficult not to accept his claim of
God planning his rise to power for the purpose of salvation (but the
reader should take notice that the narrator has not endorsed Joseph's
view explicitly). Pharaoh is quick to accept his interpretation (41.38)
and his brothers do not have any objection after his disclosure.[72] Therefore, few readers would question his credibility as a spokesman for God
as well as for the narrator. However, his disclosure of God's action for
Pharaoh can also be subversive to his credibility and can pose a threat
to the legitimization of his dreams of domination. Since he has asserted
several times that the famine is sent by God, it is then difficult to distinguish his dreams from Judah's pit since the latter is a crime and the
former a natural disaster. The protagonist prevents anyone from setting
up this distinction unless one disregards part of his words about God's
intentions. That is indeed what many readers do when they take the
famine as a natural one.[73] They seem to believe in all his words to
Pharaoh, but on a close inspection, only the part that predicts of the
coming famine is accepted as accurate.[74] His disclosure of God's inten-

---

72. The failure of wise men in interpretation is seen as a support for Joseph's
authority of interpretation. Westermann, *Joseph*, p. 45, thus comments, 'The narrative is clear and simply organized. It derives its suspense from the failure of the
Egyptian wise men to interpret the dreams (vv. 8 and 24b), who are thus put in an
unfavorable light.'

73. See footnotes 37-42.

74. Regarding Joseph's interpretation of Pharaoh's dreams, many readers focus
only on the aspect of prediction. E.g. Morris, *The Genesis Record*, p. 581, comments, 'God would indeed fulfill its predictions, and would do so beginning very
soon'; Westermann, *Joseph*, p. 46.

tion to send the famine is entirely neglected or suppressed even though he repeats it three times in such a short space (41.25, 28, 32). In contrast, the prediction and fulfilment of Joseph's rise to power and his claim of God's intention for it are inseparable for those who accept his claim.[75] In the case of Pharaoh's dreams, the coming famine is interpreted by Joseph as God's action. This understanding is rejected by those who prefer to see it as a natural disaster. For them, to question part of his interpretation is not necessarily to deny the accuracy of his prediction. However, this rejection has serious implications for Joseph's credibility.

His interpretation of Pharaoh's dreams is always regarded as authoritative, but an important part of it (i.e. his claim that the famine is sent by God) is rejected as untrue against the plain meaning of his repeated assertions. He is thus no longer a reliable source of God's intentions. Significantly, the rejection is carried out covertly without acknowledgment. To deny part of his interpretation of Pharaoh's dreams while not exposing its fault openly is to satisfy two necessities: first, it prevents damaging his claims of divine providence and domination (45.5-11), if the problem of God being the source of both the famine and its relief can be avoided; secondly, if his repeated assertions are rejected openly, his credibility will be tarnished irrevocably. Therefore, his fault has to be rejected but not exposed.

This suppression, if intended to avoid exposing Joseph's contradiction, would still undermine his credibility. His series of claims in this story depends crucially on his interpretation of Pharaoh's dreams. It is ironic that his repeated assertions about God's intentions are effectively rejected at a place in the narrative where his authority of interpretation is supposedly most secure. Joseph is enthusiastic to ascribe the author-

---

75. A rare exception is Leupold, *Exposition*, pp. 956-57, who does not regard Joseph's dreams as 'divinely inspired'. He suggests, 'they are out of Joseph's ambiguous thoughts but are divinely controlled so as to express what afterward actually transpired'. This amounts to a rejection of Joseph's claim to a divine purpose for his dreams even though they become reality. In the case of Joseph's accurate interpretation of the dreams of Pharaoh's two officers (40.1-23), most readers do not link the fulfilment of each to God's specific will. There is also no attempt by Joseph to involve God in their future. Their fates are either due to their own merit or to Pharaoh's arbitrary decision on the occasion of his birthday. The separation between the prediction of a future event and God's intention in it also makes it possible for those readers who perceive the famine as simply a natural disaster foretold by God.

ity of his interpretation to God. To Pharaoh's chief butler and baker, he says, 'Do not interpretations belong to God?' (40.8). Later he affirms to Pharaoh, 'It is not in me; God will give Pharaoh a favourable answer' (41.16). His effort to attribute the source of his interpretation to God serves to enhance the authority of his interpretation. But this effort to boost God's image and his credibility backfires. God's justice is unwittingly put into doubt by Joseph's effort to stress his power to bring about the famine. It is not that God's power is unfulfilled, but its very fulfilment puts in grave doubt its justice. This in turn brings damage to Joseph's credibility as a reliable spokesman of God.

Joseph's prediction for various dreams in this story is very accurate. It is hard for anyone not to come to a similar conclusion as Joseph's about God's intention for his dreams. The fulfilment of the brothers' bowing down (42.6; 43.26-28; 50.18) also gives support to Joseph's claim of God's plan for his dreams. Furthermore, God's sanction of Jacob's descent to Egypt (46.2-4) seems to form part of Joseph's disclosed divine plan to preserve his family (45.5-11).[76] Fretheim notices the parallel between these two speeches: 'Both move from self-identification to the quelling of fear to an announcement, only this time regarding the future. While parallel in form, Joseph's word to his brothers and God's word to Jacob are complementary in content.'[77] Therefore, there is evidence in this story that the narrator may agree with Joseph's perception of the divine intention.

However, if the narrator intends to promote the ideology of slavery for salvation, it is counterproductive to allow Joseph to claim that God has made the famine. If Joseph does not really mean it, allowing his repeated wrong assertions will jeopardize the clarity of the message. The impression of juxtaposing Judah and God is not easily eradicated once it is registered. The appearance of error is sometimes as important as the actual error itself. It is especially damaging because the real cause of the famine cannot be determined with certainty due to the absence of the narrator's explicit confirmation. The doubt over the similarity between Judah's pit and Joseph's dreams will linger on without resolution.

76. It is the only place where God appears and speaks in this story. Cf. Humphreys, *Joseph and his Family*, p. 119.
77. Fretheim, *Genesis*, p. 652. See also Ackerman, 'Joseph, Judah, and Jacob', p. 108.

In the end, the reader is not even sure if Joseph means what he says. Does he really mean to say that it is a God-sent famine? Or does he exaggerate the role of God in his attempt to impress Pharaoh? Joseph's intention is difficult to ascertain and so is the narrator's viewpoint on his words. Yet by posing these two options, my objective is not to determine his real intention with certainty. It is rather to chart their consequences for his credibility. If Joseph means what he says, it is difficult to envisage that the narrator would agree with Joseph's description of God's actions because of their close parallel with Judah's rationalization and imposition. If Joseph does not mean what he says, his repeated false assertions will undermine his credibility. Therefore, taking his words in their plain meaning or not, either way will tarnish his image as a reliable spokesman of God and the narrator. Any attempt to distinguish Joseph's dreams from Judah's pit using the distinction between natural cause and crime will only expose the incoherence of Joseph's words. Joseph's claim that the famine is sent by God has consequences for our evaluation of the overall picture of God's intentions presented by the protagonist. His claim of being destined by God to lord it over others depends on his credibility as God's reliable spokesman. If these two claims are contradictory and one of them has to be rejected, then everything he says about God's intentions has to be reexamined. The assumption of the coalescence of the perspectives of Joseph and the narrator will then be an open question rather than a foregone conclusion.

Summary

In contrast to the narratives of the previous patriarchs, God rarely appears as a participating character in the Joseph story. However, the name of God has frequently been in the mouth of the characters in this story. Confronted with the fact of the discovery of the silver cup in Benjamin's sack, Judah knows that it is hopeless for the brothers to defend themselves against the Egyptian lord and thus he says,

> What shall we say to my lord? What shall we speak? Or how can we clear ourselves? God has found out the guilt of your servants; behold, we are my lord's slaves, both we and he also in whose hand the cup has been found (44.16).

Joseph has planted the silver cup in Benjamin's sack; the brothers are innocent. However, one may interpret Judah's confession of guilt as referring indirectly to their previous crime of selling Joseph. The narrator may indeed intend to make a juxtaposition between the brothers' past crime and the present accused crime. The purpose is to create a sense of poetic justice that a crime done in secret has to be confessed in public.[78] The characters themselves are not aware of such association. Redford comments that Judah's confession 'bears a meaning the speaker is quite unaware of'.[79] This interpretation is by no mean certain. When falsely accused of spying, the brothers at once associate the distress of their present situation with their guilt in inflicting distress upon Joseph (42.21-22). When they discover that the money they have used to buy food in Egypt has been put back in one of their sacks on their first journey home, they are terrified and say, 'What is this that God has done to us?' (42.28). The brothers have a strong feeling that God is somehow working against them in return for their past crime. It is therefore possible, against Redford's assertion, that Judah's confession might consciously refer to their previous crime. However, Judah's confession may be only a tactic to appease the Egyptian lord who has claimed to be a God-fearing man (cf. 42.18). It is a manoeuvre rather than a true description of what God has done as confessed by Judah.

Another dubious appeal to the name of God is made by Joseph's steward. When he replies to the anxiety of the brothers concerning the money found in their sacks in the first journey, he says, 'Rest assured, do not be afraid; your God and the God of your father must have put treasure in your sacks for you; I received your money' (43.23). This is of course a total lie because it is Joseph, not God, who orders the planting of the money in their sacks (42.25).[80] Joseph's steward has not employed the name of God in a truthful way. Whether Judah is sincere in confessing the brothers' crime against Joseph cannot be ascertained. These two examples do not implicate Joseph's declaration of God's intentions in one way or another. But they should serve to warn readers to be cautious of any appeal to the name of God by the characters in this story. All Joseph's claims may be justifiable individually. How-

78. Redford, *Biblical Story of Joseph*, pp. 72-74, remarks, 'one of the distinguishing features of the Joseph story which sets it apart from all other Patriarchal Tales is the pivot of irony upon which the entire plot turns'.

79. Redford, *Biblical Story of Joseph*, p. 74.

80. White, 'Where Do You Come From?', p. 264, recognizes that the steward 'deliberately plays upon the popular tendency to see in the uncanny the action of the divine'.

ever, on relating them together, their problems become apparent. His claims in ch. 45 do not accord well with his claims in ch. 41. What he says about forgetfulness as caused by God is simply wrong. It becomes more problematic when he alleges that God plans salvation from the famine which he himself created. The more he says about God's actions and intentions, the more questions he raises.[81]

Undoubtedly, Joseph has the last word in this narrative, but the narrator's reticence towards it cannot be seen as a tacit endorsement. Judging from the discrepancies in his various claims, it is possible that the narrator juxtaposes Joseph's justification of his dreams of domination with Judah's rationalization of the pit of slavery in order to provide an ironic ending to this story. The climactic good/evil judgment in 50.20 by the protagonist dramatizes the tension and ambiguity further in this interesting story of parallels and reversals.

81. Sailhamer, *Pentateuch as Narrative*, p. 207, like other readers, believes 'every detail of the narrative' can demonstrate the 'truthfulness' of Joseph's final words to his brothers (50.20).

Chapter 4

READERS' RESPONSES TO JOSEPH'S CLAIMS

Joseph's justification of his dreams is a classic case of justifying one's own interest (as a lord) to those who are being subordinated in the name of the interest of all (salvation of many lives). At first sight, Joseph's ideology is not easy to justify. However his words have succeeded in persuading generations of readers, ancient or modern. This chapter looks at how the incoherence of Joseph's claims and the narrator's critical stance towards them elude the scrutiny of many readers. The first part surveys the responses of the biblical scholars, and the second part focuses on the treatment of the Joseph story in its literary character by several literary scholars.

Avoidance of Challenging Joseph's Claims

Outdated Ideology

For some readers, the ideology of Joseph's claims does not require the reader's criticism, because a proper interpretation of the ancient texts does not concern itself with judging past ideology against present moral standards.[1] However, the positive image of Joseph as a wise courtier

---

1. Lothar Ruppert, *Die Josephserzählung der Genesis: Ein Beitrag zur Theologie der Pentateuchquellen* (Munich: Kösel, 1965), p. 155, e.g., considers that it is out of place to adopt a moral judgment and condemnation of the policy of Joseph with a Christian-humanist standard ('Eine sittliche Be- und Verurteilung des Verfahrens Josephs ist fehl am Platze, da der Ersterzähler und wohl auch J an eine solche Bewertungsmöglichkeit gar nicht gedacht haben dürften; auch würde sie fremde, d.h. christlich-humanistische Maßstäbe anlegen'). Aalders, *Genesis*, p. 256, suggests that any evaluation of Joseph's measures must be based on 'the principles of moral conduct that are taught in Scripture as a whole' and not on the 'present-day political insights and standards'. Ephraim A. Speiser, *Genesis* (AB, 1; Garden City, NY: Doubleday, 1969), p. 353, also argues against the making of 'censorious comments' by 'modern moralizers' on 'the enslavement of the Egyptian peasant'

and righteous model recurs persistently across the ages and in different religious traditions (Jewish, Catholic, Protestant and Islamic). Therefore, the line separating different ages in moral and ideological judgment (positive as well as negative) is not as sharp as some suggest. Admittedly, people in an ancient culture would react differently from modern readers to the idea of domination of one person over others.[2] Commenting on the legitimacy of royal authority of Israelite kingship, Keith Whitelam gives us a picture of the ancient Israelite hierarchical ideology:

> David and his successors…were forced to offer a world view or construction of reality that not only gave legitimacy to their authority and its corrective social structure but also offered the general population order, prosperity, security and fertility, and so on, in return for loyalty and subservience (cf. Pss. 72; 89; etc.)…despite the exploitative nature of social relations, such symbols of power also signified the important benefits of peace and stability without which the vast majority of the population, dependent upon the uninterrupted cultivation of their crops, faced the very real threat of famine and death.[3]

In Genesis, all patriarchs or would-be patriarchs play the role of a ruler who is required to look after the welfare of his family. Abraham pursues and defeats the four kings, and rescues the family and possessions of his cousin Lot from their previous abduction (15.14-16); Jacob

---

because it shows 'little understanding of either history or literature'. First, the Pharaoh is viewed by his people as a god who owns all things in Egypt. Secondly, private ownership of land appears to have been sanctioned in the Middle Kingdom, but the need for a stronger government at the beginning of the New Kingdom after the expulsion of the Hyksos would seem to have made the pharaohs reassert their titular rights. He concludes that the 'agrarian changes' may reflect actual socio-economic developments and there is no evidence that Egyptian society would have found such changes to be anything other than 'constructive'. In reply, it must be noted that the changes involve more than the loss of the land but also 'the enslavement of the Egyptian peasant'. The Egyptians are driven by starvation to give up their freedom and property. Such changes may be beneficial to the pharaohs but to the Egyptian people, they must be anything but 'constructive'.

2.   Walter Russell Bowie, *Genesis* (IB, 1; Nashville: Abingdon Press, 1952), p. 811, comments that 'autocracy was taken for granted' in ancient times and that 'Joseph should have been an autocrat in Egypt did not surprise any one'.

3.   Keith W. Whitelam, 'The Defence of David', *JSOT* 29 (1984), pp. 61-87 (64). Westermann, *Joseph*, p. x, considers the Joseph story as political propaganda or justification compiled during the reigns of David and Solomon.

refers to an unknown battle that he has fought to capture more land to
give to his children (48.22); apparently being resentful of the lack of
leadership of their father, Simeon and Levi take upon them the responsibility of defending the 'moral integrity' of the family and stage a surprise attack on the city of Shechem (34.25-31). During the long period
of fraternal conflict, both Judah and Reuben step forward to offer sug-
gestions for rescuing their family members (Joseph and Benjamin).
Thus Joseph is not alone in this story in shouldering the obligation of a
patriarch to look after the welfare of his family members. In this case, it
is their survival from the threat of famine and death, which is an important motif in the legitimization of hierarchical ideology as Whitelam
describes it above.

In an ancient agricultural society, the privilege of occupying the
dominating role in a family brings with it an important responsibility,
that is, the provision of food for the family members, especially for the
little ones.[4] Therefore, Judah entreats Jacob to allow Benjamin to come
down to Egypt to acquire food with them, 'that we may live and not
die, both we and you and also our little ones' (43.8).[5] After the disclosure scene, Joseph urges his brothers to bring down their 'little ones',
'wives' and 'father' (45.19) so that he can provide them with food
according to the number of their 'little ones' (47.12). Later, assuaging
his brothers' resurfaced fear, Joseph reassures them again, 'do not fear,
I will provide for you and your little ones' (50.21). The narrator directs
our attention to Joseph's persistent efforts to play the role of patriarch
in protecting and providing for his family members, especially the little
ones.[6] To the Egyptians whom he enslaves for Pharaoh, he also says, 'at
the harvests you shall give a fifth to Pharaoh, and four fifths shall be

4.   Ackerman, 'Joseph, Judah, and Jacob', p. 98, describes 'Judah's stress on
the survival of "the little ones"—the next generation—that finally moves Jacob to
risk the death of his last beloved son, Benjamin'.
5.   Sailhamer, *Genesis*, pp. 265-66, parallels these words of Judah to his father
(43.8) with Jacob's previous similar words in telling his sons to go down to Egypt
to buy grain 'that we may live and not die' (42.2). With another similar plea by the
Egyptians to Joseph, 'Why should we die before your eyes?' (47.15, cf. 47.19),
Sailhamer suggests that these repetitions represent a thematic strategy in the narrative. Its purpose in the end is to stress that 'Joseph's wisdom is seen as the source of
life for everyone in the land'.
6.   Westermann, *Genesis 37–50*, p. 205, observes the 'continual concern for the
children' in this narrative.

your own, as seed for the field and as food for yourselves and your households, and as food for your little ones' (47.24).[7]

For those who are given protection and provision, there is a price of loyalty and subservience which they have to pay. In the light of an understanding of the ancient culture, it is important to recognize that the hostile reaction of Joseph's brothers to Joseph's dreams may not be a rejection of the social structure implied in the hierarchical ideology. Westermann, however, considers the brothers' anger at the dreams as representing a rejection of the idea that 'one brother should lord it over the others'. He suggests that the storyteller of this narrative is 'writing in a time when the kingdom had taken firm root, but he is looking backwards to a time of patriarchs who knew no kingdoms—a time when the nomads abhorred the very idea of such a political state (see Joshua 9!)'.[8] There are indeed differences in social structure and ideology between a patriarchal society and a kingdom. But suggesting that there is no hierarchical power structure of one member over the other in a patriarchal society does not accord well with the evidence in the text. Jacob as a patriarch exercises almost absolute power over his family members. Without his permission, even in danger of death for all, no one can take away his favoured son. Reuben, as the eldest son who is normally due to succeed as the patriarchal head of the family, would allow his two sons to be killed if he could not bring Benjamin back (42.37).

The brothers' rhetorical questions to Joseph do not necessarily represent a rebellion against hierarchical ideology. They are simply angry at the younger brother's apparently presumptuous gesture of usurping the privilege accorded to the elder in the norm of their time. Therefore, it is fair to suggest that the characters (both the brothers and the enslaved Egyptians) whose lives and livelihood depend on their protector and provider do not challenge the idea of subservience for survival. While those being subordinated do not actively pose a challenge to their situation, it does not imply that those who rule have no need to defend their power to dominate others. Sheer might[9] alone is not sufficient for estab-

---

7.   While the house of Jacob and its little ones are freely provided for, the house of Egypt and its little ones have to exchange their property and freedom for food.

8.   Westermann, *Joseph*, p. 10.

9.   Whitelam, 'The Defence of David', p. 61, states, 'The manipulation of the force of arms alone has seldom, if ever, been sufficient for a ruler or regime to ensure or maintain control over a particular area and its population.'

lishing the authority of the ruler. Whitelam thus comments, 'Religion has been used frequently as a most effective means of legitimizing and establishing power.'[10] Joseph becomes a powerful lord over his brothers and the Egyptians. He has absolute power over their lives. But he still has to justify his position. The brothers' angry reproach to him ('Are you indeed to reign over us? Or are you indeed to have dominion over us?' cf. 37.8) is later transformed into their full acquiescence, 'Behold, we are your servants (slaves)' (50.18). Their change is more probably due to their fear of his power rather than to their acceptance of his explanation of the purpose of his dreams. Joseph's reassurance and promise of provision of food for them and their little ones are especially revealing (50.21). Provision of food requires prostration. The physical gesture of bowing down indicates a hierarchical relation between them.

Under the shadow of the powerful lord and the burden of their guilt, it is understandable that the brothers do not and could not question his claim. No ideology can be taken for granted; some sorts of explanation have to be given for its defence and propagation. If Joseph himself attempts to justify his dreams, the reader is entitled to examine this justification. Objective interpretation prevents us from judging the culture which is quite different from ours. However, it does not prevent us from examining whether his justification is coherent or not, especially in the light of the textual evidence and the narrator's stance. By appealing to the purpose of salvation, Joseph unwittingly repeats Judah's rationalisation of survival at the price of subservience. My previous chapters have attempted to prove that Joseph's justification weakens rather than strengthens his privileged position.

Confronting Joseph's Behaviour rather than his Belief

Joseph has been subjected to criticism for a long time. Most readers criticize his behaviour towards his brothers and the Egyptian people. Their criticisms are seldom directed at his claims. Commenting generally on the behaviour of the characters in Genesis, Wenham cautions us that their deeds may not be endorsed by the narrator:

> Thus though the writers rarely put into words their moral approval or disapproval of their heroes' actions, they are not by recording their deeds always endorsing or exonerating them. On the contrary, the narrator

10. Whitelam, 'The Defence of David', p. 64.

expects his readers to share his moral outlook and like him to be shocked that the fathers of the nation should behave in such ways.[11]

In Joseph's case, Wenham does not hesitate to criticize him as a 'spoiled brat', 'precocious and uppity teenager'.[12] In contrast, Joseph's words enjoy his unreserved endorsement:

> During his slavery and imprisonment, the narrator had said that the Lord was with Joseph (39.2, 21, 23). Now Joseph makes the same point himself; four times he describes himself as God's agent: 'God sent me before you to preserve life' (45.5; cf. vv. 7-8); 'God has made me lord of all Egypt' (45.9). Even his steward makes the same point, 'Your god... must have put treasure into your sacks', even though he presumably knew it had been put there on Joseph's order (43.23; cf. 42.25). The statements about God's overruling of human affairs are undoubtedly the keys to understanding the whole Joseph story.[13]

The narrator reports the fact that the Lord is with Joseph, but this does not automatically endorse whatever Joseph says at various points. The narrator also reports that God is with the previous three patriarchs: Abraham (21.22), Isaac (26.3, 24, 28) and Jacob (28.15). They all tell lies on various occasions: Abraham (12.13; 20.5), Isaac (26.7) and Jacob (27.20). The truthfulness of the words of the patriarchs cannot be guaranteed simply because the narrator once affirms that God is with them. The reader has to judge their words both in themselves and in their own contexts. Mentioning the name of God does not itself confirm their truthfulness. For example, when Jacob lies to his father, he says, 'Because the Lord your God granted me success' (27.20). Similarly, acting under his master's order, the steward's lie about God's intention could only jeopardize rather than support Joseph's claim.

Humphreys recognizes the need to judge Joseph by his 'words and deeds',[14] but in the end he only criticizes Joseph's harsh treatment of his brothers and father. When Joseph speaks of the divine perspective in 45.5-8 and 50.18-21, he considers it as a real change, a change of 'not giving up his power, but subjecting it to a greater authority'.[15] It is

---

11. Gordon J. Wenham, 'The Gap between Law and Ethics in the Bible', *JJS* 48.1 (Spring 1997), pp. 17-29 (18).

12. Wenham, *Genesis 16–50*, pp. 357, 431.

13. Wenham, *Genesis 16–50*, p. 432.

14. Humphreys, *Joseph and his Family*, p. 181.

15. Humphreys, *Joseph and his Family*, p. 91. Similarly, White, 'Where Do

much harder to disagree with Joseph's claims than with his behaviour. However, it is also not easy to justify his claims. At no point in the narrative does the narrator give his explicit support. The narrative principle is clear that a character's speech is not as reliable as the report of the narrator. However, the narrator's approval of Joseph's words is generally assumed by many readers even though they disapprove of his actions.

Manipulating his brothers ruthlessly. The negative image of Joseph portrayed by generations of readers results mainly from his poor relationship with his brothers. The seed of their conflict is planted when Joseph brings an 'ill report' of them to their father (37.2). They probably are not aware of his action[16] and it is Jacob's favouritism towards Joseph through a special item of clothing given to him that initiates their hatred. Joseph infuriates them further by reporting his first dream of ruling over them (vv. 6-7).[17] Their enmity towards him is verbally expressed twice (vv. 4, 8), yet he seems to be oblivious to their feeling and tells them the second dream. Whether he intends it or not, his actions provoke his brothers' anger. However, at his father's request, he goes to find them to see how they are.[18] The ways he handles his dreams can be perceived negatively as being insensitive of his brothers'

You Come From?', p. 258, sees a change in Joseph from 'the egoistic favorite son' to 'a self-effacing agent of divine knowledge'.

    16. Cf. Niehoff, *Figure of Joseph*, pp. 28-29; Adele Berlin, *Poetics and Interpretation of Biblical Narrative* (Bible and Literature Series, 9; Sheffield: Almond Press, 1983), p. 48.

    17. Morris, *The Genesis Record*, p. 536, suggests that 'even if the dream came from the Lord, it was for his own encouragement, not for their edification, and he was very unwise to insist on telling it to them'. However, John Peck, 'Note on Gen. 37:2 and Joseph's Character', *ExpTim* 82 (1970/71), pp. 342-343 (343), regards Joseph's dreams as 'prophetic oracles (as in the rest of the story)', so that he is 'under divine constraint to deliver his message'; von Rad, *Genesis*, pp. 351-52, also defends Joseph's action by asserting that 'a vision was for the ancients so important and obligatory that a demand to keep it tactfully to oneself would not have occurred to them'. But in Genesis, the characters do not report their visions in this way. It seems that Rebekah has not reported (25.22-23) her vision to Isaac. Abraham, Isaac and Jacob each has received divine visions or dreams, but there are no reports of their sharing them with others. The chief butler and chief baker only tell their dreams when they are asked by Joseph. Pharaoh calls for the magicians to interpret his dreams only because he is troubled by them.

    18. Goodnick, 'Character of Joseph', p. 220.

feelings;[19] or positively as being totally innocent and honest.[20]

For many readers, Joseph's earlier interaction with his brothers forms a bad impression of him, but he is criticized most for subjecting his brothers to a long and tormenting test. He is portrayed as 'a ruthless, arbitrary despot' in the ordeal he puts his brothers through.[21] He is accused of 'toying'[22] with them and such tormenting by false accusation 'does not fit easily with the belief that Joseph is being presented as an ideal administrator and the archetypal Wise man'.[23] For Holbert, Joseph's 'famous theological dictum' in 50.20 cannot 'obliterate the cruel game he has played' on others.[24] Coats's verdict on Joseph's test is also unambiguous: 'Revenge may well characterise properly the process of Joseph's trial with his victim.'[25] Even though Brueggemann finds Joseph in ch. 37 as 'a naïve and guileless boy', he also contrasts his ruthless behaviour with his previous noble conduct in chs. 39–41:

> he is a noble and effective man of integrity who is not intimidated by the royal woman (39), the royal officers (40), or even the Pharaoh (41). But in 42–44, he is now a ruthless and calculating governor. He understands the potential of his enormous office and exploits his capacity fully. He not only manipulates the scene but seems to relish his power to intimidate and threaten.[26]

However, Wenham defends Joseph's actions and asserts that 'he may have appeared the heartless foreign tyrant to his brothers'. In his opinion, the narrator makes it plain that this is not the way he views it: Joseph's repeated weeping (42.24; 43.30; 45.1-2, 14-15) demonstrates

---

19. Lerner, 'Joseph the Unrighteous', p. 279, criticizes Joseph for being 'incapable of consideration for his brothers' in 'relating to them his dreams of dominion'. Joseph's 'insensitivity' eventually 'led to his enslavement and exile'.

20. Goodnick, 'Character of Joseph', p. 219, stresses Joseph's honesty rather than his insensitivity, 'The extent of his guilelessness and obliviousness to the reactions of others is also exposed by his presenting a second dream to his brothers after they had just asked him, cynically, whether he intended to rule over them. What character traits of Joseph can we discern at this time? Evidently, honesty, openness, sincerity, and a moral outlook.'

21. Miscall, 'The Jacob and Joseph Stories as Analogies', p. 33.

22. Josipovici, 'Joseph and Revelation', p. 75.

23. Turner, *Announcements of Plot in Genesis*, pp. 154-55.

24. Holbert, 'Joseph and the Surprising Choice of God', p. 40.

25. Coats, *From Canaan to Egypt*, p. 85. Cf. Alter, *Art of Biblical Narrative*, p. 163; Savran, *Telling and Retelling*, p. 87.

26. Brueggemann, *Genesis*, p. 337.

that he is only putting on 'a hard front' in order to solicit from them a 'sincere repentance'.[27] Instead of reporting the unspecified evil in 37.2, Joseph's test is seen as a divine instrument of punishment and correction for the brothers' evil against him. Von Rad suggests that Joseph 'constructed a situation in which it had to become evident whether they would act as they once had done or whether they had changed in the meantime'.[28] He considers the outcome as desirable because Judah's words had shown that the brothers had changed. And they obviously intend to treat Rachel's younger son quite differently from the way they had formerly treated the elder son.[29]

Similarly, Schimmel praises Joseph's concern with the moral rehabilitation of his brothers. 'Joseph's piety,' he comments, 'resides in this—he would rather see his enemies purified of their sinfulness than punish them for it.'[30] Joseph's action is recognized as harsh, but it indeed has a good effect on his brothers.[31] But by cheating their father, the brothers can also be seen as instruments to punish Jacob's previous cheating of his father Isaac. Nobody would condone the brothers' action even if it has a punitive effect on Jacob. Joseph's own word of divine providence of good overriding evil also serves to highlight the

27. Wenham, *Genesis 16–50*, pp. 431-33.

28. Von Rad, *Genesis*, p. 388. But the situation is not necessarily parallel. The brothers kill/sell Joseph on their own initiative, whereas they are forced to defend Benjamin. In the former case they are indeed guilty, but they are totally innocent in this test. And if they fail to protect Benjamin, their inactions are excusable if not justified.

29. Von Rad, *Genesis*, p. 392. Alter, *Art of Biblical Narrative*, p. 161, describes Joseph's action towards the brothers as 'an ultimate test of the nature of their brotherhood with Joseph, a bond which they have denied by selling him into slavery and which they will now be forced to recognize in a new way'; Ackerman, 'Joseph, Judah, and Jacob', p. 94, considers Joseph's intention is to prove 'their truthfulness' and 'to learn whether they are grown and changed—whether there is the possibility of reestablishing brotherhood with them'.

30. Schimmel, 'Joseph and his Brothers', p. 63. Barnhouse, *Genesis*, p. 188, also asserts that Joseph's treatment of the brothers 'was best for them'; Luther, *Lectures on Genesis: Chapters 45–50*, pp. 16-17, comments, 'indeed he has played a game with them that is sad and bitter enough; but he has done so with the greatest love and natural affection, since he was afraid that they had killed his aged father and his youngest brother'.

31. Turner, *Announcements of Plot in Genesis*, p. 159, comments that 'the narrative provides no support for the view that Joseph treated his brothers harshly in order to ascertain or provoke their repentance'.

fact that the good effect of the brothers' action will not eradicate their responsibility.[32] He does not exempt his brothers from their responsibility in selling him to slavery; he only asserts that God can work beyond and against human motives. This principle should be applicable to himself as much as to his brothers. Therefore, the good effect of Joseph's action upon the brothers does not exempt him from the responsibility for his action. If his treatment of them is harsh, his action should be judged accordingly.[33]

Joseph is also viewed as having no intention to hurt or take revenge on his brothers because he forgets all his suffering. Ackerman therefore comments, 'Like the reader, Joseph remembers not the betrayal or suffering wrought by his brothers, but his dreams.'[34] Niehoff also says, 'It nevertheless seems that the narrator does not attribute feelings of revenge to Joseph. Otherwise he would have made him remember his brothers' earlier brutality against him.'[35] The narrator reports only Joseph's remembering of his dreams. The reader is not told whether Joseph remembers his suffering or not.

Enslaving the Egyptians oppressively. The ways Joseph treats the Egyptians in his relief programme also attract a lot of discussion from readers in assessing his character. First, there are many disapproving comments. Janzen discusses the dilemma the Egyptians face when 'Joseph points to their cattle as barter' (47.16). The livestock will die without food in a famine, while if they are bartered the family loses its

32. Holbert, 'Joseph and the Surprising Choice of God', p. 41, speaks of human responsibility even under divine providence, 'The author of the Joseph narrative knows of a God of providing, a God who is with the chosen ones. But that author also affirms that human beings can choose within that providential care.'

33. Fritsch, 'God Was with Him', p. 28, notices Joseph's 'unusual' treatment, but he still defends him: 'The explanation for this unusual treatment of those who had harmed him is clearly brought out when Joseph says: "This do, and live; for I fear God" (42.18). Here is the key to Joseph's unique character. His impeccable conduct, whether as a slave or prisoner, or in Pharaoh's court, or in relation to his brethren, is attributed to the fact that he feared God, or to put it another way, that God was with him.'

34. Ackerman, 'Joseph, Judah, and Jacob', p. 87.

35. Niehoff, *Figure of Joseph*, p. 38. Sailhamer, *Pentateuch as Narrative*, p. 216, points out the relation between Joseph's remembering of his dreams and his test, 'Thus, the reader is advised that Joseph's schemes and plans against his brothers were motivated by the dreams of the earlier narratives and not by revenge for what his brothers had done to him.'

breeding base for future livestock. Even the famine will end soon, 'the rebuilding of their livestock will be slow and costly'.[36] The dilemma reappears when the famine does not end in the following year. If they do not barter the land, they will die of starvation, and the land itself will become 'desolate' and 'die' (v. 19), but if they lose it, they will have no basis at all for self-sufficiency. They are caught in 'a seller's market'.[37] Janzen suggests that the example of Naboth's loss of his vineyard (1 Kgs 21) encourages one to view Joseph's action with 'grave disapproval'. He is especially critical of the fact that 'the priests were not forced into the same situation as the rest of the people'.[38] Pointing out 'the narrator's threefold notice that Joseph married Asenath, daughter of the priest of On (41.45, 50; 46.20)', he considers that Joseph's 'special arrangement' for the priests appears to be a result of his convergence with the established interests in Egypt.[39] Instead of being an

---

36. Janzen, *Genesis 12–50*, p. 179. In contrast, Morris, *The Genesis Record*, p. 639, gives a more positive emphasis, 'the money and animals became the property of Pharaoh, or, in effect, owned by the central government. This arrangement actually benefited both the people and the animals, since they would have been unable to keep the animals alive during the famine.' Leupold, *Exposition,* pp. 1133, 1134, even considers that it 'really was a relief for the people in famine days to have the care of their cattle taken off their hands'. It is hard to imagine that the loss of one's property is purely a 'relief' and not rather a distress instead. Therefore, his suggestion that Joseph 'apparently' restores their livestock afterward is merely an attempt to lessen the harshness of his action.

37. Janzen, *Genesis 12–50*, p. 179. While Lerner, 'Joseph the Unrighteous', p. 278, suggests that Joseph 'sells back the food to its producers at an exorbitant price', most other readers stress that the tax later charged (a fifth part of the product) for their use of the land is 'very low by contemporary standards'. Cf. Arthur S. Herbert, *Genesis 12–50* (Torch Bible Commentaries; London: SCM Press, 1962), p. 147; Fretheim, *Genesis*, p. 654; Bush, *Notes on Genesis*, p. 367; Franz Delitzsch, *A New Commentary on Genesis*, II (trans. Sophia Taylor; Minneapolis: Klock & Klock Christian Publishers, 1978), p. 352. Leupold, *Exposition,* p. 1138, also remarks that what Joseph 'has done profits him nothing'.

38. Janzen, *Genesis 12–50*, p. 179.

39. Janzen, *Genesis 12–50*, p. 181. Delitzsch, *A New Commentary on Genesis*, p. 352, on the one hand remarks that 'Joseph preserved, in the first place, the interest of the king and respected the privileges of the priests, but abolished the free peasant class'; on the other hand he considers that 'Joseph undoubtedly had in view no less the good of the country than that of the king, when changing the disproportionately divided landed property into uniformed parcels of copyhold liable to rent.' Nevertheless, he quotes G.B. Niebuhr's view that 'the history of Joseph is a dangerous model for crafty ministers'.

evidence of his 'moral stature' (for not making money for himself), Joseph's effort to gather up all the money in Egypt and Canaan to Pharaoh's house (47.14) demonstrates his 'singular devotion to Pharaoh'.[40]

The concentration of Pharaoh's power by stripping the Egyptian people of their property and freedom is seen by many as having direct consequence for the future enslavement of the Israelite people. Almost all those who are critical of Joseph's action draw the same conclusion:

> In short, Pharaoh becomes very rich and powerful indeed, and the cause of all of it is Joseph, the Hebrew. Yet, the irony may cut even deeper. Because of Joseph's policies, the possibility of Pharaoh's control of labor comes into being; later, another, less generous, Pharaoh will use this policy to enslave the Hebrews. Thus one could say that Joseph, of all people, made the bondage of Israel possible.[41]

> In a society stripped of political morality, sudden mass enslavement and the murder of all male children can become feasible options of policy. It was under Joseph's initiative that the entire Egyptian population became enslaved to Pharaoh. Could the Jews, then, complain if they were required to serve Pharaoh's slaves? Ironically, they were forced to build treasure cities, doubtless to store wealth brought to the Pharaohs through Joseph's initiatives.[42]

> One is tempted to suggest that, long before there arose a new king over Egypt who had all too successfully forgotten his painful past, and in so doing had forgotten also the old Joseph. As we shall see, the forgetting is

40. Lerner, 'Joseph the Unrighteous', p. 280. Instead of being accused of aligning him with the privileged few, Joseph is said to make Pharaoh all-powerful in order to destroy the 'aristocracy' or 'hierarchy' of Egypt. Cf. Barnhouse, *Genesis*, p. 216; W. Gunther Plaut (ed.), *The Torah: A Modern Commentary* (New York: Union of American Hebrew Congregations, 1981), p. 299. Herbert, *Genesis 12–50*, pp. 146-47, explains that 'there was a constant struggle between the king and his feudal nobles', and through Joseph's skilful administration, the king 'was able to seize the opportunity to regain his domination over the land'. However, the text clearly states that 'all the Egyptians' come to beg for food (45.15) and sell their land (v. 20). Even if the struggle is only between the nobles and Pharaoh, Joseph's fighting for Pharaoh, since both are part (or top) of the aristocracy, does not excuse the way he carries out his policy.

41. Holbert, *The Storyteller's Companion to the Bible*, p. 194. He also suggests that 'it is Joseph who cajoles his family to live in Egypt, thus providing the possibility of their future enslavement' (see 'Joseph and the Surprising Choice of God', p. 41).

42. Lerner, 'Joseph the Unrighteous', p. 281.

not permanent. Yet while it lasts, it initiates sweeping social changes which will come back to haunt Joseph's descendants later.[43]

In the end, we must believe either that the later Hebrews had bad luck in their ruler or that Joseph's actions on behalf of his Pharaoh set the stage for institutional developments that allowed the next vicious leader to come along.[44]

Joseph had set his people up for a tragic repetition of his own disaster at seventeen years of age.[45]

In contrast to the Egyptians, who were reduced to serfdom, the descendants [of] Israel 'gained possessions, and were fruitful and multiplied exceedingly'. Were the seeds of future ethnic jealously sown right here?[46]

While some readers consider Joseph's enslavement of the Egyptians as 'inexcusable behaviour',[47] many others attempt to defend or explain his actions. Joseph's policy is seen as a 'fair' and 'legitimate' transaction.[48] Some argue that if the grain were given away as a 'handout', it would have rewarded 'indolence and shortsightedness'.[49] And it might have broken down the people's 'morale' if they did not pay for what they got.[50] Kidner comments:

> It was axiomatic in the ancient world that one paid one's way so long as one had anything to part with—including, in the last resort, one's liberty. sraelite law accepted the principle, while modifying it with the right of redemption (Lev. 25.25ff).[51]

43. Janzen, *Genesis 12–50*, p. 182.
44. Wildavsky, *Assimilation versus Separation*, p. 159.
45. Watt, 'Joseph's Dreams' p. 69.
46. Longacre, *Joseph: A Story of Divine Providence*, p. 53.
47. Lerner, 'Joseph the Unrighteous', p. 281. 'The Torah', Lerner asserts, 'does not condone Joseph's 'obviously inexcusable behavior' (p. 278).
48. Luther, *Lectures on Genesis: Chapters 45–50*, p. 121, comments that Joseph demands 'a fair price' for the grain he sells and the taking of the land from the people is not a 'seizure' but 'a legitimate transaction'. They do not 'lose the use of their farms' but pay a tax of the fifth part of the produce. In contrast, Bowie, *Genesis*, p. 810, does not see it as a fair deal. He argues that the record does not say Joseph buys the grain. He thinks that it is more probable that Joseph taxes them and later requires them to buy back what they have produced.
49. Morris, *The Genesis Record*, p. 591.
50. Leupold, *Exposition*, p. 1134.
51. Kidner, *Genesis*, p. 211.

Wenham quotes the same law to support Joseph's action:

> The OT law itself does not envisage the destitute simply being bailed out
> by the more well-to-do. Rather, if possible, members of a family should
> help their destitute relatives, just as Joseph did, by buying their land and
> employing them as slaves.[52]

Instead of focusing only on Joseph's 'fair' treatment of the Egyptians, it
is important to compare it with his 'free' provision for his family. In
that case, the above reasons given by these readers will generate more
problems than answers to the justification of Joseph's action. First,
Joseph breaks the Old Testament law by bailing out his family. Secondly, the 'handout', according to some of these readers, will break his
own family's morale. In this perspective, Joseph's action is not 'fair' in
treating the Egyptians better than his family.

There are some attempts to shift the blame to the Egyptians. They are
'reckless' in not laying up provision for themselves against the famine.[53] Either they are guilty of not heeding the warning of the famine,[54]
or they 'could not be relied on' to store up for themselves because of
their nature of looking after only 'their immediate needs'.[55] In Bush's
word, they 'reap the consequences of their improvidence'.[56] Another
way to minimize the negative impression of Joseph's action is to try to
play down the change of the status of the Egyptians. Barnhouse defends
Joseph against the accusation of making Egypt 'a nation of slaves' by
insisting that 'the Egyptians were not slaves' but 'free tenants' who
paid a reasonable 20 per cent income tax.[57] Bush suggests that the
Egyptians voluntarily[58] sell themselves as Pharaoh's 'servants or

52. Wenham, *Genesis 16–50*, p. 452.

53. Bush, *Notes on Genesis*, p. 294.

54. Cf. Luther, *Lectures on Genesis: Chapters 45–50*, p. 121; Bush, *Notes on
Genesis*, p. 294.

55. Morris, *The Genesis Record*, p. 583.

56. Bush, *Notes on Genesis*, p. 363.

57. Barnhouse, *Genesis*, p. 217. For the same term 'tenant' used to designate the
new status of the Egyptians, see also Sarna, *Genesis*, p. 321; Kidner, *Genesis*,
p. 211.

58. Many readers stress the fact that it is the Egyptians who 'initiate the idea of
their own enslavement (v. 9) and even express gratitude when it is implemented'
(Sarna, *Genesis*, p. 323; cf. Morris, *The Genesis Record*, p. 640; Leupold, *Exposition*, p. 1135; Skinner, *Genesis*, p. 500). Both Egyptians and Judah (later the brothers) offer themselves as slaves, one slavery is implemented and the other is not. The
onus of responsibility of turning the Egyptians to slaves remains Joseph's as he

bondmen'[59] but 'this part of the bargain must have been, to a certain extent at least, remitted'. The reason for this is because the people are allowed to own four parts of the crop (47.24), and that is not consistent with a state of 'absolute slavery'. Therefore, they later only become Pharaoh's 'tenants and tributaries'. The only change in their status is that they should pay tax for using the lands—a condition with which they are 'perfectly satisfied'. He concludes that 'there is not the smallest reason for accusing Joseph of injustice or cruelty in this transaction'.[60]

Wenham acknowledges that the Egyptians are indeed enslaved, but, commenting on their gratitude to Joseph (47.25), he remarks, 'Ancient slavery at its best was like a tenured employment, whereas the free man was more like someone who is self-employed. The latter may be freer, but he faces more risks.' He argues that slavery 'under a benevolent master could be a quite comfortable status (cf. Joseph with Potiphar)'.[61] The two examples he discusses provide an interesting contrast. While the Egyptians express gratitude to their 'benevolent master' for their 'comfortable status', the story reports Joseph's recollection of his experience of slavery as 'affliction' (41.51-52) and 'evil' (50.20). His experience in Potiphar's house serves as a poignant reminder that slaves are

declares to them, 'I have this day acquired you and your land' (47.23). Bush, *Notes on Genesis*, p. 363, argues that Joseph has no choice but enslaves the people because 'the corn was not Joseph's but Pharaoh's'. It is as if Pharaoh were able to anticipate this shift of responsibility when he commands his people who come to him for food, 'Go to Joseph; what he says to you, do' (41.55).

59. Fretheim, *Genesis*, p. 654, seizes on the textual problem in 47.21 and argues that 'the language of "slavery" appears insufficiently nuanced' and the people become 'tenant farmers' even though 'it deprives them of some freedom'. For the textual problem, see Chapter 2, footnote 57.

60. Bush, *Notes on Genesis*, p. 367.

61. Wenham, *Genesis 16–50*, p. 449. Bush, *Notes on Genesis*, p. 295, also uses the people's gratitude as a witness to Joseph's 'uprightness' in his dealings with them. For similar emphasis on their gratitude, see Ross, *Creation and Blessing*, p. 687; Fretheim, *Genesis*, p. 654. The salvation of the Egyptians is no doubt extraordinary and gratitude has indeed been expressed by them to their saviour. It is equally true that not only the scale of the enslavement of a whole nation, but the nature of a nation enslaving its own citizens except the priests (who are a powerful elite in ancient societies) is also unprecedented. Hurowitz, 'Joseph's Enslavement of the Egyptians', p. 360, comments, 'The major innovation of the biblical author is that he has converted a private situation in which individuals sell themselves or their children to other private individuals into a national event in which an entire population (the Egyptians) sells itself to a public figure (Joseph and Pharaoh).'

entirely at the mercy of their masters and 'benevolent masters' can turn ugly (cf. Potiphar and his wife). The material condition of the enslaved Egyptians arranged by Joseph is indeed not harsh, neither are his experiences as a slave, being put in charge of Potiphar's house and the prison. Therefore, emphasizing the material aspect could neither justify his action, nor explain why he repeats the enslavement, which once embittered him so much, on others.

Wildavsky in his book *Assimilation versus Separation* provides a thorough criticism of Joseph's actions towards the Egyptians. 'By timeless standards,' he remarks, 'Joseph's implementation of administrative wisdom cannot be condoned.'[62] He condemns Joseph for taking 'all the resources of the Egyptian population', 'making Egyptian landholders into serfs to Pharaoh', and worst of all, uprooting them from their land in order 'to remove people's attachment to their ancient land as well as to demonstrate to them that they are no longer in possession'.[63] In his judgment, Joseph's administration is 'a vast cruelty'. More importantly, he observes that 'Joseph's rationale for his behavior as chief administrator must have been the same as the one he later gave to his brothers, namely, that all this was part of a divine plan to keep the Hebrew people alive.'[64] The idea that 'Joseph's harsh treatment is necessary for the survival from famine'[65] is condemned as violating the moral law 'in the name of survival'.[66] And he criticizes 'Joseph's invocation of divine purpose' as making 'God as an accomplice to immoral behavior'.[67] The fallacy of the rationale of survival at the price of subservience is aptly identified and rebuked, but he also suggests that it is possible to interpret Joseph's invocation 'in a more favorable way':

> The two principal instances [45.7-8; 50.20] in which Joseph invokes the will of God do not directly concern his own actions but rather those of his brothers. It could be argued that Joseph's purpose in making his assertions about *divine providence* is, first, to comfort his brothers with-

---

62. Wildavsky, *Assimilation versus Separation*, pp. 147, 152. See also his essay 'Survival Must Not Be Gained through Sin: The Moral of the Joseph Stories Prefigured through Judah and Tamar', *JSOT* 62 (1994), pp. 37-48.

63. For similar comment on the relocation, see Luther, *Lectures on Genesis: Chapters 45–50*, p. 124.

64. Wildavsky, *Assimilation versus Separation*, p. 142.

65. Wildavsky, *Assimilation versus Separation*, p. 14.

66. Wildavsky, *Assimilation versus Separation*, p. 144.

67. Wildavsky, *Assimilation versus Separation*, p. 142.

out denying their guilt and, second, to express a sense of a larger meaning encompassing the events of their lives. That human beings are
responsible for their actions, so that divine providence does not cancel
out the guilt of Joseph's brothers, while God directs the larger outcomes
of events.[68]

Wildavsky is able to put into doubt the rationale behind Joseph's
actions to dominate others (his dreams); nevertheless he cannot resist
the temptation to accept Joseph's assertions of divine providence
behind the brothers' action to sell him into slavery (his pit). As I have
argued in Chapter 2, if Joseph's suffering is directed by God for a
larger purpose of salvation, then his dreams of domination have to be
fulfilled in order to realise this purpose promised in the divine providence. Wildavsky will be inconsistent if he rejects Joseph's domination
while accepting his claim of divine providence.

Finally, Wildavsky criticizes Joseph's actions in 'making foreigners
[Egyptians] aliens within their own country' as immoral.[69] The root of
the problem, in his assessment, is that, as Pharaoh's administrator,
Joseph becomes 'Egyptianized in food, clothing, hair, customs, marriage, and ultimately power relationships'.[70] He is guilty of being corrupted by foreigners. Commenting on the enslavement, Wildavsky
exclaims, 'Had Pharaoh done this by himself, we might not think anything of it... But for Joseph to be the main actor, not an accomplice,
tries our understanding.'[71] The criticism of the 'un-Hebraic character'[72]
of Joseph's actions due to Egyptianization is a cultural bias that simply
contradicts the narrative details in this story. That begins with the sons
of Jacob selling one of their own into slavery well before they and the
victim have contact with the Egyptian people; and it ends with the mass
enslavement of the Egyptian people by a member of this Hebrew family.[73] The scale of enslaving a whole nation is extraordinary, but one

---

68. Wildavsky, *Assimilation versus Separation*, p. 158 (my italics).
69. Wildavsky, 'Survival Must Not Be Gained through Sin', p. 38.
70. Wildavsky, 'Survival Must Not Be Gained through Sin', p. 48. He contrasts
Joseph with Moses and considers that as 'exact (binary) opposites, each the mirror
image of the other—Joseph, who grows up a Hebrew, becoming Egyptianized,
Moses, who grows up Egyptian becoming Hebraized' (p. 38).
71. Wildavsky, *Assimilation versus Separation*, p. 142.
72. Wildavsky, *Assimilation versus Separation*, p. 125.
73. In addition to opposing Egypt to Israel, Brueggemann, *Genesis*, pp. 356-58,
sets up an opposition of empire/family as a basis for expounding the view that the

cannot describe the Egyptian people as being corrupted by this family, because the practice of slavery is certainly not foreign to their culture. Also, it is difficult to find evidence in this story to support the claim that the Egyptians corrupted Joseph and this family.[74] To regard the enslavement of the Egyptian people as a result of Egyptianization is really a way of blaming the victims for the victimization they suffer.[75]

Dual portraits of Joseph due primarily to his ambiguous behaviour. On the whole, there are two opposed images of Joseph in the history of interpretation. One is positive and the other is negative. The former view usually sees Joseph starting out as a spoiled youth but through the suffering he emerges as a mature man. Commenting on Joseph's resistance to the sexual advance by Potiphar's wife, Niehoff speaks of the change in Joseph from treating his family 'recklessly' to becoming 'an exemplary figure with regard to religious morals'.[76] Referring to his noticing of the anxiety of his fellow prisoners (40.6-7), she writes, 'Joseph's sensitivity to human and political realities, which he put to ill use in his youth, is now shown in fuller maturity.'[77] Finally, his sensitivity grows stronger than ever at the recognition scene (45.1-3) where he is described as 'a delicate and sensitive person who shows consideration for his brothers' feelings'. From the perspective of Joseph's sensitivity, Niehoff's portrait of him evolves from an insensitive brother to a very friendly one. Such an 'amiable image', she remarks, 'is the final and remaining impression which the reader receives of Joseph's character'.[78]

Humphreys takes the narrator's gradual unfolding of Joseph's emotion as his interpretative strategy. He describes him as always the centre

'people of promise' are in danger of being compromised by the imperial policies of oppression 'after the lead of Joseph'.

74. As an example to illustrate that the Hebrews are capable of committing murder and enslavement, the text reports the slaughter of all the males of the city of Shechem and the capture of all their little ones and their wives (34.25-29).

75. Brueggemann, *Genesis*, p. 358, also shifts the blame to the Egyptians and remarks, 'Joseph's Israel lived dangerously near the brink of Egyptianization'; similarly, Sarna, *Understanding Genesis*, p. 222, warns of the same danger, 'Against this external counter-pressure to assimilation is opposed an inner drive towards Egyptianization on the part of Joseph.'

76. Niehoff, *Figure of Joseph*, p. 34.

77. Niehoff, *Figure of Joseph*, p. 36.

78. Niehoff, *Figure of Joseph*, p. 38.

of attention of both the reader and the other characters. But his emotion and motive are hidden at first and are only gradually revealed later. As more and more of his deeds and words betray his inner self, Joseph is also perceived as evolving from a 'spoiled' insensitive youth to a mature man.[79] However, Goodnick is against seeing any sudden change in Joseph's character. He maintains that there is a consistently positive pattern of personality growth in the character of Joseph from childhood onwards, with relatively little change over the course of his later life.[80] Goodnick works from a psychological perspective of childhood development and he considers that Joseph always acts innocently to gain the affection of his father and brothers.

Coats judges the characters in Joseph's story according to their attitude towards the future. He considers that the restored relationship in Jacob's family does not depend on a mutually accepted attitude towards the past, but a workable attitude towards the future. And it requires a mutual commitment for survival in the face of a common crisis (i.e. famine). In his view, all parties act out of no real choice, but the need to act out of commitment for the future. In offering himself in Benjamin's place, Judah has no choice but commits himself out of 'the circumstances of the occasion, not Joseph's loving care, or a prior moral awakening, or an essential element of Judah's character'. Jacob also has no choice but commits his most prized possession, Benjamin, only because of having no food and no chance for getting it.[81] Joseph commits himself to self-revelation, neither out of getting repentance nor revenge from his brothers for their past crime. It is because of the famine, the survival of the family in the future:

> It seems to me to be crucial that the reconciliation does not orient toward the past, toward the violations or revenge as just payment for the violations. It orients toward the future. A famine is at hand. And the brothers need each other in spite of themselves.[82]

---

79. Humphreys, *Joseph and his Family*, pp. 87-88. Richard Elliott Friedman, 'Who Breaks the Cycle? Deception for Deception', *BR* 2.1 (1986), pp. 22-31, 68 (30), also remarks, 'Joseph changes from what one could say is a thoughtless teenager to a sensitive, powerful man'; Watt, 'Joseph's Dreams', p. 68, 'Joseph's infantile narcissism has undergone a radical transformation' to become an 'agent of God's providence'.

80. Goodnick, 'Character of Joseph', p. 215.

81. Coats, *From Canaan to Egypt*, p. 84

82. Coats, *From Canaan to Egypt*, pp. 85-86.

Coats's perspective on this story is orientated toward the future. In the light of this perspective, all parties are perceived as guilty for their past acts, but the chief burden of guilt falls on Joseph. Joseph is then described as a spoiled child, pampered by his father, insensitive to his brother's feelings about him. He is good to Benjamin and his father, but he is not excused for his harsh treatment of the brothers even if it effects a just punishment for their sin.[83]

Joseph's actions throughout his life draw consistent criticism from Holbert. At home he is pictured as the 'arrogant', 'boastful' teenager who dreamed that the moon and the stars would bow down to him. Later, in Egypt, he is the 'scheming, plotting, disguised governor of Egypt' who 'manipulated the lives of his family like some cruel god'.[84] All Joseph's acts are measured against the possible harmful effects on his father and brothers. His treatment of his brothers is harsh and therefore his motive is evil, boastful and arrogant. Most agree that Joseph's acts in some way are harsh, but Holbert dwells on this longer and downplays their positive effects on the confession of his brothers. He disagrees with other positive views of Joseph's character. On von Rad's assessment, he remarks, 'When I read von Rad's analysis of the character of Joseph, I can hardly keep from wondering whether von Rad is reading the same narrative I am reading.'[85]

Readers throughout all ages have responded differently to Joseph's harsh test of his brothers and his enslavement of the Egyptians. It is difficult to arrive at a consensus. Whatever portrait they create of Joseph in this story, they mainly employ Joseph's actions as their building blocks to construct a character from the text. Those who prefer a positive view focus mainly upon Joseph's piety in resisting the sexual temptation from Potiphar's wife. The forgiveness given to his brothers is an important positive factor in Joseph's character too. Those who prefer a more cynical portrait will first focus on his reporting his dreams boastfully to his brothers with a certain degree of arrogance. And his long tortuous test of his brothers finds no favour from his critics. His action to enslave the whole Egyptian nation meets with condemnation from some readers, while many others attempt to justify it.

---

83. Coats, *From Canaan to Egypt*, pp. 80, 82, 85.
84. Holbert, 'Joseph and the Surprising Choice of God', p. 40.
85. Holbert, 'Joseph and the Surprising Choice of God', p. 34.

Attempting to divorce Joseph's behaviour from his belief. Joseph's behaviour elicits different responses. In contrast, there is a general acceptance by readers of his belief in divine providence and in his destiny—chosen by God as a lord to save lives. The acceptance is at least in the sense that Joseph's perspective is the same one held by the narrator, and Joseph is his mouthpiece. In the previous chapters, I have attempted to challenge his important speeches (concerning their incoherence and unreliability as representing the narrator's perspective) to Pharaoh and his brothers. As for his actions, my approach is to locate the basis of his behaviour in his belief. My conclusion is that Joseph's actions in subjecting his brothers and the Egyptians in subservient roles are perfectly compatible with his belief in the idea of subservience for survival. Admittedly, the assessment of the degree of ruthlessness in his domination is debatable and readers may come to a different conclusion. However, it is questionable to divorce Joseph's behaviour from his belief, that is, to assess his actions without setting them in the context of his claims of a divinely inspired domination over his subjects, and of their necessary subservience for their survival. This failure to evaluate the consequence of his belief on his actions can be shown through Turner's criticism of Joseph's actions.

In evaluating Joseph's behaviour in his test, Turner agrees with Ackerman's suggestion that one of the motives of his test is to bring his dreams to fulfilment.[86] While Ackerman considers Joseph's effort successful, Turner points out that the obeisance of father and mother in the second dream never materializes.[87] On the one hand, he does not object to Joseph's dreams of 'superiority over his brothers'.[88] He has argued for the divine origin of the dreams, and describes Joseph as being 'destined for great things'.[89] On the other hand, what annoys him is Joseph's attempt to fulfil his destiny through his test. And he thinks that it explains 'Joseph's bizarre behaviour toward his brothers'.[90] In his

86. Turner, *Announcements of Plot in Genesis*, p. 160 n. 1. Sternberg, *The Poetics of Biblical Narrative*, pp. 289, 291-93, however, considers that it is Joseph's 'anxiety' about 'Benjamin's survival', rather than his wish to fulfil the dreams, that prompts him to demand the brothers to bring Benjamin down.
87. Turner, *Announcements of Plot in Genesis*, p. 166.
88. Turner, *Announcements of Plot in Genesis*, p. 166.
89. Turner, *Announcements of Plot in Genesis*, pp. 147-48.
90. Turner, *Announcements of Plot in Genesis*, p. 154.

view, Joseph is neither a complete villain nor a complete saint.[91] He retains genuine love for his family, but in trying to realize his dreams he still 'wants to have the best of both worlds: he wants to be reunited with his family but on his own terms, with himself their superior'.[92] Joseph is thus portrayed negatively by his attempt to take matters (the fulfilment of dreams) into his own hands.[93] Concerning the promise of God, he advocates a kind of human inactivity to allow God to do more, rather than attempting to fulfil God's promise by human effort.[94] But why are the attempts to fulfil (or to report) something destined by God criticized by readers? It is especially puzzling if the dreams are said to be important for the survival of many lives.

Apparently, it is always Joseph's manner of handling the dreams, and not the dreams themselves, which is under attack. If his dreams are of divine origin, then he is only attempting to fulfil them on divine terms and it is not on 'his own terms' as Turner sees it. Joseph may be blamed for the dubious means he employs to fulfil his dreams of superiority over his brothers, or one can criticize human effort to fulfil the divine plan, but he certainly cannot be blamed for the terms set forth in his dreams if they are of divine origin.

In contrast to Turner's criticism of Joseph's effort, Ackerman argues that Joseph 'must play a role in bringing the dreams to fulfillment' and it will then enable him to 'learn the divine purpose for his life'.[95] Both readers share the same view of Joseph's motive, but they have opposite opinions of his effort to fulfil the divine plan. It is no wonder that they also have different assessments regarding the outcome of Joseph's

91. Turner's work focuses on the non-fulfilment of God's previous promises (or announcements) in Genesis; his portrait of Joseph is directly shaped by this perspective.

92. Turner, *Announcements of Plot in Genesis*, p. 164. Alter, *Art of Biblical Narrative*, pp. 163-64, proposes a similar motive: 'or is he chiefly triumphant, moved to play the inquisitor in order to act out still further the terms of his dreams, in which the brothers must repeatedly address him self-effacingly as "my lord" and identify themselves as "your servants"?' Alter finally comments that the narrator's refusal to supply specific connections between Joseph's remembering of his dreams and his test is a 'characteristic biblical reticence'. Skinner, *Genesis*, p. 475, suggests that there may not be 'a consistent ethical purpose on Joseph's part' and that 'the official Joseph is an inscrutable person, whose motives defy analysis'.

93. Turner, *Announcements of Plot in Genesis*, p. 169.

94. Turner, *Announcements of Plot in Genesis*, pp. 179-80.

95. Ackerman, 'Joseph, Judah, and Jacob', p. 88.

attempt. Since not all parts of Joseph's dreams are fulfilled,[96] Turner's interpretation of the failure of Joseph's effort is more accurate. But in terms of the meaning of the dreams, Ackerman may be correct to suggest that Joseph's attempt to play the role of a lord over his brothers (and even over his father) may finally help him understand 'the divine purpose for his life'. The reason why he is destined to rule over others is then announced after his attempt to bring his dreams to fulfilment in ch. 45. Ackerman not only discusses Joseph's role as a lord; he also gives sufficient attention to the brothers' role. 'Joseph's dream sequence,' he claims, 'establishes the pattern for his course of action after his brothers come to Egypt: obeisance of all the brothers is of first importance.'[97]

Turner is uneasy about Joseph's attempt to reunite with his brothers 'on his own terms, with himself their superior', but Ackerman interprets Joseph's action as not only permissible, but even as required of him according to his dream sequence. Ackerman thus brings Joseph's new-found theological conviction of domination in line with his behaviour. Stressing Joseph's obligation to rule, his comment that the brothers 'naturally refused to see anything providential in a plan that would cast them down before any brother'[98] comes close to being a criticism of their refusal to align their understanding with the destiny of their subordination. Ackerman recognizes the inevitable link between Joseph's belief and behaviour but it is not easy for other readers to blame the brothers for their refusal of their 'obeisance' as he does.

In summary, there is general tendency for most readers to criticize Joseph's actions rather than questioning his claims about God's intentions. The following sections on the studies done by some literary

96.   Ackerman, 'Joseph, Judah, and Jacob', pp. 87, 92, 108, observes the 'unusual description of Joseph's thoughts in 42.9' connecting the remembering of the dreams and the test. When Benjamin came down and 'did obeisance' (43.26) before Joseph, Ackerman sees 'the first dream has been completely fulfilled. He considers that the second dream was fulfilled when Joseph 'appeared unto him (Jacob)' (46.29) like a theophany and when Jacob 'bowed down the head of the bed' (47.31) even 'the object of the verb left ambiguously unstated'. These ambiguities do not give a clear indication that Jacob did bow down before Joseph. As Turner points out, the absence of Rachel makes the fulfilment of dreams 'inherently impossible'. For a detailed discussion on Rachel's role, see Turner, *Announcements of Plot in Genesis*, pp. 145-51.

97.   Ackerman, 'Joseph, Judah, and Jacob', p. 88.

98.   Ackerman, 'Joseph, Judah, and Jacob', pp. 95-96.

scholars show that they do not deviate from this tendency in construct-ing their portraits of Joseph.

Literary Paradoxes of the Pit and Dreams and their Unravelling

Donald A. Seybold is a literary scholar who attempts to demonstrate the artistic achievement of the Joseph story.[99] Since his analysis of the lit-erary pattern in this story is excellent and my argument relies heavily on his insight, his article deserves the following detailed discussion. At the beginning of his article, he praises the artistry in this story: 'Rarely in Western literature has form been woven into content, pattern sewn into meaning, structure forged into theme with greater subtlety or suc-cess.'[100] At the heart of this artistry, he discovers a 'literary device of paradox' which stands at the centre of the narrative pattern and the final thematic significance of the story.[101] Specifically, this device is the paradox of the pit with which the following three parts of the structure of this story are closely related: (1) the three sets of dreams; (2) the four sets of Joseph's relationships in his family, Potiphar's household, prison, and Pharaoh's household; (3) and finally 'the variations on the "pit" episode which combine both narrative and symbolic purposes to become the central repositories of paradox as well as provide the links of concatenation through which the other elements combine into the final and deeper significance of the story'.[102]

One of the variations of the pit is 'the whole paradoxical purpose of his "death" as God's way of preserving the family'.[103] Joseph's 'death' is a metaphor referring to his past affliction of being thrown into a pit and sold into slavery. At first sight, it is not a particularly paradoxical idea that one has to suffer in order to help others. Furthermore, it is necessary to explore in detail how this narrative of profound paradox 'resolves itself in absolute symmetry' and how its 'predicament' is unravelled.[104]

According to Seybold, the story begins with the 'unnaturalness'[105] of

---

99. Seybold, 'Paradox and Symmetry', pp. 59-73.
100. Seybold, 'Paradox and Symmetry', p. 59.
101. Seybold, 'Paradox and Symmetry', p. 73.
102. Seybold, 'Paradox and Symmetry', p. 59.
103. Seybold, 'Paradox and Symmetry', p. 71.
104. Seybold, 'Paradox and Symmetry', p. 59.
105. Seybold, 'Paradox and Symmetry', p. 60.

a younger son being favoured over all his brothers by his father. The 'unnatural' relationship is further compounded by Joseph's two dreams depicting the bowing down of his brothers and parents before him. It leads to 'an even more unnatural act' because it provokes the brothers' plot to destroy the dreamer and his dreams.[106] How will the predicament of Joseph's dreams of domination, which Seybold considers as unnatural and responsible for his downfall, be resolved? First, he describes the act of throwing Joseph into the pit as 'an alternative to murder', while the pit becomes 'a refuge which allows Joseph's life to be preserved'. Thus, it is 'an ambivalent one which ultimately (through subsequent events) becomes a paradox central to the story's outcome and meaning'.[107] The pit is paradoxical because it 'prefigures' Joseph's enslavement and incarceration: they are 'destructive to the individual', but 'less destructive than the alternative of death which Joseph faces from his brothers and from Potiphar'.[108] In summary, the unnaturalness of dreams leads to the unnaturalness of imprisonment in pit/prison, which are in turn an alternative to even more unnatural acts—murder and the death penalty. Secondly, he parallels the same problem of an 'unnatural and untenable situation' in Joseph's dreams with that of the pit/prison:

> his brothers and his father will bow down before him. If such an unnatural situation can somehow be simultaneously natural, we will have a paradox as compelling and necessary as that inherent in the pit/prison.[109]

The 'unnatural' subservient relationship between Joseph and his family can become 'natural' because, as a paradox like the pit/prison, it provides a way to avoid the more unnatural alternative of death.[110] Thus

---

106. Seybold, 'Paradox and Symmetry', p. 61.

107. Seybold, 'Paradox and Symmetry', p. 61.

108. Seybold, 'Paradox and Symmetry', pp. 62-63. He further comments, 'That the pit/prison which stood ambiguously between freedom and death is operating paradoxically is also clear: it is the place where Joseph is both condemned and saved' (p. 64).

109. Seybold, 'Paradox and Symmetry', p. 65. The dreams are thus as 'unnatural' and 'paradoxical' as the pit. In effect, they are only one of the subtle mutations of the pit.

110. Seybold, 'Paradox and Symmetry', p. 67, deduces his idea of the change of the unnatural to the natural from the Judah/Onan/Tamar story (Gen. 38): 'Preservation of the family and propagation of the tribe are natural, and wasting the human seed or failing to impregnate the woman is unnatural. Incest is paradoxically natural

Seybold reasons that Joseph 'will need to commit an unnatural act (make his brothers and parents subservient) in order to do the natural thing (keep his family from being destroyed).[111] Since the outcome of Joseph's dreams is good, the 'unnatural situation' of his domination over his family not only becomes natural but 'good'. He further stresses that it is good, 'especially since it is what God wants'.[112] After the transformation of 'the unnatural' to 'the natural', to 'good' and finally to what God wants, Seybold declares, 'The paradox is perfect and profound.'[113] However, he adds that 'paradox is only the result of the human perspective and our limited understanding of the ways in which God operates'.[114] The literary device of paradox is instrumental in helping Seybold to naturalize the unnatural. It is interesting to note that its significance is greatly reduced once its aim of illustrating God's plan is achieved.

In terms of content, Seybold's justification of domination and subservience (in both dreams and pit) for the sake of survival does not differ from that of other readers,[115] but it is endowed and embellished with greater literary significance:

> The younger son can dominate an older one when it is necessary to preserve the family... Always in the Joseph story the structures of preservation supersede those of waste, even when preservation demands one tradition be temporarily violated. The profound paradoxes of the story are a direct result of the tensions created by acts and events which are both natural and unnatural at the same time. Dreams become reality, subservience becomes dominance, prisons become places of preservation. The major operative patterns, symbols, and structures of the Joseph narrative are orchestrated into a symphony whose movements, themes, and motifs are tonal variations of the same structuring key.[116]

under such a compelling natural law. If the unnatural can in some cases be natural, if such a paradox can hold in this case, it can very possibly hold in the case of Joseph's dreams.'

111. Seybold, 'Paradox and Symmetry', p. 68, in effect regards everything unnatural in this story as natural in view of the ultimate unnaturalness of death.

112. Seybold, 'Paradox and Symmetry', p. 66.

113. Seybold, 'Paradox and Symmetry', p. 69.

114. Seybold, 'Paradox and Symmetry', p. 72.

115. E.g., Wenham, *Genesis 16–50*, p. 493; Longacre, *Joseph*, p. 43; Bush, *Notes on Genesis*, p. 234; Ackerman, 'Joseph, Judah, and Jacob', p. 107; Ross, *Creation and Blessing*, p. 687.

116. Seybold, 'Paradox and Symmetry', p. 73.

The structuring key is the paradox of 'subservience preferable to freedom in order to preserve the family': the subservience of the brothers to Joseph is paradoxically necessary for their survival; the pit and prison are paradoxical as less destructive than death for Joseph. These profound paradoxes operate through a large number of repetitions of literary patterns, symbols and structures of this story.[117] Above all, they are 'in absolute symmetry' and 'in faultless symmetry', an artistic aspect Seybold stresses in the first and last paragraph of his article:

> The result is a narrative of profound paradox that first reveals then resolves itself in *absolute symmetry*. To look closely at the major patterns of paradox is to discover how the literal level of the narrative fully engenders the meaning and how *pattern* finally unravels predicament.

> Further, this analysis makes very clear the literary forms of repetition, pattern, and character that operate in the story and give it an elegance and eloquence quite apart from its religious, historical, or theological significance. And most important, it demonstrates that a close look at the narrative shows structures that allow the narrative *pattern* to speak its final significance in *faultless symmetry*.[118]

In his conclusion, Seybold admits that he is concerned more with the literary pattern of this story than its religious content. However, the literary pattern and symmetry somehow help to unravel the predicament (presumably a moral one) of the paradoxes.

Many readers have double standards in that they praise Joseph's dreams of domination while condemning the brothers' casting him into a pit/slavery as a virtual murder.[119] However, Seybold explicitly parallels the paradoxical nature of the brothers' action with that of Joseph's dreams. According to his description, through the intervention of 'Reuben' and 'some Midianite traders',[120] Joseph is first thrown into a

---

117. The Joseph story is famous for its unusual amount of doublings and repetitions. Ackerman, 'Joseph, Judah, and Jacob', pp. 85-113, also provides a literary analysis of these features in this story. Redford, *Biblical Story of Joseph*, pp. 138-86, has a detailed discussion of the discrepancies of the repetitions in terms of source analysis.

118. Seybold, 'Paradox and Symmetry', pp. 59, 73 (my italics). Redford, *Biblical Story of Joseph*, pp. 71-72, also notices many instances of symmetry in the plot and setting of this story.

119. Cf. Alter, *Art of Biblical Narrative*, pp. 167, 176; Ackerman, 'Joseph, Judah, and Jacob', pp. 86, 99.

120. Seybold, 'Paradox and Symmetry', pp. 60-61. The exegetical decision to

pit and then sold into slavery in Potiphar's house. He considers it a better alternative to death, but he neglects to mention that Judah gives the similar excuse of opting for slavery instead of death for his brother (37.26-27).[121] Judah's rationalization suits Seybold's parallels and thesis exceedingly well, but it will pose a challenge to his conclusion that the unnatural can be transformed into the natural or that subservience for preservation is acceptable. From the victim's viewpoint, slavery may be less destructive than death, but to justify its necessity is difficult. Seybold's mentioning of Judah's rationalization could easily contradict his attempt to justify the paradox of subservience as a better alternative to death. Joseph as a character in the story cannot be blamed for his ignorance of Judah's words when he justifies his domination on similar grounds.[122] However, Seybold as a reader cannot be excused, especially since he is a reader with high literary sensitivity to narrative repetitions. If he is able to construct the 'profound paradox' and 'structuring key' through various subtle literary parallels, patterns and symbols (pit, prison and clothing), it is extraordinary that he fails to notice Judah's explicit assertion of the same idea, which he attempts to establish from these patterns.

While Judah's assertion best captures the principle that Seybold deduces from the various literary patterns and parallels in this story, the mass enslavement of the Egyptians in exchange for their survival is a

choose only one source out of the possible two (Reuben–Midianites and Judah–Ishmaelites) may enable Seybold to avoid comparing Judah's rationalisation with his understanding of the paradox of pit. For a brief discussion of these two sources, see Alter, *Art of Biblical Narrative*, pp. 166-68.

121. Seybold, 'Paradox and Symmetry', p. 70, admits that 'Joseph's brothers and his captors have always opted for the alternative that allowed Joseph to live and Joseph will not do otherwise to his brothers.' But he immediately suggests that the purpose of Joseph's test is to teach the brothers to 'ally themselves with the pre-servers rather than the wasters'. If the brothers have always opted for preservation, they have nothing to learn from Joseph in this respect. Joseph's test only gives one more illustration of what they have always believed. The best model is Judah: he sells Joseph to save his life (37.26-27); he requests Jacob to risk his another favourite son to avoid the death of the whole family (43.8); finally, he offers himself in place of Benjamin to be a slave in order to save his Jacob's certain death of losing his remaining favourite son (44.22, 31).

122. Seybold, 'Paradox and Symmetry', p. 71, omits Judah's rationalisation, but he seizes on Joseph's similar justification in 45.5-11 and considers it as 'the controlling deep structure of the entire narrative'.

concrete, if not the best, illustration of these literary patterns. Joseph's relief policy could be used to support his theme that the unnatural can be transformed into the natural, especially since the Egyptians gratefully accept enslavement for their salvation. However, Seybold simply ignores it. Maybe its dubious aspect still poses a problem for him in justifying Joseph's claim and action.

Finally, Joseph's famous theological dictum in 50.20 is also conspicuously absent in Seybold's construction of the paradox of turning the unnatural into the natural.[123] He considers Joseph's speech in 45.5-7 as demonstrating his final acknowledgment of the usefulness of his pit/ prison experiences as God's way of preserving the family. However, he fails to point out that at the end Joseph also condemns them as evil in unequivocal terms. The pit/prison experiences remain evil and never become natural as Seybold attempts to suggest. Joseph's speech about divine providence, as understood by other readers, 'does not cancel out the guilt' of his brothers.[124] The idea that God is overriding human evil for a good purpose is not in Seybold's discussion at all. In fact, for him there is no human evil but 'the unnatural' that requires transformation to 'the natural'. As previously mentioned, his analysis is concerned more with the literary significance of this story than its moral judgment. The literary beauty of the recurring patterns of subservience for preservation somehow enables the predicament of these profound paradoxes to be unravelled. The operative terms he employs in this operation are mostly of formal literary qualities: 'paradox', 'contradiction', 'ambiguity' and 'ambivalence'.[125] Significantly, when a value judgment cannot be avoided, he opts for the opposition with less emphasis on value judgment—natural/unnatural instead of good/evil. The latter is the choice made by Joseph and other readers. Its use would probably make it harder for Seybold to transform the pit/prison and dreams from

123. Most readers treat Joseph's words in 45.5-11 and 50.20 as complementing each other to form his view on God's plan and intention. Cf. Josipovici, 'Joseph and Revelation', p. 78; Miscall, 'The Jacob and Joseph Stories as Analogies', p. 38; Longacre, *Joseph*, p. 43.

124. Wildavsky, *Assimilation versus Separation*, p. 158. See also von Rad, *Genesis*, p. 438; Wenham, *Genesis 16–50*, p. 433.

125. By stressing the ambivalent and paradoxical nature of the pit/prison and the dreams, he can naturalize their predicament without being accused of ignoring their problematic nature.

unnatural to natural. This may explain why he avoids Joseph's final moral verdict on the pit.

Setting the pit as the symbolic centre of Joseph's story, he is excellent in pinpointing the crucial message of the story. More importantly, he makes a good case for establishing the link between the pit (and its variations), Joseph's dreams and the test. Joseph's words in 45.5-11 about the necessity of his pit and dreams are best illustrated by Seybold's analysis of other literary patterns and parallels in this story. He presents a clear picture of their similarity and paradoxical nature in respect of sacrificing freedom for preservation. However, it is significant that he omits those parallels that focus more on the ethical aspect. He tracks down the recurring instances of subservience for survival, but ignores Judah's explicit articulation of this principle and its classic application in Joseph's enslavement of the whole Egyptian nation. Most of all, he avoids Joseph's unequivocal condemnation of the evil of the pit. The discovery of these omissions weakens his argument that 'the unnatural' can be turned into 'the natural'.

A Fictional Experiment in Knowledge

Robert Alter analyses the Joseph story in his book *The Art of Biblical Narrative* in a chapter entitled 'Knowledge and Narrative'.[126] He calls the story a 'fictional experiment' in knowledge. All major characters in it have something to learn. Even Joseph 'the magisterial knower' has a lot to learn because at the outset he as yet does not know the true meaning of 'his own destiny'. His prophetic dreams 'might well seem at first the reflex of a spoiled adolescent's grandiosity, quite of a piece with his nasty habit of tale-bearing against his brothers and with his insensitivity to their feeling, obviously encouraged by his father's flagrant indulgence'. The brothers are plainly ignorant of 'Joseph's real nature and destiny, of the consequences of their own behaviour, of the ineluctable feelings of guilt they will suffer because of their crime, and climactically, of Joseph's identity when he stands before them as viceroy of Egypt'. And 'the heretofore shrewd Jacob on his part is just as blind as his old father Isaac was before him'[127] in provoking conflict among their sons by his excessive love for Joseph.

Alter recognizes that the process of coming to knowledge is not an

126. Alter, *Art of Biblical Narrative*, pp. 155-77.
127. Alter, *Art of Biblical Narrative*, p. 159.

easy one. He comments, 'There is a horizon of perfect knowledge in biblical narrative, but it is a horizon we are permitted to glimpse only in the most momentary and fragmentary ways.' Only 'through a variety of technical procedures, most of them modes of indirection', could the reader discern any 'meaningful pattern' intended by the narrator.[128] In his description, the story of knowledge centres on Joseph's hiding of his identity when the brothers come to bow down before him and his disclosure after his test. The 'magisterial knower' embarks on a journey to enable his ignorant brothers to come to terms with the divine knowledge. The final result of this fictional experiment is a passage from ignorance to knowledge of self and other, and of God's ways:

> In the purposeful reticence of this kind of narration, the characters retain their aura of enigma, their ultimate impenetrability at least to the human eyes with which perforce we view them. At the same time, however, the omniscient narrator conveys a sense that personages and events produce certain stable significance, one which in part can be measured by varying distances of the characters from divine knowledge, by the course through which some of them are made to pass from dangerous ignorance to necessary knowledge of self and other, and of God's ways.[129]

Perfect Knowledge in Fragmentary Ways

When Joseph reveals his identity to his brothers, he discloses God's purpose of 'sending' him down before them to Egypt and making him a lord there in order to save their lives and those of many others as well. As my previous chapters have demonstrated, the declaration of a salvation purpose for his dreams only serves to parallel his justification with Judah's previous rationalization. Joseph's knowledge of self is clear to himself, but to the reader the narrator presents a more ambiguous picture than his simplified version of past events. Before his disclosure, the painful experience of enslavement drives him to attempt to rid himself of the past hardship and all his father's house by naming his first-born Manasseh ('to forget', see 41.51). To forget by an act of commemoration is a clear sign of a divided self. Even after the disclosure and his understanding of his destiny, the ambiguity inside him does not go away. A slave once tormented by past enslavement now becomes a

---

128. Alter, *Art of Biblical Narrative*, p. 158.

129. Alter, *Art of Biblical Narrative*, pp. 158-59. Goodnick, 'Character of Joseph', p. 224, also sees Joseph's test of the brothers as helping them to search within, 'he wondered whether they had lived through these same 20 years to arrive at a deeper self-understanding, to regret what they had done'.

master enslaver of a whole nation. It can only be explained as the result of a self deeply ambivalent within. The whole ordeal that Joseph inflicts on the brothers hinges on their complete acquiescence in Jacob's favouritism of the younger over the elder. Before and after the disclosure he consistently shows special favour towards Benjamin (43.34; 45.22). But when Jacob favours Ephraim (the younger) over Manasseh (the elder) in bestowing the blessing, it 'displeased' him (48.17). Therefore, all the signs inform us of a person who has not come to terms with himself.

The narrator also does not present Joseph as a person who comes to a true knowledge of others. At the outset, Joseph never knows, or cares to understand, the cause that provokes his brothers' crime. As for the encounter with the brothers, it is correct for Alter to assert that 'the narrator...began the episode [of initial questioning of the brothers] by emphatically and symmetrically stating Joseph's knowledge and the brothers' ignorance'.[130] The brothers are ignorant of the identity of this Egyptian lord during the test. In the final confrontation, Judah 're-proaches' the Egyptian lord for ignoring the death threat to Jacob by demanding that Benjamin leave his father.[131] Therefore, Joseph's test exposes his own ignorance as much as that of the brothers. Moreover, at the end of the story, Joseph seems to be surprised by the brothers' fear of his possible revenge after the death of their father. However, Judah's previous plea for mercy is entirely based on the possibility of the death threat to him. Once he is gone, they are naturally feeling vulnerable,[132] and they attempt to use the words of their dead father to fend off possible revenge from Joseph (50.15-21).[133] The text does not allow

---

130. Alter, *Art of Biblical Narrative*, p. 165.

131. Cf. O'Brien, 'Contribution of Judah's Speech', pp. 444-45.

132. Schimmel, 'Joseph and his Brothers', p. 64, notes 'The brothers, then, aware of the incompleteness of their repentance, have good reason to fear the emergence of hostility on the part of Joseph—particularly after the death of their father, whose presence might have acted as a temporary inhibition on his vengeance.'

133. It is interesting to note that, when Isaac dies, there is no report of Jacob's fear of Esau's revenge. The text specifically states that Esau intends to kill Jacob only after their father's death (27.41). The presence of parents seems to be a factor in preventing fratricide. It also explains the brothers' attempt to kill Joseph only in a place that is far distant from their father. Westermann, *Genesis 37–50*, p. 39, comments that it is 'outside their father's domain' that 'the brothers' hate can be realized in action'.

us to know whether the brothers are lying or not,[134] but their plea surprises Joseph. It gives an impression that the parties do not fully know each other.[135]

Finally, Alter asserts that 'the omniscient narrator conveys a sense that personages and events produce certain stable significance, one which in part can be measured by varying distances of the characters from divine knowledge'.[136] This assertion makes Joseph's words about God's actions and intention the centre of reference for all other characters and events in the story. This view takes Joseph's words as God's words for granted. I have tried to put this assumption in doubt in the previous chapters. Here I merely wish to contrast Alter's understanding of God's ways with that of Joseph, in order to highlight the difficulty in asserting the certainty of knowing what God's ways are. At the end of his analysis of the Joseph story as an experiment in knowledge, Alter concludes, 'A basic biblical perception about both human relations and relations between God and man is that love is unpredictable, arbitrary, at times perhaps seemingly unjust, and Judah now comes to an acceptance of that fact with all its consequences.'[137] Judah may come to an acceptance of God's ways as 'unpredictable, arbitrary' and 'seemingly unjust', but this understanding is not what Joseph presents in his various claims. It is completely contradictory to his emphasis on God's ways as a divine good overriding human evil intention (45.4-11; 50.20-21). Alter in effect takes Joseph's words as divine knowledge while changing his emphasis in an opposing direction. Whose view of God's ways is right? Can the characters in this story and readers outside it be certain of the knowledge of God's ways? Alter reads the story as a model of narration and knowledge, which, however complex at the beginning and the middle, will come to an end with a definite sense of closure. The Joseph story is indeed a fictional experiment in knowledge, but there is no such easy transformation from ignorance to definite knowledge as Alter hopes to find.

---

134. Josipovici, 'Joseph and Revelation', comments, 'Did Jacob really issue such a command before he died? We will never know.'

135. Holbert, *The Storyteller's Companion to the Bible*, p. 195, suggests that 'Joseph still has not understood the depths of their fear.' In contrast, Goodnick, 'Character of Joseph', p. 228, considers that 'they still misread his motives and projected their own feelings'.

136. Alter, *Art of Biblical Narrative*, pp. 158-59.

137. Alter, *Art of Biblical Narrative*, pp. 174-75.

The Linear Reading

If one reads a narrative in a linear way, the question of what will happen next in the unfolding of the plot is usually given considerable attention. How does the tension of the story in the beginning evolve during the narration? How is it resolved in the end? White interprets the Joseph story in this way and asserts, 'In the standard rhetorical narrative we must assume that the plot is constructed from the viewpoint of its ending that is known by the narrator from the outset.'[138] Whether reading forward or backward, the tendency is to focus on how the plot is developing. Applying this to Joseph's dreams, which are fulfilled at the end of the plot, many readings are therefore focused on the '*if*',[139] '*when*' and '*how*' of their fulfilment, as Redford succinctly summarizes:

> The brothers' reaction ['Are you indeed to reign over us? Or are you indeed to have dominion over us? (37.8)'] to the dreams sets the whole plot in motion, and from this point on all interest focuses on the '*if*', '*when*', and '*how*' of fulfillment.[140]

It is interesting to note that the question '*why*' the dreams have to be fulfilled is mysteriously circumvented by some readers, whereas Joseph himself places great emphasis on it. On the one hand, he explains *why* he was 'sent' by his brothers or by God (45.5-7); on the other hand, he explains *why* he has to be made a lord to rule over others (45.8-11). In contrast, Joseph seems to show little interest on the questions of '*if*', '*when*' and '*how*' in the fulfilment of his dreams. Understandably, due to the painful experience, he even tries to forget the dreams of ruling over his brothers when he actually becomes a lord in Egypt (41.50). Only the encounter with the brothers seems to cause Joseph to struggle to understand why he has been 'sent' by God and why he has to be lord over his brothers. His claim to knowledge of the divine plan in 45.4-11 seems to solve his puzzlement concerning his fate brought about by his dreams.

138. White, 'The Joseph Story', p. 60.

139. Turner's book, *Announcements of Plot in Genesis*, on the Joseph story puts more emphasis on 'if' the dreams are literally and fully fulfilled or not, pp. 143-73. Bob Becking, 'They Hated Him Even More', *BN* 60 (1991), p. 44, focuses on the 'literary tension' created by Joseph's dreams and comments that 'the reader of the story is left with two questions. Will the situation referred to actually occur and will the brothers and/or the father try to prevent them?'

140. Redford, *Biblical Story of Joseph*, p. 71 (my italics).

Of course, in any approach to reading, the question '*why*' can always be asked along with '*if*', '*when*', and '*how*' in the plot development. But why is it so seldom asked in the reading of Joseph's story? Joseph gives the story its ending with a repeated answer (three times in ch. 45 and once more in ch. 50) why his dreams have to be fulfilled: it is in order to save lives. If readers too readily accept this at the beginning of their reading process, they may tend to focus less on the purposive aspects of the dream (the why?) than on questions about 'if', 'when', and 'how' the dreams are fulfilled. After all, nobody in the narrative objects to his claims; he indeed saves many lives as he claims. Those who benefit by his actions would of course have no incentive to question their benefactor. Joseph returns good for the evil of his brothers.[141] Pharaoh is indebted to Joseph's effort to gather such huge wealth for him. The Egyptians suffer comparatively more than the other characters during the famine, but they at least owe their lives to Joseph. Interestingly, they are the only ones who express openly their gratitude to Joseph (47.25).

The Sense of Ending

For many readers, the ending of a story is a privileged vantage point from which one can resolve the 'disparate levels of knowledge'.[142] Since Joseph provides a comprehensive review of the series of past events while the narrator does not, his disclosure speech at the end becomes the dénouement of the story.[143] With the benefit of 'retrospective observation', the reader is said to 'be in a position to understand' the divine plan.[144] Humphreys suggests that 'it is only at the end of the novella, in hindsight, that Joseph can detect the benevolent hand of providence' and through his acknowledgment the reader can recognize

141. White, 'Where Do You Come From?', p. 271, asserts, 'The absence of direct discourse from the brothers' response to Joseph's interpretation suggests the negation of their own viewpoint and their absorption into the divine (authorial) perspective.'

142. Humphreys, *Joseph and his Family*, p. 51, states, 'the resolution... involves the final coming together of what have been disparate levels of knowledge, as well as placing the family's story in a larger context shaped by a providential understanding of what is doing'.

143. Von Rad, *Genesis*, p. 432, notes, 'The statement about the brothers' evil plans and God's good plans now opens up the inmost mystery of the Joseph story.'

144. Yairah Amit, 'The Dual Causality Principle and its Effects on Biblical Literature', *VT* 37.4 (1987), pp. 385-400 (392).

it too.[145] Wenham considers the Joseph story as a 'witness to the invisibility of God's actions in human affairs: only in retrospect can man see what God has been doing'.[146] Similarly, White suggests that the actions of the mysterious divine 'can only be understood retrospectively from the end to which they lead'.[147] Brueggemann explains why God's intentions are kept until the end before their disclosure: 'The narrative is also about the hiddenness of God. The narrator has found a mode of storytelling appropriate to the theme. The story hints and implies. Only very late does it make anything explicit.'[148]

The 'privileged reading' position is not only from the end of a story, but for Robert E. Longacre it is also from 'above the story'. In his book, *Joseph: A Story of Divine Providence*, he embarks on a systematic application of discourse analysis in his study of this story. He argues that there is an 'overall plan and global purpose of a story' that exercises 'a control in the composition of the story'. The assumption of his methodology is that 'the whole legislates the parts, while, in turn, a study of the parts is necessary to the comprehension of the whole'. He admits that this argumentation is *necessarily circular* but not a 'vicious' one, if the overall design and the detail are brought into plausible harmony with sufficient care.[149] Then he claims, 'We are told in the story itself and in an echo of the story in Gen. 50.20 that this is a story of *divine providence*'. Joseph's claim becomes a 'macrostructure' with which one may analyse the parts of the story.[150] The presupposition that there is a 'whole' that can serve to control the interpretation of the parts is controversial. Moreover, the way he determines Joseph's claim as such a 'whole' is questionable.

He posits a contrast between the 'above-the-story and within-the-story points of views'. We as readers 'stand with the narrator above the story and realize that God is working things out for Joseph, for his family, and for the preservation of everyone'. On the other hand, he

145. Humphreys, *Joseph and his Family*, pp. 125, 128.
146. Wenham, *Genesis 16–50*, p. 432. See also Cohn, 'Narrative Structure', *JSOT* 23 (1983), pp. 12, 14.
147. White, 'Where Do You Come From?', p. 271.
148. Brueggemann, *Genesis*, p. 293. He also suggests, 'Not only the brothers, but Joseph as well, are unaware until the end of the ways of God in keeping the dream' (p. 289).
149. Longacre, *Joseph*, pp. 42-43 (his italics).
150. Longacre, *Joseph*, p. 43 (his italics).

describes how the narrator portrays 'Joseph as *within* the story' suffering degradation, disgrace and imprisonment.[151] Then he suggests that Joseph somehow comes to stand above the story:

> Joseph's remarks in 45.5-8 and 50.19-21 also reveal that the central participant of the story has now caught up with its unfolding macrostructure. Enough of the story has gone past that he now, like the narrator and us, can stand above the story and view it as a whole. So, as we have seen, it is from these remarks of Joseph that we obtain in semifinished form the statement of the macrostructure.[152]

If we rely on Joseph for this macrostructure, we cannot really be said to be standing 'above' the story and the protagonist to know about God's plan. Furthermore, to portray Joseph as standing 'above' the story, like the narrator and readers, is only a way, in metaphorical sense, to justify the decision to take his claim as a 'whole' to control the interpretation of the story. Characters are only a literary construct[153] by a narrator and they can never in principle stand above the story like readers. Whether reading from 'above' or from 'the end of' a story, the assumption is that it will arrive at a closure. I find the following warning about the 'privileged reading' position from Josipovici helpful:

> The point is that where in works of art in the West there is usually a place at which interpretation stops and the truth appears, the Hebrew Bible does not seem to work like that. Just as we get parataxis instead of subordination at the level of syntax, so, in the narrative, we are always denied a point of view above the action. And when we think we have found at last a place from which to interpret we find that it too is subject to conflicting interpretation.[154]

In modern narrative theories, the sense of closure is no longer as highly regarded as before. Instead, the emphasis of reading is shifted to the ongoing reading process which prevents 'the formation of any "finalized hypothesis" or overall meaning'.[155] Under this influence,

---

151. Longacre, *Joseph*, pp. 47-48 (his italics).

152. Longacre, *Joseph*, p. 51.

153. Rimmon-Kenan, *Narrative Fiction*, p. 36, comments that 'in the story character is a construct, put together by the reader from various indications dispersed throughout the text'.

154. Josipovici, 'Joseph and Revelation', p. 82.

155. Rimmon-Kenan, *Narrative Fiction*, p. 121, also adds a remark that it is mainly modern texts that are characterized by the new emphasis on non-closure. However, there are other readers, like the ones I am going to discuss, who attempt

Hugh C. White adopts a speech-act approach to studying the relation of the direct discourse of the characters to the indirect discourse of the narrative framework in the Joseph narrative.[156] He utilizes two categories of literary presentation developed by Stanley Fish in his analysis: 'The rhetorical presentation is closed, the end corresponding to the beginning, whereas the dialectical approach is open.'[157] He proposes a correlation between the former and the narrator's discourse, and between the latter and the discourse of the character. The goal of his analysis is to trace the process of a narrative 'consuming itself', which 'will take the form of the content of the closed perspective of the narrative framework being taken up into the direct discourse of the characters and subordinated to the ongoing dialogical process which prevents the narrative from achieving closure.'[158]

According to White, the central tension of the plot is defined in terms of broken communication between the brothers ('the brothers could not speak shalom to him', cf. 37.4) and its restoration ('and afterward his brothers spoke with him', cf. 45.15). The concluding statement of the narrator in 50.21b ('Thus he comforted them and spoke of the concerns of their heart') serves as the 'formal closure' of the major unifying theme of the Joseph narrative.[159] This formal closure in the narrative framework is made possible by Joseph's direct discourse about the divine plan in 50.20. Thus, White reckons that 'even the most encompassing explanation [the formal closure in 50.21b] is subordinated to (and thus "consumed" by) the open dialogical process [50.20]'.[160] Furthermore, he considers that the transmission of the patriarchal promise of land from Joseph to his brothers (in the form of an oath by the characters, cf. 50.24-25) constitutes a most significant ending of this narrative. And it opens a future which extends beyond the end of this narrative.[161] The future of this promise and of these quarrelsome brothers is open to the eyes of faith. He then concludes, 'Every system utilized by the narrator to explain the actions of his characters, including the drive

to read the biblical narrative in this new direction.

156. Cf. White, 'The Joseph Story', pp. 49-69; *idem*, 'Where Do You Come From?', pp. 232-75; *idem*, 'Reuben and Judah', pp. 73-97.

157. White, 'The Joseph Story', p. 54.

158. White, 'The Joseph Story', p. 55.

159. White, 'The Joseph Story', pp. 58, 66.

160. White, 'The Joseph Story', p. 68.

161. White, 'The Joseph Story', pp. 56, 57.

ward the restoration of broken communication between Joseph and his brothers, is thus finally subordinated to the uttered promise and its open future.'[162]

White prefers the open dialogical process to the rhetorical closure. But the fulfilment, and thus closure, of the patriarchal promise of the land cannot in theory be achieved at the end of this narrative and is necessarily open beyond it. Instead of pondering the future relationship of these quarrelsome brothers, it is more meaningful to challenge the closure posed by Joseph's speeches concerning the events within this narrative (i.e. enslavement, famine, salvation and God's intention). In this aspect, White admits that the rupture of the previous closure by the brothers' scepticism (50.15-18) indicates that 'the perspective of the brothers has obviously not been totally eclipsed by Joseph's theory of a cosmic plot'.[163] However, he does not question Joseph's version of the events at all. On the contrary, he attempts to demonstrate that the dream as a narrative device allows 'the narrator to enter in symbolic form into the consciousness of a character, i.e. knowledge of the end of the story'.[164] Joseph's 'interpretive comments' (45.5, 8) are proof of 'the opening of Joseph to the perspective of the author', and his consciousness 'is virtually assimilated into that of God'.[165] Despite White's effort to advocate a reading strategy that prevents closure, Joseph's interpretation (as far as God's intentions is concerned) is already taken by him as the 'formal closure' of the meaning of the story even before the protagonist recognizes it. Therefore, instead of being subordinated to (or 'consumed' by) the 'dialectical approach', the 'rhetorical closure' in White's scheme is in fact a solid foundation for the 'ongoing dialogical process'.

However, the assumption that the end will bring closure is not shared by all. And not everyone agrees with Joseph's interpretation, even

162. White, 'The Joseph Story', p. 68.
163. White, 'Where Do You Come From?', p. 274.
164. White, 'The Joseph Story', p. 60, also observes that the dreams are not attributed to God as their source, but exert influence on events as they become speech acts. It means that the response of the brothers to the report of Joseph's dreams actually shapes the course of events and leads eventually to their fulfilment.
165. White, 'Where Do You Come From?', pp. 269, 270. He also suggests that the duration of Joseph's self-control in hiding his emotion and identity is the aspect of this narrative segment not known by Joseph, which prevents the total coalescence of the narrator's perspective with that of Joseph (p. 260).

though he has the last word in this story. Zornberg is critical of Joseph's obsession with 'metaphysical certainty'[166] and expresses reservation about the credibility of Joseph's disclosure speech:

> He speaks many words, achieving the purpose—not of knowledge—but of giving his brothers and his father a narrative—questionable, not entirely credible—a redescription of the meaning to their lives.[167]

Zornberg does not explain which part of Joseph's narrative is questionable and why. He simply suggests that Joseph's speech seems replete with 'theological propositions', but in fact Joseph 'is not making sententious, theoretical statements'. He considers that Joseph is only 'talking about his personal perspective on his own life... in order to provide his brothers with the only stratagem that will help them to scotch their own shame'.[168] Instead of questioning Joseph's claims of divine providence and domination, he turns to discuss the 'problem of knowledge' when the father receives the news of his 'dead' son. He reasons that Joseph will have difficulty persuading his father, through his brothers, to believe his survival and rise to power.

Similarly, Josipovici challenges Joseph's disclosure speech without confronting it directly. He remarks, 'I therefore want to read rather carefully a passage where a revelation seems to occur. It is not the revelation of God to man, but of Joseph to his brothers.'[169] In his view, revelation in both tragedy and comedy in Western literature 'seems to mean the knitting up of the plot and the discovery of the truth at last'. In contrast to the notions of 'closure' and 'final understanding', he asserts that the 'particular mode of narration of the Hebrew Bible'[170] does not seem to work like that. Commenting on Joseph's self-revelation, he states:

> The story of Jacob's children, in other words, is going to be *his* story. And I use the term advisedly, for it is not the narrator but *Joseph* who sees their lives in terms of a story or a drama with an initial prophetic dream, a catastrophe, a miraculous recovery, a revelation and a final reconciliation as all come to accept the truth of the prophetic dream.[171]

166. Zornberg, *Genesis*, p. 351.
167. Zornberg, *Genesis*, p. 344.
168. Zornberg, *Genesis*, p. 345.
169. Josipovici, 'Joseph and Revelation', p. 75.
170. Josipovici, 'Joseph and Revelation', pp. 76, 87, 77.
171. Josipovici, 'Joseph and Revelation', p. 83 (his italics).

He suggests that Joseph's understanding of *his* story is similar to the pattern, found in the case of David and Saul, which starts 'with a fairy-tale opening and then subject[s] it to reality in the form of real failure and death'.[172] In other words, he does not consider Joseph's interpretation of his own dreams as accurate. He considers that 'it will be Judah's seed which will inherit and not Joseph's'.[173] Therefore, in his view, the narrative delivers its final irony and Genesis 50 has to be thought about again: 'God did mean it for good, but even Joseph could not see what good it was that God meant.'[174]

Josipovici comes to this conclusion because he considers that it is wrong to 'artificially divide Genesis from Exodus and both from Judges and Samuel and Kings'.[175] It is possible to relate Joseph's dreams to the future tribal relationship in the later Israelite history. However, what Joseph declares in his interpretation is about God's plan for the salvation of many through his enslavement and lordship. The significance of his dreams over his brothers for the future tribal history is not in his disclosure speech. In fact, he only mentions his lordship over Egypt, not over his brothers. And the 'good' he refers to is again not about the future but about the past action of God to turn the brothers' evil to the ways to salvation. Josipovici still considers one brother ruling over the others as 'good'. The problem for him is not whether it will or should happen but who will occupy the privileged role in the hierarchy. In this aspect, the 'good' he perceives does not differ significantly from Joseph's understanding.

Summary

When a story ends, many readers expect a resolution to the enigma that appears at the beginning of the story, especially if it is an ancient story. For example, Berlin declares:

> The story is resolved when the disharmony is resolved. Joseph sees his brothers as they come to see themselves (42.21ff); later he reveals himself to his brothers, i.e., they see him as he really is... Thus at the end of the story, all points of view coincide. All characters are reconciled and reunited, and the ambiguity is eliminated.[176]

172. Josipovici, 'Joseph and Revelation', p. 84.
173. Josipovici, 'Joseph and Revelation', p. 85.
174. Josipovici, 'Joseph and Revelation', p. 85.
175. Josipovici, 'Joseph and Revelation', p. 85.
176. Berlin, *Poetics*, p. 51. Humphreys, *Joseph and his Family*, p. 51, also sug-

Humphreys is also confident of a resolution for this story: 'The exposition to the novella spoke of discord. The conclusion demonstrates harmony and trust.'[177] However, as previously mentioned the brothers' fear of Joseph's revenge resurfaces once their father is gone.[178] They have to appeal for mercy again by quoting the words of their dead father (50.15-17).[179] Since neither Joseph nor the reader can be sure of the truthfulness of their appeal, it is difficult to determine whether the harmony between them is based on trust or mistrust. Joseph is kind in reassuring and comforting his brothers, but, as long as he recognizes only their evil and no fault of his own in the conflict,[180] it can only be seen as a 'tempered reconciliation' rather than a complete one.[181] The question of brotherhood and reconciliation is indeed a central theme of this story, yet there is no simple resolution to it. Jacob has not relented of his favouritism, Joseph is still unaware of his fault and the brothers are at the mercy of Joseph's power. Instead of giving us a simple verdict, this story is better seen as giving us a chance to experience the problem of brotherhood and reconciliation.[182] It can be done by continuously adopting the viewpoint of each character in turn. We will then be drawn to question and evaluate the characters from each other's perspective. By what means can one arrive at true brotherhood and reconciliation? What are the causes of the problems? What should one do to avoid and resolve this tragic conflict? These questions can be posed

gests that the perspectives of Joseph and his brothers are joined when they join in embrace.

177. Humphreys, *Joseph and his Family*, p. 86.

178. See footnote 133.

179. Josipovici, 'Joseph and Revelation', p. 79, observes that the brothers do not even dare to speak directly to Joseph but through a messenger, and this suggests that they have never ceased to fear Joseph's revenge.

180. Holbert, *The Storyteller's Companion to the Bible*, p. 195, criticizes Joseph for emphasizing the brothers' sin against him while saying 'nothing about his cruel sin against them as master puppeteer in Egypt'.

181. Ackerman, 'Joseph, Judah, and Jacob', p. 109. Josipovici, 'Joseph and Revelation', p. 81, also suggests that 'the brothers are less than convinced by Joseph's protestations of love and forgiveness'. If there is reconciliation, 'it is only a partial and qualified one, at least on the part of the brothers'. See also White, 'Where Do You Come From?', pp. 274-75.

182. This emphasis of reading as an experience is influenced by Stanley E. Fish's interpretative strategy. See his book *Is There a Text in This Class? The Authority of Interpretive Communities* (Cambridge, MA: Harvard University Press, 1980), p. 67.

but one should resist the temptation to come to a neat conclusion. Alter reminds his readers that they can only see with human eyes with a limited vision:

> for in this characteristic biblical perspective no simple linear statement of causation can adequately represent the density and the multiplicity of any person's motives and emotion. Joseph is not unknowable either to God or to the narrator but he must remain in certain respects opaque because he is a human being and we, the readers of the story, see him with human eyes.[183]

In contrast, Joseph is not satisfied with such uncertainty. He is a master interpreter and succeeds extremely well in predicting future events. The narrator reports the fulfilled events for us to verify his prediction. But in terms of the significance of these events, especially God's intentions behind them, the narrator does not provide us with a corresponding confirmation. But the impulse to ascribe unequivocal meanings to the course of events is undeniably enormous for this successful interpreter. While the narrator remains consistently reticent, Joseph does not restrain himself from giving authoritative assertions of God's intention behind every major event. Knowledge gives him immense power, and he exercises it with extraordinary results in saving and enslaving many lives at the same time. A slave-saviour becomes a master-enslaver. Joseph's story is a parable of knowledge—not of its certainty but of its elusiveness. This story heightens as much as clarifies the confusing human condition and the inscrutable divine will behind it. Unfortunately, many readers (biblical scholars or literary critics) are taken in by Joseph's claims and unaware of their incoherence as I have outlined in previous chapters. Joseph is not a perfect hero and he is subjected to criticisms throughout the ages. They are usually targeted at his behaviour rather than his belief. This is a failure to confront the symptom while neglecting the source of the problem. However, one of the sources of his conflict with his brothers is favouritism (parental or divine) which does not go unnoticed but is a thorny issue to deal with. The final chapter will reflect on its role in the family strife in this story.

---

183. Alter, *Art of Biblical Narrative*, p. 164.

Chapter 5

FAVOURITISM FUNCTIONS AS BOTH CURSE AND CURE

The Joseph story is about the conflict between Joseph and his brothers. There are two incidents that give rise to the conflict: Jacob's favouritism towards Joseph (37.3-4) and Joseph's dreams of lordship over his family (37.5-11). This chapter will discuss how and on what grounds the problem of favouritism, parental and divine, is resolved in this story.

Paternal Favouritism

The narrator mentions that Jacob loves Joseph more because he has been born to him in his old age (37.3). The reader is later informed by Judah that Jacob's emotional attachment to Joseph and Benjamin is due to the love of his wife Rachel (44.27). For some readers, Joseph's better moral behaviour is another factor that explains Jacob's special love. Contrasting with his 'treacherous, murderous, and incestuous' brothers, Barnhouse considers that Joseph's 'courage and righteousness justified Jacob's choice'.[1] These opposite traits first appear when Joseph brings an 'evil report' (Gen. 37.2) of his brothers to their father. According to Lowenthal, Joseph wants the brothers to be 'worthy of God's Covenant' and it is 'his ardent concern for the family's future under God' that motivates his action.[2] Goodnick thinks that Joseph's report is truthful because there is no mention of any rebuke by his father as there was in relation to Joseph's dreams. Furthermore, he is considered 'reliable' by his father because he is later 'sent to bring other reports' about the brothers.[3] However, it is improper to verify Joseph's report from his father's response, or the absence of it. Westermann rightly remarks that there is no clear evidence to conclude 'whether the bad report about the

1. Barnhouse, *Genesis*, p. 156.
2. Lowenthal, *The Joseph Narrative in Genesis*, pp. 15-16.
3. Goodnick, 'Character of Joseph', p. 219.

sons of the maidservants was justified or not'.[4] If his report is indeed reliable, Joseph's image is still not necessarily positive for some readers. Morris comments, 'No doubt the reports were true, and Jacob needed to know them, but it is questionable whether Joseph should have become a talebearer in this way.'[5] Alter evaluates him as a spoiled adolescent because of his 'nasty habit of tale-bearing against his brothers'.[6] Even Fritsch, who pictures Joseph as 'one of the most perfect characters' in the Old Testament, whose conduct is a model for all to follow, considers this tale-bearing as a fault in Joseph's character.[7]

Some readers praise Joseph's action from the perspective of his concern for his family, while others focus on his tale-bearing as a manifestation of Joseph's insensitivity to his brothers. However, the events in the next two chapters present a less ambiguous picture. Joseph's resistance to sexual temptation contrasts sharply with Judah's immoral indulgence. The Hebrew word רעה ('ill, evil, wickedness') used in 37.2 to describe the 'evil report' is the same word Joseph later uses to refer to the great 'wickedness' of sexual immorality that he will not do before God (39.9). Joseph's moral integrity is thus an indirect accusation with Judah's immoral conduct, and it can also serve as an indirect confirmation of the truthfulness of his 'evil report'. Joseph may not be perfect, but he is undoubtedly more virtuous than his brothers. Favouritism provokes family conflict,[8] however justifiable it seems to be in hindsight.[9] It is then imperative to observe how the conflict is going to be resolved and how the favouritism will be tackled.

When the story returns to Jacob's family after Joseph's rise in Egypt,

4.   Westermann, *Genesis 37–50*, p. 36.

5.   Morris, *The Genesis Record*, p. 535.

6.   Alter, *Art of Biblical Narrative*, p. 150. Brueggemann, *Genesis*, p. 299, notes, 'for the boy is too young, not able to do much, confined to domestic chores. It is easy, then, to resent, to become a tattler.' Niehoff, *Figure of Joseph*, p. 117, quotes the suggestion of the Midrash *Genesis Rabbah*: 'Joseph's three troubles, namely his brothers' assault, their sale of him and the advances of Potiphar's wife, are in reality divine punishment for each of his slanders.'

7.   Fritsch, 'God Was with Him', pp. 23-24.

8.   Ackerman, 'Joseph, Judah, and Jacob', p. 96, observes that 'the theme of favoritism producing conflict runs throughout the book of Genesis', in the rivalries between Isaac and Ishmael, Jacob and Esau, and finally Joseph and his brothers.

9.   Ross, *Creation and Blessing*, p. 601, explains why the brothers are not chosen by contrasting their 'envy and hatred' with Joseph's 'faithfulness and honesty'.

the narrator directs the reader's attention again to Jacob's favouritism.[10] The father transfers his affection from Joseph to Benjamin. He does not send Benjamin to Egypt with his brothers because he is afraid to lose another favourite son. The cause of the family conflict reappears but the brothers quietly depart without any sign of complaint. Jacob's grief at the loss of Joseph may help to dissipate their past hatred and jealousy. Jacob's favouritism prompted the conflict in the past, but Joseph should not be blamed for the fault of his father.[11] When Joseph demands that the brothers bring down Benjamin, his role in perpetuating the favouritism becomes more evident.[12] Both Jacob and Joseph focus on Benjamin and they say similar words to the brothers: When Jacob sends them to find food without Benjamin, he says, 'that we may live and not die' (42.2); afterward, when Joseph requires them to bring Benjamin down, he says, 'you will live…and you shall not die' (42.18-20). The brothers are caught in a 'dilemma'[13] between the demands from both the father and his favourite son. Joseph and his father are apparently unaware of each other's action. The text at this stage does not indicate that he is informed of his father's favouritism towards Benjamin.

Is Joseph Concerned for Brotherhood and his Father?
Some argue that Joseph's test is motivated by his concern for brotherhood and his father. For example, Goodnick suggests that Joseph's goal is to 'create stronger bonds and harmony among all the brothers, with his own father as the respected patriarch over all'.[14] Lowenthal also considers that 'Joseph decides to purge them first with a "show" of anger, God's anger and God's retribution', in order 'to actualize through their true repentance their potential brotherliness'.[15] Fritsch

---

10. Alter, *Art of Biblical Narrative*, p. 161, considers Jacob's withholding of Benjamin as 'a repetition of the privileged treatment he once gave Joseph'.

11. Bush, *Notes on Genesis*, pp. 223-24, argues that Joseph should not be blamed for 'accepting this token of his father's love', because 'it was not his province to affect wisdom superior to that of his aged parent'.

12. Ross, *Creation and Blessing*, p. 657, notes, 'Benjamin's favored status appears early in the chapter with Jacob's hesitancy to let him go, and it is prominent at the end in the treatment by Joseph.'

13. Brueggemann, *Genesis*, p. 340.

14. Goodnick, 'Character of Joseph', p. 228.

15. Lowenthal, *The Joseph Narrative in Genesis*, p. 70. Sternberg, *The Poetics of Biblical Narrative*, p. 296, considers that the brothers' 'change of heart from

recognizes Joseph's 'despotic unconcern for the hapless victims [his brothers]', but he defends him by stressing 'his love for Benjamin, the youngest brother, and his concern for his aged father'.[16] But Coats criticizes Fritsch for missing the emphasis of the story. He asserts that the alienation in the family is neither 'between Joseph and Benjamin', nor 'between Joseph and his overprotective father'. Instead, it concerns the troublesome relationship between Joseph and his brothers.[17]

If Joseph really wants the brothers to affirm brotherhood, Judah does not agree to this concern. He offers to take Benjamin's place as a slave, but there is no expression of love for Benjamin in his speech. He mentions his father (44.19) at the very beginning of his speech, and then his last word of appeal falls squarely on the frailty of his father (44.34). Within his speech, there are 14 occurrences of the word 'father' and only 6 occurrences of the word 'brother(s)'.[18] The emphasis of the whole speech is on the father rather than on the brotherhood in general or Benjamin in particular. It is his appeal to the death threat to the old father that prompts Joseph to reveal himself. Joseph's immediate inquiry about his father's well-being confirms the effectiveness of Judah's emphasis.[19] Among the brothers, Judah may be the one who

fraternal enmity and vindictiveness to solidarity...make them worthy of him at the end of the course'.

16. Fritsch, 'God Was with Him', p. 28. Brueggemann, *Genesis*, p. 340, suggests that Joseph 'is not a man without passion. But his passion is not for his brothers, not for the well-being of his family, not even for his father. His overriding passion is for Benjamin... That yearning sets Joseph on a collision course with his father, who cannot bear to release the beloved son of his old age.'

17. Coats, *From Canaan to Egypt*, pp. 82-83.

18. Father (44.19, 20, 20, 22, 22, 22, 24, 25, 27, 30, 31, 32, 32, 34, 34); Brother (44.19, 20, 23, 26, 26, 33). Cf. Arnold Ages, 'Why Didn't Joseph Call Home?', *BR* 9 (1993), pp. 42-46 (44). Quoting J. Strahan, *Hebrew Ideals*, Lowenthal, *The Joseph Narrative in Genesis*, p. 101, notes the final word of Judah's speech is 'father': 'Judah uses the word most sacred to him, "father", fourteen times in his plea for his brother, and it is his final, climactic word which gathers into itself all the pathos of his appeal.' Significantly, it is also the last word Joseph speaks to the brothers when he detains Benjamin: 'as for you, go up in peace to your father' (44.17). Judah immediately picks up Joseph's last word and reiterates it throughout his speech and ends the speech with 'father' as his last word: 'I fear to see the evil that would come upon my father' (44.34). The fear of evil is shrewdly placed opposite to Joseph's word of peace.

19. Cf. Humphreys, *Joseph and his Family*, p. 84. In contrast, Savage, 'Literary Criticism and Biblical Studies', p. 95, considers that human action is secondary

can truly understand Jacob's agony of losing his sons. It is probably his experience as a father who lost two sons that prompts him to utter this expression of the love between Jacob and Benjamin: 'his life is bound up in the lad's life, when he sees that the lad is not with us, he will die (44.30-31)'.[20] Abraham experienced the possibilities of losing two sons (21.11; 22.2). Rebekah worried about losing two sons in one day (27.45). Jacob lamented the loss of Joseph and has expressed his fear of losing his second son Benjamin. Reuben was willing to have his two sons put to death if he cannot bring back Benjamin (42.37). But none of them actually lost his sons, except Judah. It is no wonder that the description of the father's emotional attachment to his son is from Judah. However, it does not mean that Judah necessarily condones Jacob's favouritism.[21] There is a clear sign of disapproval when he rebukes his father for risking the lives of the whole family for the sake of the safety of Benjamin alone (43.8-10).[22]

Since Judah bases his appeal on his concern for the father, it is then tempting to assume that Joseph's test is consciously designed to inspire their love for the father. Humphreys thus comments on Joseph's test: 'this provokes the fullest evidence of a change in the brothers, with Judah taking the lead in his plea for Benjamin's life for his old father's sake. Joseph's first public show of deep private emotion is the result.'[23]

The brothers indeed care for their father more than they did in the past. But at the beginning of the test they pleaded with Joseph not to bring down Benjamin for their old father's sake. It is Joseph who ignores their plea until he is finally confronted by Judah's impassioned speech.[24] He then has a change of heart, reveals himself and asks after

under divine providence, so he agrees with Redford and comments, 'Redford is right. Judah's earnest persuasion will not alter the outcome of events.' But Judah's actions are always effective in persuading his brothers (37.26-27), his father (43.1-14) and Joseph.

20. For a similar observation, see Zornberg, *Genesis*, p. 326.

21. Alter, *Art of Biblical Narrative*, p. 175, speaks of Judah's acceptance of favouritism: 'It is a painful reality of favoritism with which Judah, in contrast to the earlier jealousy over Joseph, is here reconciled, out of filial duty and more, out of filial love.'

22. Speiser, *Genesis*, p. 330, comments, 'Judah does not hesitate to speak up forcefully, and even accuse Israel of dangerous indecision'; cf. Coats, *From Canaan to Egypt*, p. 40.

23. Humphreys, *Joseph and his Family*, p. 90.

24. Instead of focusing on Judah's speech as a sign of his profound trans-

the well-being of his father. Does Joseph want the brothers to care for his father through the test? It may well be the opposite. It is Joseph's test that deals a 'crushing blow' to his father.[25]

Joseph Demands the Brothers' Acquiescence in Favouritism

The brothers have previously informed Joseph of Jacob's favouritism towards Benjamin and the threat to their old father if Benjamin is gone. Joseph already 'knows what is happening', while his father 'knows nothing but cares and grieves his loss'.[26] It is a test about favouritism. Holbert summarizes succinctly its nature: 'To bring the younger brother, left alone with a doting father, that is Joseph's test. Joseph knows about Jacob's favoritism; he had earlier lived with it.'[27] Sternberg explains Joseph's strategy as turning back 'the wheel of time to the original crime against himself, with the circumstances reproduced and the ten ranged against Benjamin...who has taken his brother's place as paternal favorite'.[28] The aim of the test is to see whether the brothers have 'come to terms with the father's preference'.[29] 'To exacerbate the brothers' jealousy', Sternberg further suggests, 'Joseph now

---

formation, Mark A. O'Brien in his article, 'Contribution of Judah's Speech', pp. 429-47, considers his speech as one playing a key role in the characterization of Joseph. He argues that it exposes Joseph as a character who is as much in need of transformation as his brothers because Judah confronts him with the danger to their father in his demand of Benjamin.

25. Holbert, 'Joseph and the Surprising Choice of God', pp. 38-39, remarks on the cruelty of Joseph, 'He also must know what his request will mean to his father; it will be a crushing blow, and yet he asks it coolly and coldly with no apparent remorse.' Referring to the question Joseph asks the brothers in 43.27, Holbert further comments, 'Joseph first asks: "Is it *shalom* with your father, the old man of whom you speak? Is he still alive?" Who more than Joseph knows that it can hardly be *shalom* with the Old Jacob? This little pleasantry is in reality a cruel jibe, which may more accurately mean, "How is the old man bearing up under the strain? Is he dead yet?" But they respond with the appropriate pleasantry, "It is *shalom* with your servant, our father; he is still alive". Everyone in this room knows it is not *shalom* with Jacob, yet all say it; a more terrible scene can hardly be imagined' (his italics).

26. Brueggemann, *Genesis*, p. 336.

27. Holbert, 'Joseph and the Surprising Choice of God', p. 38.

28. Sternberg, *The Poetics of Biblical Narrative*, p. 303.

29. Sternberg, *The Poetics of Biblical Narrative*, pp. 302-303. Alter, *Art of Biblical Narrative*, p. 161, also suggests that the dénouement of the story will hinge on the brothers' ability to accept with full filial empathy their father's preference.

shows him special favor during the banquet—"Benjamin's portion was five times as much as any of them"—rubbing it in through the contrast with the order of natural seniority in which he has taken care to seat them.'[30] However, Joseph's special treatment recurs after the test. He gives every brother a festal garment, but Benjamin is given five festal garments and three hundred shekels of silver (45.22). His special treatment of Benjamin is thus not merely a part of the test. It is an inclination which he retains throughout the course of his interaction with the brothers, and he never recognizes it as insensitive.

Sternberg considers Joseph's strategy successful in inducing the brothers to acquiesce in 'the old father's sentiments' which 'receive not just a mention but repeated and preferential treatment'.[31] Westermann comments, 'He [Joseph] hears too that the brothers now speak differently of the preferential love for the children of this particular wife.'[32] So Joseph's effort to resolve the conflict by repeating, and thus reinforcing, favouritism does not go unnoticed. If there is anything inherently wrong with favouritism, one can no longer blame the father alone for inciting the conflict. The favourite later plays an active role in reinforcing not only the father's fault, but his own special status as well.

Furthermore, it is important to observe the way the narrator presents Joseph's knowledge of his father's plight, and its effect on the reader's perception of Joseph's insistence of favouritism.[33] Savage notices that Judah's speech 'recapitulates the negotiations between Joseph and his brothers and sets these in the context of Jacob's *age* and his *love* for his [two favourite] sons'.[34] The narrator withholds Joseph's previous knowledge of this vital piece of information from the reader until Judah appeals to Joseph on these two factors.[35] Once Judah reveals that

30. Sternberg, *The Poetics of Biblical Narrative*, p. 303. Ross, *Creation and Blessing*, p. 656, also suggests that 'Joseph was deliberately favoring Benjamin over his brothers, providing them with reason for jealousy and preparing them for the opportunity to rid themselves of Benjamin as they had Joseph.'

31. Sternberg, *The Poetics of Biblical Narrative*, p. 307.

32. Westermann, *Genesis 37–50*, p. 136.

33. Savage, 'Literary Criticism and Biblical Studies', p. 95, focuses rather on the change of attitude by the audience towards the brothers: 'The audience's detached, triumphal enjoyment of the picture is replaced by their being drawn, finally, into the affectivity displayed by Jacob's family. The audience cares what happens to them.'

34. Savage, 'Literary Criticism and Biblical Studies', p. 95 (my italics).

35. For a detailed comparison between Judah's recollection (44.19-23) and the

Joseph has been told of Jacob's favouritism for Benjamin, and that the old father will die if Benjamin is gone, this disclosure will modify the reader's former perception of Joseph.[36] At first, he seemed to enforce favouritism unwittingly while being unaware of the danger posed to the old father. Now the reader discovers that Joseph deliberately forces the brothers to yield to Jacob's favouritism in the perfect knowledge of the risk to the well-being of his old father.[37] The narrator's use of recapitulation exposes a troubling aspect of Joseph's test. If he does not know his father's frailty without Benjamin, then he is only guilty of hurting his father unknowingly.[38] But he has already been warned of the danger,[39] so it is not harsh to criticize his action as 'playing with death'.[40]

Joseph may indeed care for Benjamin and his father, but he cares for himself more. Longacre describes the choice of Benjamin in the test as an '*echo* or *reflection*' of Joseph himself.[41] He is using Benjamin only in order to force his brothers to accept their father's favouritism. So he

previous events (42.7-20, 29-38; 43.2-10), see Westermann, *Genesis 37–50*, pp. 135-36.

36. This concept of making and remaking of a portrait is borrowed from Wolfang Iser's reading theory of the 'illusion-making and illusion-breaking' and 'forming of *gestalt* and remodification of it'. It is based on an assumption that any configurative meaning will be continuously modified when new perspectives are incorporated in the reading process. See his book, *The Act of Reading: A Theory of Aesthetic Response* (Baltimore: The Johns Hopkins University Press, 1978), pp. 118-28.

37. Wenham, *Genesis 16–50*, p. 404, observes that 'Joseph's determination to bring his younger brother down to Egypt is pitted against Jacob's reluctance to let Benjamin out of his sight.'

38. Turner, *Announcements of Plot in Genesis*, p. 155, observes that Jacob's words serve as an accusation against Joseph's action: 'by imprisoning Simeon and demanding Benjamin's presence in Egypt, he puts his frail father through torture, as can be seen in Jacob's words to his sons: "You have bereaved me of my children: Joseph is no more, and Simeon is no more, and now you would take Benjamin; all this has come upon me" (42.36).'

39. O'Brien, 'Contribution of Judah's Speech', p. 439, suggests that 'Joseph's desire for power over his brothers lead[s] him to disregard their warning about the effect his demand would have on his father.'

40. Turner, *Announcements of Plot in Genesis*, p. 162. Savran, *Telling and Retelling*, p. 87, regards Joseph's detaining of Benjamin as a 'cruel act' in the light of 'Jacob's frailty', and asserts that it 'cannot be part of a divine sponsored master plan but must be a reflection of Joseph's personal desire for revenge'.

41. Longacre, *Joseph*, p. 50 (his italics).

is guilty of caring more about his status as a favourite son than about the well-being of his father and Benjamin. It may not be a sin requiring to be confessed, but it is a serious flaw in his character that he should be aware of. Unfortunately, not only is Joseph ignorant of his problem, but some readers concur totally with Joseph's perspective in his insistence on acceptance of his status by the brothers. For example, commenting on Judah's citing his father's words: 'My wife bore me two sons', Lowenthal considers that Joseph would be glad to hear that 'the brothers have overcome their grudge about the father's having favoured Rachel over their own mothers'.[42] If Joseph really wants the brothers to accept, without resentment, 'the father's compensatory transference to Rachel's orphans of his affection for them', [43] it does not occur to Lowenthal that it is highly insensitive for Joseph to harbour such an attitude.

Sternberg understands rightly that Judah's action in adducing the father's favouritism as the grounds for self-sacrifice breaks down Joseph's last defences. But he seems to adopt Joseph's strategy whole-heartedly by asserting: 'That the sons of the hated wife should have come to terms with the father's attachment to Rachel ("my wife") and her children is enough to promise an end to hostilities and a fresh start.'[44] Humphreys simply excuses the favouritism as 'an inescapable fact of life' that must be accepted and understood.[45] Fretheim even declares that 'Favoritism per se does not constitute the problem; rather, the problem involves the way in which favoritism manifested itself publicly, on the part of both chooser and chosen.'[46] If favouritism is not

---

42. Lowenthal, *The Joseph Narrative in Genesis*, p. 99. Alter, *Art of Biblical Narrative*, pp. 170, 175, criticizes Jacob for being 'oblivious to the feelings of his ten sons' by speaking in a way 'as though only the sons of Rachel, and not they, were his sons'. But he praises Judah's ability to bring himself to quote sympathetically Jacob's extravagant statement that his wife bore him two sons.

43. Lowenthal, *The Joseph Narrative in Genesis*, p. 99. Jacob's special love for Joseph did not begin when Rachel died. When Jacob faced a possible attack from Esau, he arranged Rachel and Joseph at the very end of his convoy (33.2).

44. Sternberg, *The Poetics of Biblical Narrative*, p. 308.

45. Humphreys, *Joseph and his Family*, pp. 46, 47.

46. Fretheim, *Genesis*, p. 602. Similarly, Westermann, *Genesis 37–50*, p. 37, makes a distinction between the father's predilection and preference: 'it is not the father's predilection for Joseph that arouses the brothers' hatred; it is something else. Jacob presents Joseph with a distinctive garment; it is this gives rise to open conflict...the consequence of predilection is preference. The predilection becomes

a problem itself, it is difficult to understand why its manifestation in public would change its basic nature. It is more reasonable to argue that publicity in this case only makes a bad situation worse.

It is one thing to require the brothers to understand their father's favouritism, but it is quite a different matter for the favourite to demand that the brothers accept his special status. Intricately, Joseph's action produces both effects. The aim of Joseph's action is, according to Feuer, to test the brothers: 'will the brothers sacrifice another brother, as they once threw Joseph in the pit and sold him into slavery out of jealous rage at the favored status of Rachel's children?'[47] The cause of the crime, the favoured status, is accurately identified, but Feuer aligns himself mainly with Joseph's viewpoint in tackling the brothers and their crime. On the one hand, Joseph is credited with staging a successful 'potential re-enactment of their crime' to enable 'his brothers' repentance' and 'regeneration'. On the other hand, trapped by Joseph to offer himself in Benjamin's place, Judah is said to 'have learned the importance of family cohesion, even at the cost of allowing Rachel's child to retain his favored status'.[48] Both ways, Joseph's positive influence on the 'moral status' of the brothers receives total endorsement. The 'favored status' as the cause of the family strife now becomes the cost of the family cohesion that brothers have to learn to endure. Unfortunately, Joseph's active role in imposing this cost escapes critical assessment.

Targeting the brothers' crime and their repentance will only be dealing with the symptom but not the cause of the family conflict. Joseph's test is indeed a step further. It strikes at the root of the problem (parental favouritism) by requiring the brothers' complete acquiescence. However, instead of eliminating the favouritism, it is an odd attempt to resolve the conflict with more favouritism, effectively treating the cause as the solution, the curse as the cure. Ironically, yielding to Joseph's demand is simultaneously a sign of their repentance. It satisfies the justice of confronting their long-hidden crime. However, the injustice of favouritism, which provoked the conflict in the first place, is not rebuked but reinforced.

public and so the father shares the blame for the conflict that it unlooses.'

47. Feuer, 'Happy Families', p. 274.
48. Feuer, 'Happy Families', p. 275.

Avoidance of Confronting Divine Favouritism

The conflict in Jacob's family erupts due to paternal favouritism, but most readers are aware that its tragic effect is intensified by divine favouritism. For example, Redford rightly comments that 'the principal device used to occasion the brothers' jealousy is the dream which portends Joseph's rise to power'.[49] Sarna points out that the coat given to Joseph by Jacob is 'a hated symbol of favoritism and a cause of discord', and further asserts that Joseph's dreams are 'even more potent a source of disharmony'.[50] Ackerman also asserts that 'divinely inspired dreams, given to a younger son who wears a special garment, continue and intensify the theme of divine and parental favoritism that produces conflict'.[51] Joseph's dreams as the primary force to drive the family to 'conflict and fear' is thus well recognized.[52]

Becking realizes that the brothers' hatred, provoked by the love of Jacob, is increased by Joseph's dreams, but he asserts that '[t]he primary emphasis in the story is not on the dreams as such; but on the growing alienation between Joseph and his brothers'.[53] He is not alone in shifting the attention from the principal cause of the conflict to other aspects of the conflict itself. Many readers focus their analyses on the process from the breakdown of the family's unity to its restoration, and evaluate Joseph's merit or fault in manipulating the brothers to achieve their repentance and reconciliation.[54]

49. Redford, *Biblical Story of Joseph*, p. 89.

50. Sarna, *Understanding Genesis*, p. 212. See also Baldwin, *Genesis 12–50*, p. 159; White, 'Reuben and Judah', pp. 86, 88.

51. Ackerman, 'Joseph, Judah, and Jacob', p. 97. Youngblood, *The Book of Genesis*, p. 244, points out that Joseph's two dreams 'strained the relationship between himself and his brothers'.

52. Brueggemann, *Genesis*, p. 343. It is significant to note that when the brothers plot to murder Joseph, they take away his coat that signifies his father's favouritism, but their spoken rationale for getting rid of Joseph is due to his dreams (cf. 37.19-20). Ross, *Creation and Blessing*, p. 596, rightly observes that Joseph seems rather 'oblivious' to the brothers' jealousy over his dreams.

53. Becking, 'They Hated Him Even More', p. 47.

54. E.g., Ackerman, 'Joseph, Judah, and Jacob', pp. 95, 97-98, interprets the plot of the story as the breakdown of communication, caused by divine favouritism, and its restoration as occurring when the brothers are able 'to approach him (45.4)' and to 'speak with him (45.15)'. See also George W. Coats, 'Strife and Reconciliation: Themes of a Biblical Theology in the Book of Genesis', *HBT* 2 (1980), pp. 15-

Von Rad remarks that Joseph's dreams can be understood in two ways, 'either as real prophecies or as the notions of a vainglorious heart'.[55] But he is quick to affirm their prophetic substance as unmistakable and he condemns the reactions of Jacob and the brothers as negative. At the beginning of his article, Ackerman asks,

> had special favor been thrust on the youth, or did he grasp after it by tattling on his brothers? Did the dreams indicate divine choice, or were they the ambitious imaginings of a lad who would play the role of deity?

He cites the recurring motif of 'God's presence with Joseph in Egypt' as evidence for the divine origin of the dreams.[56] He then devotes the rest of his article to describing how and why Joseph 'must play a role in bringing the [two] dreams to fulfillment'.[57] His argument is that since Joseph's rise to power is a divine choice and 'human beings cannot thwart the divine purpose', a 'wise' and 'appropriate' human response is required to complement and complete the divine activity.[58] In contrast, Turner considers that it is wrong for Joseph to try to fulfil the dreams instead of waiting for providence to work it out for him.[59] But he also argues that the dreams are not merely 'Joseph's own psychology' but 'divine revelation'.[60] He considers that the lack of reference to the divine in 37.5-11 cannot be offered as conclusive proof for denying the divine nature of Joseph's dreams. Moreover, he argues that 'Joseph's successful interpretation of them lends credence to his judgment regarding their source.'[61] The important matter for these readers is

37; Schimmel, 'Joseph and his Brothers', pp. 60-65; Ackerman, 'Joseph, Judah, and Jacob', pp. 85-113; Fritsch, 'God Was with Him', pp. 21-34; Sternberg, *The Poetics of Biblical Narrative*, pp. 285-308.

55. Von Rad, *Genesis*, p. 351.

56. Ackerman, 'Joseph, Judah, and Jacob', p. 86. Westermann, *Joseph*, p. 11, considers that Joseph's dreams, rather than being simply the product of his 'ambition', are probably 'a hidden sign from God' because of Jacob's reaction to keep the matter in mind. White, 'Reuben and Judah', p. 88, asserts that the 'providential force' of the dreams goes beyond the human emotions, i.e. Joseph's arrogance and the brothers' envy, it has precipitated. In another article, 'The Joseph Story', p. 61, he argues that the dream is not a deception but a totally unmotivated intrusion by the narrator into the consciousness of a character.

57. Ackerman, 'Joseph, Judah, and Jacob', p. 88.

58. Ackerman, 'Joseph, Judah, and Jacob', pp. 86, 94-95, 112.

59. Turner, *Announcements of Plot in Genesis*, p. 165.

60. Turner, *Announcements of Plot in Genesis*, p. 144.

61. Turner, *Announcements of Plot in Genesis*, p. 146. For his detailed argument

to decide the source of the dreams. Once the source is determined as being from God and not as arising out of human ambition, the problem of favouritism, and its disastrous effect on the peace of the family, seem to become less critical and can be explained away more easily.

Joseph's Destiny is Justified for the Common Good

Many readers observe that the text presents Jacob's old age as a reason for his favouritism (cf. 37.3).[62] This reason is regarded as softening 'the arbitrariness of Jacob's preferential treatment'.[63] Later, Judah's speech is motivated by 'the deepest empathy for his father, by a real understanding of what it means for the old man's very life to be bound up with that of the lad'.[64] However, the excuse of old age cannot be used to justify the divine favouritism. Instead, Joseph offers the need for survival as the sole reason for his dreams.[65] It is generally accepted as a valid reason by many readers. Thus, the 'divine favoritism' is honestly acknowledged by Ackerman but its necessity is duly defended:

> Full reconciliation, however, cannot take place until they can resolve the issue that had partially instigated that crime: divine favoritism. Only when Joseph explains that the dreams indicated a specially ordained family role rather than a personally privileged divine love are the brothers able to approach him.[66]

Joseph's status as favourite is now justified as being not for personal gain but for the welfare of the whole family. 'As the brothers learn that the divine favoritism they had once hated involved the risking/descent of the chosen one so that Israel might live,' Ackerman further asserts, 'they can now perceive Joseph's dreams of ascendancy in a new light'.[67] There is a price for Joseph to be paid before the rise. The

---

for the divine origin of Joseph's dreams, see pp. 144-47.

62. Cf. Goldin, 'Youngest Son', p. 34; Westermann, *Joseph*, p. 5.

63. White, 'Reuben and Judah', p. 85.

64. Alter, *Art of Biblical Narrative*, p. 175.

65. David J.A. Clines, *Interested Parties: The Ideology of Writers and Readers of the Hebrew Bible* (JSOTSup, 205; Sheffield: Sheffield Academic Press, 1995), pp. 200-201, discusses the problematic nature of God's choice of Israel from among all the nations. He observes that the Pentateuch itself sees no problem for this 'exclusivity' and it even 'makes a point of there being no rationale' for God's choice (cf. Deut. 7.7).

66. Ackerman, 'Joseph, Judah, and Jacob', pp. 98-99.

67. Ackerman, 'Joseph, Judah, and Jacob', p. 107.

implication is that his ordained role is no longer as enviable as it first appeared.

In the name of salvation, some readers justify Joseph's ruling over his brothers as his 'career'.[68] He is only serving as 'the agent of destiny, as God's instrument, in the large plan of the story'.[69] The brothers are blamed for failing to recognize his 'true destiny'.[70] According to Fritsch, the dramatic climax comes 'when the hero gets his just revenge on those who have tried to impede his inevitable rise to fame and glory'.[71] However, the 'careers' of the brothers being subjugated are either ignored or played down.[72] In contrast, Joseph's viewpoint is always given preference:

> Joseph insists that God rather than he is the shaper of the familial destiny.[73]

> Now his political power is beyond measure, and he does rule over the whole family as his adolescent dreams had foretold. However, as he himself points out, his power emanates from God, and whatever happens is for the common good (Gen. 45.4-8).[74]

However unfair it is, the strikingly different fates for both parties are justified in the name of the 'common good'. Ross considers Joseph's claim to ruling over his brothers is only a matter of leadership, in that everyone has to submit to God's sovereign choice. The brothers' reaction of envy and hatred is 'understandable',[75] but 'disastrous to the unity of the nation and so could not be left unchecked'.[76] The cause of

---

68. Cf. Wenham, *Genesis 16–50*, p. 432; Ackerman, 'Joseph, Judah, and Jacob', p. 95, also refers to the dominant theme of this story as 'the providential care of the family of Israel through Joseph's career'.

69. Alter, *Art of Biblical Narrative*, p. 139.

70. Alter, *Art of Biblical Narrative*, p. 163.

71. Fritsch, 'God Was with Him', p. 27. However, Joseph's dreams are not only the dreams of glory, but also the dreams of prostration. Glory for the dreamer will inevitably also mean nightmare for those who are subjugated in this story.

72. Sternberg, *The Poetics of Biblical Narrative*, p. 285, thus suggests that 'Joseph's rough handling of his brothers causes the reader no undue worry about their ultimate fate' because his dreams foretell 'a happy ending'.

73. Feuer, 'Happy Families', p. 277.

74. J. Robin King, 'The Joseph Story and Divine Politics: A Comparative Study of a Biographic Formula from the Ancient Near East', *JBL* 106 (1987), pp. 577-94 (593).

75. Ross, *Creation and Blessing*, p. 601.

76. Ross, *Creation and Blessing*, p. 657.

family strife is no longer the favouritism but the reaction to it. Thus, Joseph's effort to test the brothers for jealousy is deemed necessary. It pleases Ross that the brothers finally 'accept their lot gratefully and without jealousy'. '[I]n spite of the favouritism to Benjamin,' he concludes, 'the brothers displayed a greater maturity about their lot in life'.[77] To lessen the unfairness of Joseph's privileged position, Ackerman warns of the danger of misuse of power: 'The last thing that Joseph can do, if he wants to reestablish his place as brother in the family, is to overwhelm his brothers with his power.'[78] Similarly, Westermann senses that the narrator wants to issue such a warning 'to the powerful not to lay false charges against the powerless'. This is a criticism against the deceitful ways in which Joseph treats the brothers in his test, especially in the light of his own suffering experience with his master's wife.[79]

Blaming Human Favouritism rather than Divine Favouritism
Although many readers acknowledge the dreams as the source of the family conflict, they tend to criticize not the dreams themselves but the ways Joseph handles them. Joseph is criticized for reporting the dreams in a 'childish boasting' way.[80] He is thus portrayed by many as 'insensitive',[81] 'arrogant and boastful'[82] towards his brothers. Alter suggests that Joseph's insensitivity to his brothers' feelings in reporting his dreams is encouraged by his father's indulgence.[83] But he rightly observes that the dreams and Joseph's reporting of them are targets for the brothers' hatred.[84] Goldin attributes the cause of the family conflict to both factors too: 'he not only dreams outrageous dreams of power, he

77. Ross, *Creation and Blessing*, p. 662.
78. Ackerman, 'Joseph, Judah, and Jacob', p. 95.
79. Westermann, *Genesis 37–50*, p. 249.
80. Westermann, *Genesis 37–50*, p. 38.
81. Cf. Lerner, 'Joseph the Unrighteous', p. 279; Josipovici, 'Joseph and Revelation', p. 84.
82. Holbert, 'Joseph and the Surprising Choice of God', p. 40. Morris, *The Genesis Record*, pp. 534-35, describes Joseph's character as 'morally pure', yet it 'was marred by spiritual pride to a degree which his brothers finally found impossible to tolerate'.
83. Alter, *Art of Biblical Narrative*, p. 150.
84. Alter, *Genesis*, p. 210, considers that it is misguided to construe 'they hated him yet more for his dreams and for his words' (37.8) as a hendiadys ('for speaking about his dreams').

delights in telling them to his family. It is no wonder the brothers decide to kill him.'[85] So it is inaccurate to emphasize Joseph's act of reporting the dreams while neglecting the problem of the dreams themselves.[86]

Many tend to focus on the problem of human favouritism rather than the divine favouritism that is implied by Joseph's interpretation of his dreams. Wenham does not hesitate to state clearly that 'Jacob's favoritism turns normal sibling rivalry into deadly hatred' and that the father 'is blind to the effects of his actions on his sons'.[87] He further remarks, 'So by sending dreams providence *seems* to be making a bad situation worse, though *doubtless* Joseph's cockiness in relating them to his brothers and father made their impact even worse than might otherwise have been the case.'[88] The problematic nature of the divine favouritism is clearly overshadowed by the certainty of human faults.[89]

If the dreams sent by providence still seem to have some undesirable results for Wenham, Kidner affirms them without reservation as 'God's design' and 'divine sovereignty'. He condemns the paternal favouritism

85. Goldin, 'Youngest Son', p. 39. Holbert, *The Storyteller's Companion to the Bible*, p. 169, remarks, 'Joseph begins to dream, and can hardly wait to reveal the content of these dreams to his brothers'; White, 'Reuben and Judah', p. 87, also notices that 'the description of the act of reporting in the narrative framework alerts the reader to the significance of that action in itself, apart from the content of the dream', but he stresses more the problem of the reporting than the content of the dreams.

86. Bush, *Notes on Genesis*, p. 225, is uncertain 'whether Joseph acted wisely in telling his dream', but he suggests that 'it was evidently done in all the simplicity of a child-like heart, without the remotest idea of inflaming a resentment already too strong'. He also asserts that 'Joseph was secretly directed by an overruling Providence in relating it', because, in his view, 'the dream was obviously suggested by God himself'. In contrast, Josipovici, 'Joseph and Revelation', p. 84, finds Joseph's insistence on his present power and glory in his disclosure speech 'rather unpleasant'. Again, the element of pride and triumph in Joseph's words is censured while the problem of dreams of power and glory themselves escape criticism.

87. Wenham, *Genesis 16–50*, p. 359. White, 'Reuben and Judah', p. 85, describes Joseph's action as 'tattling on his brothers', but he reckons that Jacob is 'largely responsible for his son's behavior'. Humphreys, *Joseph and his Family*, p. 92, speaks of 'the injustice in this parental favouritism, natural as it is'.

88. Wenham, *Genesis 16–50*, p. 359 (my italics).

89. Coats, 'Strife and Reconciliation', p. 32, also lays the blame squarely on Joseph and his father: 'The braggart Joseph and his doting father intensify the hostility of the siblings.'

as 'ostentatious and provocative'. Jacob is criticized for learning nothing from his early experience of favouritism suffered at the hands of his parents. By giving Joseph a coat of many colours, '[it] would bear an even heavier crop of hatred and deceit than it had yielded in his own youth'.[90] But later the father is praised for having 'learnt by now, as his sons had not, to allow for God's hand in affairs, and for His right of choice among men'.[91] Feuer judges that 'Joseph brings his brothers' wrath upon himself by his arrogant recounting of his dreams as much as his father does by tactless favoring of the boy',[92] but there is a 'triumphal quality of Joseph's assertion of God's plan'.[93]

Stigers recognizes that the manifestation of parental partiality is 'unwise',[94] and that 'the divine purpose in Joseph reinforc[es] the parental preference'. Since God's 'method is employed against human disapproval', it seems to him that there is no need to excuse 'the manner by which Yahweh would preserve His people'.[95] The culprits, according to Stigers, are rather the brothers whose 'conduct was direct defiance of the message of the dreams'. They are criticized for 'fighting against God and His providence' and for their inability 'to undergo the humiliation indicated in the dreams!'[96] Similarly, Bush asserts that 'Joseph was destined to high honor' and 'it pleased God now to favor him'.[97] However, he criticizes Jacob for acting 'unwisely in distinguishing Joseph from his brethren', even though he is well aware that by honouring Joseph over the brothers, God 'provoked them the more'.[98] Again, the brothers bear the major burden of guilt:

> 'We will not have this man to rule over us.' Such is our native pride and stoutness of spirit, that we cannot bear the thought of being subject to those who have been our equals or inferiors. But let us remember that 'promotion cometh not from the south, nor from the east, nor from the west; it is the Lord that putteth down one, and setteth up another; and who shall stay his hand, or say unto him, What doest thou?'[99]

90. Kidner, *Genesis*, p. 180.
91. Kidner, *Genesis*, p. 181.
92. Feuer, 'Happy Families', p. 279.
93. Feuer, 'Happy Families', p. 278.
94. Stigers, *A Commentary on Genesis*, p. 270.
95. Stigers, *A Commentary on Genesis*, p. 271.
96. Stigers, *A Commentary on Genesis*, p. 274.
97. Bush, *Notes on Genesis*, p. 224.
98. Bush, *Notes on Genesis*, pp. 223, 225.
99. Bush, *Notes on Genesis*, pp. 225-26.

Youngblood apportions blame to each family member for their role in the conflict: Jacob's 'favoritism and insensitivity' bring 'him and his sons to grief, leading [him] from joy to sorrow, Joseph from freedom to slavery, and the brothers from contentment to jealous rage and violence'; the brothers are full of 'hatred, murderous intent, and deception'; finally, Joseph's 'latent pride' and 'naïveté' in reporting the dreams are major causes of the conflict.[100] As for the dreams themselves, Youngblood totally aligns himself with Joseph's perspective in asserting that their 'ironically unexpected fulfilment' is a divine providence in turning human evil to good purpose.[101]

Westermann observes the curious displacement of hostility: 'the hatred of those who have been slighted is targeted far more vehemently against the favored one than it is against the one who does the favoring, even when the favored one should not be blamed'.[102] He explains that 'the brothers' fear and respect for their elders' prevent them from directing their hatred at Jacob.[103] Dealing with the family relationship, the brothers' error of blaming the recipient of favouritism is rectified by many of the readers mentioned above. All parties in the family, the father and the sons, are now judged according to their part in the strained relationship. However, when confronting divine favouritism, these readers repeat the brothers' error of targeting their criticism on the favoured one rather than the one who favours. Thus, Joseph is criticized for reporting his dreams,[104] or for attempting to fulfil them.[105] The brothers are criticized for failing to recognize, or for opposing, the

---

100. Youngblood, *The Book of Genesis*, pp. 244, 247.

101. Youngblood, *The Book of Genesis*, p. 283.

102. Westermann, *Joseph*, p. 8.

103. Westermann, *Joseph*, p. 7. It is also significant to notice that the bond between Joseph and his brothers hinges mainly on their common respect for Jacob. Joseph's test and his brothers' response centre on the well-being of their old father. At the end of the story, the dead father still exerts a critical influence on their relationship as the brothers quote an unverifiable pleading of their father to Joseph (cf. 50.15-17).

104. Cf. Westermann, *Genesis 37–50*, p. 38; Goldin, 'Youngest Son', p. 39; Holbert, *The Storyteller's Companion to the Bible*, p. 169; Wenham, *Genesis 16–50*, p. 359; Feuer, 'Happy Families', p. 279; Youngblood, *The Book of Genesis*, pp. 244.

105. Cf. Turner, *Announcements of Plot in Genesis*, pp. 159-65.

divine choice.[106] But the 'divine favouritism' enjoys a considerable amount of support and defence by these readers, even though its role in intensifying the family strife is honestly admitted. Surprisingly, the reason for the 'divine favouritism' given by them does not differ from the one declared by Joseph. They just echo, maybe more elaborately, his claims of divine providence and divine domination for salvation.[107]

In discussing the parental favouritism, Westermann refuses to allocate the exact share of guilt to those involved:

> Instead, the fault should be located in the fact that Jacob's special love for Joseph is openly proclaimed in the form of this gift [a long robe with sleeves]. The gift, which acts as a document of Jacob's favoritism, sparks an incident for which everyone, including Jacob, shares some portion of guilt. It is the storyteller's purpose to point out exactly this. This action by which they then all come to share guilt cannot simply be blamed on the error of any single person; the incident is somehow self-powered, because no matter how we try to assign blame, some of it always remains unallocated. The things that happen here are as fundamentally inexplicable as the events described in Genesis 3.[108]

He detects a 'parallel' between the brothers' reaction with that of Cain in the primaeval story: 'Cain didn't direct his hatred toward God, who favored Abel; instead, he hated the person who was favored, Abel himself.'[109] In connecting the human favouritism with the divine one, he regards the nature of favouritism as 'somehow self-powered' and 'fundamentally inexplicable'. It seems that he wants to avoid criticizing divine favouritism by not blaming anyone for paternal favouritism either.

---

106. Cf. von Rad, *Genesis*, p. 351; Alter, *Art of Biblical Narrative*, p. 139; Stigers, *A Commentary on Genesis*, p. 274; Bush, *Notes on Genesis*, pp. 225-26.

107. E.g., Humphreys, *Joseph and his Family*, p. 125, assumes that for the brothers and the reader there is no other understanding except through Joseph's perspective: 'finally the brothers come to know what Joseph and the reader know, and all come to know through Joseph's recognition that the tug and pull of this family's story must be comprehended within a larger divine design, and the design is one that seeks to preserve life'. For a similar view, see Ackerman, 'Joseph, Judah, and Jacob', p. 107; Wenham, *Genesis 16–50*, p. 432; King, 'The Joseph Story and Divine Politics', p. 593. Concerning the problematic nature of Joseph's claims, please refer to the first three chapters of this book.

108. Westermann, *Joseph*, p. 5.

109. Westermann, *Joseph*, pp. 7-8.

Favouritism Perpetuated

After a detailed analysis of the 'undoing, morally and psychologically, of the brothers' violation of fraternal and filial bonds' through Joseph's test, Alter concludes his study with a startling verdict on divine–human relations: 'A basic biblical perception about both human relations and relations between God and man is that love is unpredictable, arbitrary, at times perhaps seemingly unjust, and Judah now comes to an acceptance of that fact with all its consequences.'[110] Possibly drawing significance from Judah's speech and the erroneous human interaction in this conflict-ridden family, Alter frames the nature of divine–human relations in terms of 'unpredictable, arbitrary and at times perhaps seemingly unjust love'. To qualify 'love' as 'unpredictable', 'arbitrary' and 'unjust' is both ambiguous and provocative, especially in relation to God.[111] 'Unjust favouritism' would be a straightforward judgment, but 'unjust love' seems to be acceptance and rejection at the same time.[112] Alter's description seems to express his feeling of ambivalence towards this basic biblical perception which he finds in this story.[113]

Alter applauds the remarkable change in Judah who 'now can bring himself, out of concern for his old father, to accept the painful fact of paternal favoritism ("and his father loves him") that was the root of the brothers' hostility to Joseph'.[114] However, his acquiescence is neither purely out of 'filial duty' and 'filial love', nor entirely voluntary. It is rather a 'painful process of learning to which Joseph and circumstances

110. Alter, *Art of Biblical Narrative*, pp. 174-75.

111. Quoting Alter's insight on Judah's acceptance of the painful reality of favouritism, Josipovici, 'Joseph and Revelation', p. 83, declares that 'there is no rhyme or reason in parental love, or at least none that children can grasp, and that we cannot blame our parents for loving our brothers or sisters more than ourselves'. However, Alter does not restrict his description of arbitrariness to parental love alone; it also includes the divine love.

112. Alter, *Genesis*, p. 264, characterizes the father's love as 'outrageous favoritism', but he does not use 'favoritism' to describe divine love in this story.

113. In contrast, Greenspahn, *When Brothers Dwell Together*, p. 159, questions the divine choice more directly and remarks, 'God's lines are not always straight. Moreover, if the younger offspring who fill the Bible are God's tools, it is worth remembering that the older siblings, with whom its landscape is so littered, are also God's creatures.' Clines, *Interested Parties*, p. 210, also questions 'why in any case should one of the them "serve" the other, considering that they are brothers?'

114. Alter, *Genesis*, p. 263.

have made him submit'.[115] Joseph's test is thus no longer perceived as merely a means to confront the guilt of the brothers. Alter articulates unequivocally its other function, which is to compel the brothers to submit to both 'paternal favoritism' and 'Joseph's dreamt-of-supremacy, their necessary subservience'.[116] The brothers are said to acquiesce in paternal favouritism out of concern for their old father. What, then, is the justification for Joseph's dreamt-of supremacy and their necessary subservience? Alter offers no reason of his own, he only points out Joseph's repeated assertions 'that it is God who has singled him out for greatness as the instrument of His providential design to preserve the seed of Israel'.[117] By restating Joseph's justification without elaboration, he differs from other readers in that he has yet to internalize it as his own. Anyway, if he considers the 'love' in this story as unpredictable, arbitrary and unjust, it is fair to say that he is not entirely convinced of the justice of this favouritism, paternal or divine.

Ackerman also recognizes that 'although brothers may be reconciled, divine favouritism remains'.[118] But this notion of divine favouritism, with its propensity to provoke conflict, not only escapes his criticism; he further asserts that 'a mysterious providence has brought and will continue to bring blessing and tempered reconciliation out of favouritism and conflict'.[119] It is no wonder that he describes it as 'paradoxical' and 'surprising', since it is not what one would expect from a fair and just God.

It is difficult for anyone to accept favouritism without some reservation,[120] but it is interesting to note that Hugh White proposes a rather novel defence of its necessity. The problem of sibling rivalry, according to his view,[121] is one of the most frequently recurring motifs throughout the narratives of Genesis. It begins in the primaeval history with the murder of Abel by Cain. The problem persists in the rivalry between Isaac and Ishmael, and then in that between Jacob and Esau. White

---

115. Alter, *Art of Biblical Narrative*, p. 175.

116. Alter, *Art of Biblical Narrative*, p. 173.

117. Alter, *Art of Biblical Narrative*, p. 176.

118. Ackerman, 'Joseph, Judah, and Jacob', p. 109.

119. Ackerman, 'Joseph, Judah, and Jacob', p. 109.

120. Stigers, *A Commentary on Genesis*, p. 271, however, asserts that God can make his choice 'against all human disapproval'.

121. White, 'The Joseph Story', pp. 49-69. See also his work, 'Where Do You Come From?', pp. 232-75.

concludes that the problem 'is never satisfactorily resolved', and that the rival brother 'is simply forced outside the pale of God's blessing' in each case. In the Joseph story, the problem of sibling rivalry is again 'placed on the centre stage and explored in depth'. It is different from the previous cases in that the promise must now be transmitted to 'the prototypical form of the nation, the "Sons of Israel" '. Since no rival brother can simply be rejected, the problem of sibling rivalry, according to White, gives rise to an 'unprecedented critical problem' for 'the transmission of the promise which must take place here at the end of the patriarchal history'.[122]

The promise might be simply transmitted by Jacob to all of his sons, but White reckons that this would not deal 'forthrightly with the complex problem of rivalry which the Biblical writers had always acknowledged as having its roots in the parental habit of favouring one son above the other(s)'.[123] White asks rhetorically, 'Is Jacob then to be exempted from this pattern so evident in the tales of the previous patriarchal families?' For him the answer is negative. Suggesting that Jacob could not transmit the promise to all of his sons due to his favouritism, White offers a solution to this problem:

> The brilliant solution to this problem, one which is both continuous with the previous narratives and yet boldly new, is for Jacob to choose his favorite son for the transmission of the promise, thereby precipitating the problem of sibling rivalry. Then, in the course of the narrative, a solution to the problem will be worked out that will enable the favorite son, acting as a patriarchal type figure, to transmit the promise successfully to his brothers.[124]

White then considers Joseph's final words to his brothers in 50.24-25 as 'the climactic event, the transmission of the promise, for the first time, from one brother to another'.[125]

---

122. White, 'The Joseph Story', p. 57.
123. White, 'The Joseph Story', pp. 57-58.
124. White, 'The Joseph Story', p. 58.
125. White, 'Where Do You Come From?', p. 238, argues against the view that takes the last scenes of the Joseph story as a later appendix (cf. George W. Coats, 'Redactional Unity in Genesis 37–50', *JBL* 53 (1974), pp. 15-21; von Rad, *Genesis*, p. 433). In his analysis, these last few verses of the story have a 'profound link' with the previous events. They constitute an important ending because 'they contain the transmission of the patriarchal promise of land from Joseph to his brothers (the first such transmission from one generation to the next solely by a human agent),

There are two questionable aspects in White's interpretation. First, his suggestion of the absence of Jacob's transmission of the promise to the other sons except Joseph is open to doubt. White himself concedes that Genesis 49 contains Jacob's blessings upon them. But he argues that their blessings are of 'less importance'. Because in 48.22 they are excluded from one specific parcel of land[126] which is given to Joseph only, their blessings are not considered as the traditional patriarchal promises and blessings.[127] However, while the land given to Joseph is more specific than that given to his brothers, it does not necessarily imply they are given no land in their father's blessings. The motif of land is specifically mentioned in the blessing of two sons: Zebulun is to 'dwell at the shore of the sea...and his border shall be at Sidon (49.13)'; and Issachar 'saw that a resting place was good, and that the land was pleasant (49.15)'. Joseph in 50.24-25 is indeed acting like a patriarch in reassuring his brothers that God will lead them from Egypt to the land which was promised to Abraham, Isaac and Jacob. But this does not negate the fact that Jacob has already transmitted the patriarchal promises to all his sons before his death. Joseph's words to his brothers can be seen only as additional assurance to the promise.

Secondly, his interpretation provides an excuse for the perpetuation of the problem of favouritism in this story. In order for Joseph to transmit the promise to his brothers, the rivalry between them has to be solved. According to White, 'the problem of rivalry has not been completely expunged from the relation of Joseph to his brothers', but

> the basis for peaceful dialogue has been established sufficiently between the guilt-ridden, fearful perspective of the brothers, on the one hand, and Joseph's benign interpretation of the universal intentions of God, on the other, to permit an authentic transmission of the promise.[128]

and the extraction of an oath by Joseph from his brothers to carry his bones up from Egypt, presumably when this promise of land is fulfilled'.

126. Von Rad, *Genesis*, pp. 418-19, observes an oddity here: 'Jacob's assertion that he conquered Shechem with the sword is remarkable. This cannot refer to what was narrated in chapter 34, for there Jacob complained about his sons' deed, while here he glories in it. And how could he promise to one of his sons what his sons had conquered?' The Hebrew word 'mountain slope' (שכם) may be a word-play on the name of the Canaanite city of Shechem (cf. 48.22).

127. White, 'Where Do You Come From?', p. 272.

128. White, 'Where Do You Come From?', p. 274.

White reasons that Jacob could not be exempted from the pattern of parental favouritism, and that therefore it could not be possible for Jacob to transmit the promise directly to his other sons. The 'brilliant solution', he suggests, is for Jacob to choose his favourite son as an agent to transmit the promise to his other sons. The cause of sibling rivalry, parental favouritism, suddenly becomes necessary and even sanctioned by God to fulfil his promise.

Other readers may feel uneasy about divine favouritism as it has occurred in this story, but White considers it a desirable answer to a new problem. The importance of the transmission of the promise requires God to allow Jacob to choose Joseph to bless the whole family. The problem of the transmission of the promise envisioned by White is probably a pseudo-problem, as I have just argued. More importantly, in obliging Jacob to transmit the promise to Joseph alone, it endorses parental favouritism with an honourable motive. It is rather extraordinary to suggest the use of favouritism to resolve the obstacle which is caused by the same favouritism in the first place. But White is not alone in suggesting this. Other readers read this story with similar understanding. He only articulates it in a more eloquent scheme. The effect of Joseph's test, as understood by Alter, is a perfect example of such a move.[129]

Summary

Instead of criticizing Joseph's demand for the brothers' acceptance, Sternberg seems to suggest that Joseph is right to suspect that there is in them 'a total lack of understanding, let alone acceptance, of the paternal sentiments that have torn the family apart'.[130] Humphreys simply accepts that 'love is not nicely balanced' and 'even one who loves in an excess that must result in imbalances and pain can be understood, and must be loved, for through this love run ties that binds sons to father'.[131] These readers in effect consider that fatalistic acceptance of favouritism is the best solution to the family strife.

Similarly, the divine favouritism is the main cause of the conflict, but it also becomes in the reading of many the solution to the conflict. The dreams are seen as a 'blessing' for the well-being of the family as well

---

129. See footnote 114.
130. Sternberg, *The Poetics of Biblical Narrative*, p. 306.
131. Humphreys, *Joseph and his Family*, pp. 48-49.

as a 'curse' that disturbs its peace.[132] In a different way, Westermann restates this contradictory nature of the dreams of choosing one who will lord it over the others: it is 'the monarchy [portended by the dreams] which gives rise to the breach inasmuch as it is [also] the monarchy that enables the family of Jacob to be saved from famine and thereby heal the breach'.[133] Thus, divine favouritism is again seen as both the curse and the cure. '[O]nly at the end of a long history of hatred, blindness, deceit, and discord,' Humphreys asserts, 'Joseph and his brothers came to acknowledge a divine providential design behind and through their intentions and actions.'[134] What is left unsaid is that such a design, to favour one over others in the name of salvation, is also the culprit in this long history of family strife.

Reconciliation between brothers depends on the acceptance of the favouritism that has shattered the peace in the first place. Joseph's test in treating the cause of the conflict as its cure becomes a model for some readers to take towards divine favouritism. Divine favouritism intensifies the hatred of the brothers towards Joseph at the beginning of the story, and divine favouritism is later offered as the foundation for the reconciliation between Joseph and his brothers.

In his work 'Plato's Pharmacy', Derrida draws upon Plato's *Phaedrus*, a dialogue between Socrates and Phaedrus about speech and writing, in order to elaborate a critique of 'Western metaphysics'.[135] Drawing on Socrates' comparison of the written texts to a drug (*pharmakon*), he comments:

> This *pharmakon*, this 'medicine', this philter, which acts as both remedy and poison, already introduces itself into the body of the discourse with all its ambivalence. This charm, this spellbinding virtue, this power of fascination, can be—alternately or simultaneously—beneficent or maleficent.[136]

The ambivalence of this double meaning of *pharmakon* can be compared to the role Benjamin played in Joseph's test.[137] As a substitute for

132. Brueggemann, *Genesis*, pp. 294-95.
133. Westermann, *Genesis 37–50*, p. 103.
134. Humphreys, *Joseph and his Family*, p. 125.
135. Jacques Derrida, 'Plato's Pharmacy', in *idem*, *Dissemination*, pp. 61-171.
136. Jacques Derrida, 'Plato's Pharmacy', p. 70.
137. For a concise explanation of Derrida's concept of *pharmakon* as the medium, the movement and the play in which opposites (soul/body, good/evil, inside/outside, memory/forgetfulness, speech/writing, etc.) are opposed, see Jonathan Cul-

Joseph as the father's favourite, his role serves as an important focus to illustrate the complex responses by the characters to favouritism. By forcing the brothers to accept Benjamin as Jacob's favourite, Joseph's test in effect turns the poison (favouritism) of the family unity into its remedy. For many readers, Judah's final speech to Joseph represents nothing but a complete acceptance of this change. However, judging from Judah's rebuke to Jacob for withholding Benjamin, his acceptance of favouritism is accompanied by a serious reservation:

> And Judah said to Israel his father, '*Send* the lad with me, and we will arise and go, *that we may live and not die*, both we and *you and also our little ones*...for if we had not delayed, we would now have returned twice' (43.8-10).

Significantly, this refusal[138] to allow Jacob to cling on his favourite is justified as a matter of life or death for the whole family. That is also precisely the promise, or the threat, Joseph offers when he demands Benjamin (and thus their acceptance of favouritism) from the brothers:

> On the third day Joseph said to them, 'Do this and *you will live*, for I fear God: if you are honest men, let one of your brothers remain confined in your prison, and let the rest go and carry grain for the famine of your households, and bring your youngest brother to me; so your words will be verified, and *you shall not die*' (42.18-20).

Caught between the wishes of Jacob and Joseph, Judah's response to Benjamin's favourite status is inevitably both rejection and acceptance. On the one hand, if he does not confront Jacob's special attachment to Benjamin, he risks the death of the whole family. For Judah, favouritism is a threat (poison) to their very survival. On the other hand, for the sake of survival, he has no choice but to accede to Joseph's demand of acceptance of favouritism as a condition (remedy) for their reconciliation. If Joseph's test is designed to force the brothers to accept the father's favouritism, it also compels Judah to confront it face to face

---

ler, *Structuralist Poetics* (Ithaca, NY: Cornell University Press, 1975), pp. 142-44.

138. Indeed, Judah echoes, word for word, his father's previous hope ('that we may live and not die') with the exception that keeping Benjamin at home is no longer an option: 'And he said, "Behold, I have heard that there is grain in Egypt; go down and buy grain for us there, *that we may live, and not die*." So ten of Joseph's brothers went down to buy grain in Egypt. But Jacob did *not send* Benjamin, Joseph's brother, with his brothers, for he feared that harm might befall him' (42.2-4).

with his father. Parental favouritism, like *pharmakon*, is thus simultaneously a poison and a remedy for the family unity and survival.

Furthermore, Joseph's disclosure speech strengthens his favourite status by declaring a divine endorsement, which is justified again as being the matter of life or death for the whole family ('you and your little ones'):

> And now do not be distressed, or angry with yourselves, because you sold me here; for God sent me before you to preserve *life*... And God sent me before you to preserve for you a remnant on earth, and to keep *alive* for you many survivors...you shall dwell in the land of Goshen, and you shall be near me, *you and your children* and *your children's children*, and your flocks, your herds, and all that you have; and there I will provide for you, for there are yet five years of famine to come; lest *you* and *your household*, and all that you have, come to *poverty* (45.5-11).

> As for you, you meant evil against me; but God meant it for good, to bring it about that many people should be kept *alive*, as they are today. So do not fear; I will provide for *you and your little ones* (50.20-21).

Most readers take the silence of the brothers as an acceptance of Joseph's claim of divine favouritism. However, one has to be aware that Joseph does not persuade the brothers to accept paternal favouritism. They are rather forced by his power and deceit into submission before the disclosure of his identity. Whether they are later convinced by his justification of his status as favourite can only be a matter open to speculation. They are dumbfounded by his disclosure (45.3) and there is no guarantee that their fear of his reprisal will be gone forever (50.15-17). The absence of any rejection of his claim may therefore be due to the fact that they are simply in no position to question the powerful lord. Furthermore, Judah's rejection of Jacob's favouritism towards Benjamin in the name of the survival of the whole family— 'that we may live and not die', both we and 'you and also our little ones' (43.8-10)—provides a subtle counterpoint to Joseph's insistence upon favouritism for the same excuse.

CONCLUSION

Joseph claims to be enslaved for others. In the end, he indeed saves many lives, but he is a sad figure, a fact he never denies. He attempts to forget the past but fails (41.52). It returns to haunt him. The encounter with his brothers in Egypt triggers a series of events contrived and manipulated by him with intriguing results that makes this story one of the most unforgettable tales in the Hebrew Bible. Joseph's torture trial of his brothers and its ending are sandwiched between his several outbreaks of crying. Confronted with Judah's willingness to give up his freedom for his father's sake, Joseph blurts out his insights upon his past and God's intentions for it. His speech reveals him as an individual obsessed with his suffering and destiny. He indeed mentions the salvation of others, but such allusions are mainly used to explain his pit of suffering and dreams of glory. Similarly, his words are intended to assuage his brothers' fear and guilt, but they may also function no less as alleviation of his emotional distress created by his bitter experience. These double functions do not necessarily discredit him, for he is not a perfect human being. A sense of self-consciousness of one's need is perfectly normal even in an act of seeking the benefit of others. For example, Reuben fails to rescue Joseph and exclaims, 'The lad is gone; and I, where shall I go?' (37.30). As selfless as Judah is, as is shown in his final speech of self-sacrifice which succeeds in breaking down his brother's harsh façade, he also in the end expresses his own predicament, 'For how can I go back to my father if the lad is not with me? I fear to see the evil that would come upon my father' (44.34).

The proof of the danger of Joseph's obsession with himself is rather his subsequent policy of mass enslavement of the Egyptians. There must be something inherently flawed in his perception of past events that it is he who finally affirms and repeats rather than abhors and repeals the terror of enslavement. Seen from this perspective, it is not unfair to describe him as a tormented soul permanently made wretched by his suffering in the pit. Comparing this to the experience of African slavery, Gerald West gives an apt observation about Joseph's reaction to his past: 'As often happens, those who have themselves been treated as objects to be bought and sold do the same to others.'[1] What he refers to is Joseph's detainment of Simeon as a hostage after his own experience of slavery. However, Joseph's enslavement of the Egyptians is a far better illustration of how easily a victim can become a victimizer. My work is attempting to describe this process of tragic transformation in Joseph's experience.

Is Joseph's enslavement of the Egyptians (47.13-26) related to his claim of domination (45.8b-11)? Before this question is answered, one has to examine the ideology behind his claim. Joseph's declaration of his destiny to be enslaved and to rule over others in order to save lives seems to be a novel and unique idea that suddenly comes to full realization. However, it is built upon the more fundamental idea that the hierarchical structure of domination and subservience is necessary for survival. A survey of the various events in the story shows that every major character holds the same rationale: Reuben allows his brother to be thrown into a pit in order to save him (37.22); Judah excuses himself from bloodguilt by selling Joseph into slavery (37.26-27); Judah opts for slavery for himself in order to avoid the death of his father (44.33-34); the Egyptians give up their bodies in order to escape starving to death (47.19); at the end of the story, the brothers finally bow themselves down in submission to Joseph's domination in order to stay alive (50.18). So Joseph's new-found idea is not unique at all, but there has come about a critical shift of emphasis in Joseph's understanding. The death or slavery alternative imposed on Joseph in Judah's excuse suddenly becomes the domination for survival justification announced by Joseph in his interpretation of his dreams. The shift is mediated through their common characteristic: subservience for survival. From Reuben's tactical use of it, to Judah's excuse and model, to its discovery by Joseph as a divine principle intended by God, the rationale of subservience for survival undergoes a profound change in terms of its desirability. The idea gradually evolves from a negative or pragmatic practice to a positive normative principle. From being a rationale for an incident in a single family, it finally justifies an event in which the fate of a whole nation is involved.

1. Gerald West, 'Difference and Dialogue: Reading the Joseph Story with Poor and Marginalized Communities in South Africa', *BI* 2.2 (1994), pp. 152-70 (162).

Joseph attempts to justify his domination with the purpose of saving lives. The emphasis on salvation, which does not appear explicitly in his dreams, is understandable because he is supposedly empowered to reveal the hidden intention of God in his dreams. However, the issue is not only about salvation, but also about salvation at the price of subservience. The motif of 'bowing down' figures prominently in his original dreams,[2] being as emphatic as the motif of 'domination', if not more so. But in his interpretation, the emphasis on subservience is silently removed, leaving the motif of 'domination' alone in the foreground. In fact, the whole issue of the subjugation of the brothers to his domination is suppressed.[3] The emphasis is now on domination over Egypt. This subtle shift serves an obvious purpose: it helps to minimize the resistance of the brothers to his claim of divine domination because the price required for their salvation is tacitly suppressed. It is a strategy for maximizing attention to the benefit (i.e. salvation) while minimizing the hidden cost. It is one thing to say that God destines Joseph to be a lord to save lives, and it is quite another matter to say that his brothers are destined to be subjugated in order to be saved. The former appears acceptable to many readers while the latter is undoubtedly problematic, yet they are in reality the two faces of the same coin.

To avoid antagonizing his brothers, Joseph's strategy in shifting the emphasis of his domination over them to his domination over Egypt will in fact turn against his justification by exposing the link between his claim to fraternal domination and his policy of mass enslavement of the Egyptians. Joseph claims repeatedly that God has made him lord over Egypt (45.8- 9) and nobody can deny the fact that the Egyptians in the end become slaves through Joseph's policy, however benevolently it is executed (47.13-26). It is in his words about domination over Egypt that the burden of proof will fall upon those who try to object linking Joseph's claim and his policy of mass enslavement. Therefore, before making any judgment of his policy, one can locate its rationale in his previous claim over Egypt. Conversely, the mass enslavement of

---

2.   The Hebrew word חוה for 'bowing down' appears three times in ch. 37, twice when Joseph reports his dreams to his brothers and his father (vv. 7, 9), and once when used by Jacob to question his dreams (v. 10). The fulfilment of their 'bowing down' is also recorded in 42.6; 43.26, 28; 44.14; 50.18. The last two verses use a different Hebrew word, נפל ('fall down').

3.   Ackerman, 'Joseph, Judah, and Jacob', p. 87, however rightly asserts that the 'dream depicts [Joseph] being treated as lord rather than brother'.

the Egyptians will then enable us to know what Joseph's words of victorious domination over Egypt (as well as over his family) really meant. His dreams of domination no longer simply require a subservience of a symbolic order in the form of 'bowing down'; putting his claim and his policy together will reveal that his domination is rather a servitude of a much harsher nature.

Forced by the dire situation, the Egyptians may become resigned to the reality of their subservience in order to stay alive. In contrast, it is highly possible that Joseph acts out of his conviction of his true destiny to dominate the Egyptians by enslavement in order to save them. The fact that the Egyptians become enslaved by Joseph seems to be unavoidable in the light of his theological interpretation of his dreams of domination as divine and good. Joseph, on the one hand, is a great saviour and, on the other, is also a great enslaver. Salvation and enslavement at the same time on such a scale of magnitude are remarkable. One can trace the ambiguity to the idea of subservience for survival. One may not always be able to avoid pragmatic compromise in facing difficult situations in this imperfect world, but the readiness to accept the justification of subservience in the name of survival will no doubt contribute to the perpetuation of another undesirable situation (i.e. slavery) which all characters (including Joseph) in this story dread. Joseph as a prisoner has had a painful experience of slavery that he never really forgets or recovers from and this may be the reason why he cannot prevent himself from spreading it to others.

Joseph's strategy of prefacing his justification of domination with his suffering in the pit is a clever one. His dreams occupy a strategic position in the plot of this story as they trigger the fraternal conflict and betrayal (37.5-20) as well as his test of his brothers (42.9). However, attention given to them by readers of the narrative of his interaction with his brothers (chs. 42–44) is usually kept to a minimum in contrast to the attention given to the pit narrative.[4] On the whole, the Joseph story is best remembered as a biblical story about divine providence associated with his suffering in a pit and slavery rather than about the royal ideology signified by his dreams.[5] In his disclosure speech,

---

4.   Turner, *Announcements of Plot in Genesis*, pp. 143-69, treats Joseph's test as his attempt to fulfil the dreams. Other readers usually consider these chapters as Joseph's dealing with the pit, his coming to terms with it and his confrontation with the brothers' crime.

5.   The justification of royal ideology is associated more with those biblical

Joseph first stresses his suffering and then declares that God has turned his descent into Egypt into an occasion to bring about salvation. The effect would be entirely different and would probably encounter much stronger resistance if he declared at the outset that God requires the domination of one over the others in order to achieve salvation.

The way Joseph presents his justification is not only a matter of attempting to distract his audience's attention. More importantly, the necessity of his rise to power is carefully grafted into his assertion of the providential purpose of his suffering in the pit. Structurally, the pit and the dreams are two sides of the same coin. They share the same premise of subservience for survival, even though they are the opposite of each other in hierarchical terms: the pit of slavery versus the dreams of lordship. Sequentially, the pit and the dreams are two parts of the same mission to accomplish the shared aim to save lives. They are so inextricably intertwined that it is no longer possible to accept one without the other. Chained in a sequence, the result is in an apparent temporal as well as logical causal relationship.[6] That is, if, for whatever reason, one attempts to deny his justification of the dreams, the providential nature of his suffering as a slave for the well-being of others will be void. Without his subsequent rise to power, he will not be able to save lives as he claims. It is this illusion of the usefulness of his suffering that makes it difficult, if not impossible, to reject his subsequent glory of domination.

Ostensibly, Joseph attempts to overcome the anxiety of his brothers by stressing the 'usefulness' of their evil action, but he establishes the

---

texts relating to the Solomonic or Davidic periods. Nevertheless, the question of monarchy lies behind this story. It is represented in the story by the question, 'May and ought a brother rule over his brothers? (37.8)' Westermann, *Genesis 37–50*, p. 25, considers that this dispute and its final resolution in this story mark the transition from the patriarchal period to the monarchical state. Therefore, he suggests that the story originated during the period of David and Solomon. Gary A. Rendsburg, 'David and His Circle in Gen. 38', *VT* 36 (1986), pp. 438-46, suggests the story was written in the Israelite monarchical era by someone who intended to 'poke fun at the royal family [David]' through his ancestor Judah (p. 444).

6.   The pit-dreams sequence is also an archetypal sequence. The fall-and-rise of a protagonist is a typical mythic–literary pattern which has an unmistakably universal appeal in storytelling (ancient and modern). Ackerman, 'Joseph, Judah, and Jacob', p. 106, compares Joseph's descent–ascent motif with Baal. He points out that 'the Canaanite vegetation god who annually descends into the pit and then arises—underscores the mythic descent pattern of the hero'.

necessity of his dreams of ruling over them at the same time. Self-justification is thus hidden in a sincere effort to reassure. It encounters little resistance from his brothers; even Joseph himself may not be fully conscious of his own disguised attempt to justify the legitimacy of his domination. Can Joseph justify his claim independently without the pre-text of his pit? By comparing his insight into God's intentions with that of Reuben and by tracing the source of his new-found conviction to Judah's model, my analysis suggests that the case Joseph presents is not as convincing as it appears.

Both Reuben and God (as portrayed by Joseph) share the same attempt to save people at a price of subjugation on the part of those who are rescued (in various degrees of seriousness—pit for Joseph, bowing down for the brothers and slavery for the Egyptians). While Reuben is reacting out of a despairing crisis,[7] Joseph regards the divine measure as a premeditated positive move under divine total control. The eldest brother's secret intention in his rescuing effort fails disastrously, but he never intends his brother's freedom to be lost forever. In contrast, Joseph's domination over his brothers and the Egyptians is not per-ceived as a purely temporary one, as in Reuben's intention. The juxta-position of Reuben's excuse with Joseph's claim to divine domination for salvation reveals that the subservience in the divine measure is much harsher than that of Reuben's.

Modelling Judah's good example of sacrificing oneself for others (44.33-34) as a source of his insight for his interpretation of God's intentions is undoubtedly the supreme irony of this story. Judah is forced by Joseph's test to choose his own subservience for the sake of the survival of his father; the ironic reversal of his role as a victimizer to being a victim of his previous rationale (37.26-27) is unmistakable. Out of ignorance, Joseph mistakes the rationale, which his test has just condemned, for a divine principle to explain his suffering in the pit and his dreams of domination for the survival of many. A hideous idea becomes an honourable one. Joseph's justification of his domination is

---

7. Redford, *Biblical Story of Joseph*, p. 140, comments, 'The context of Reuben's advice is more dramatic: the lad is on the horizon and coming closer by the minute, and now there impulsive madmen have of a sudden taken it into their heads to kill him on the spot! Reuben must think quickly, must deter them at all costs'; Holbert, *The Storyteller's Companion to the Bible*, p. 170, also considers that Judah is also 'improvising' in offering another plan to the brothers.

thus a case of self-delusion due to his ignorance of what his test has achieved.

The flawed interpretation of the past becomes an imperfect blueprint for the future. 'Imperfect' is a mild word for his policy of mass enslavement which is indeed recognized as less than ideal by many readers. He certainly genuinely believes what he declares. As a result, he acts according to what he firmly believes. This explains why he could repeat the enslavement he abhors so much. In discussing the enslavement of the Egyptians, Janzen warns of the danger of a 'mind-set—the theology or worldview—within which human crises are met with a wisdom that is taken to be given by the gods but that is in fact a false wisdom'.[8] People with a strong predisposition to assert right and wrong or good and evil are more susceptible to the tendency of trans-forming an ambiguous situation into a paradigmatic one. Joseph's understanding of God's intentions (45.5-11; 50.20) is a prime example of this tendency.

Joseph's behaviour has attracted much criticism from generations of readers, but his understanding of divine providence and domination continues to escape critical scrutiny. To avoid confronting Joseph's belief (which is what makes his actions possible in the first place) is not only missing the point but in danger of committing the same mistake as his. The following example will illustrate my assertion. To 'undermine Judah's claim that by selling the boy the brothers will avoid the horror of blood-guilt', Alter suggests that the writer of the Joseph's story employs 'two disparate versions'[9] of Joseph's disappearance in order to 'intimate some moral equivalence between kidnapping and murder'.[10] This suggestion would render Judah's intention to save his brother's

8.   Janzen, *Genesis 12-50*, p. 180.

9.   Alter, *Art of Biblical Narrative*, pp. 166-68, summarizes these two versions (Reuben–Midianites and Judah–Ishmaelites): 'in E, Reuben is Joseph's advocate and concludes he is dead after the Midianites (having found the boy in the pit quite by chance) take him away; in J, Judah saves Joseph's life by proposing to sell him into slavery, the slavetraders here being identified as Ishmaelites'.

10.   Alter, *Art of Biblical Narrative*, pp. 166, 167. Ackerman, 'Joseph, Judah, and Jacob', p. 99, also accuses Judah's pious suggestion 'of not laying hand on a brother' as 'not so different from murder' and comments that 'in many ways bibli-cal law equates selling a person into slavery with murder'. Sternberg, *The Poetics of Biblical Narrative*, p. 304, points out 'the automatic causal linkage between theft (as crime) and death and slavery (as punishment), and the virtual equation of death and slavery'. For a similar observation, see Coats, 'Strife and Reconciliation', p. 32.

life by selling him into slavery an unacceptable excuse. While the crime of the brothers is unambiguously identified, Joseph's justification of delivering people from famine by the same measure of enslavement is perceived quite differently by Alter: 'The reduction of the entire population to a condition of virtual serfdom to the crown in all likelihood was meant to be construed not as an act of ruthlessness by Joseph but as an instance of his administrative brilliance.'[11] This opposite evaluation of the motives of the protagonist and the anti-hero of this story simply repeats Joseph's conviction, that is, that what others have done to him is evil while the same measure, when he inflicts it on others, is good (cf. 50.20).

It is easy to consign the hierarchical ideology of domination and subservience for the purpose of survival to the unenlightened historical past. Unfortunately, a quick dismissal will miss the opportunity to look carefully into the intriguing details of this interesting story which may not present Joseph's claim in an unequivocal way. One of the most difficult issues that prevent readers from challenging Joseph's understanding of his destiny is the divine favouritism implied in his claims. The difficulty for many readers in confronting it soon comes to a resolution (or an impasse for some) when the curse of the family conflict suddenly becomes its cure. The idea of a divine choice of the nation together with the themes of divine providence and patriarchal-hierarchical ideology are major doctrines in the Hebrew Scripture and its cultural settings, and the text-oriented approach I adopt in this study should be supplemented in the future with a historical-theological one and the scope extended outside this story. The contribution of Joseph's various claims to these doctrines are influential, but the ambiguities of the interrelation between his words have not been sufficiently scrutinized in the past, and this work is an attempt to expose the problematic nature of his claims.

As for Joseph's claim of domination, my challenge is not, in a sense, to reject it. To do so would require a value judgment upon which it would be difficult to come to a consensus. My approach is rather to expose the incoherence of his various claims, turning his words against them. First of all, it is his own claim of domination over Egypt (45.8b-11) that links his ideology with his policy, thus betraying the real nature of what his domination requires as being not merely symbolic sub-

11. Alter, *Genesis*, p. 283.

servience but real servitude. His repeated assertions that the famine is sent by God (45.25, 28, 32) are loud and clear; they become ambiguous only if one attempts to avoid paralleling God's role (as declared by Joseph) in the destruction and deliverance of a whole nation with the similar one that Judah plays towards his brother. Joseph's final verdict on the difference between good and evil (50.20) at the end of the story makes it far harder for him to prove the difference between his justification and Judah's excuse due to their similar attitude towards the idea of subservience in exchange for survival. He is of course unaware of the predicament, which he draws himself into due to his extraordinary but problematic claims, because of his ignorance of Judah's inexcusable imposition (37.26-27). This double blindness serves to call into doubt the certainty of the coalescence of the perspectives of the protagonist and the narrator in this story.

BIBLIOGRAPHY

Aalders, G. Charles, *Genesis*, II (trans. William Heynen; Bible Student's Commentary; 2 vols.; Grand Rapids: Zondervan, 1981).

Ackerman, James S., 'Joseph, Judah, and Jacob', in Kenneth R.R. Gros Louis, James S. Ackerman (eds.), *Literary Interpretations of Biblical Narratives*, II (Nashville: Abingdon Press, 1982), pp. 85-113.

Ages, Arnold, 'Why Didn't Joseph Call Home?', *BR* 9 (1993), pp. 42-46.

Alter, Robert, *The Art of Biblical Narrative* (New York: Basic Books, 1981).

—*Genesis: Translation and Commentary* (New York: W.W. Norton, 1996).

Amit, Yairah, 'The Dual Causality Principle and its Effects on Biblical Literature', *VT* 37.4 (1987), pp. 385-400.

Argyle, Aubrey W., 'Joseph the Patriarch in Patristic Teaching', *ExpTim* 67 (1956), pp. 199-201.

Bach, Alice, 'Breaking Free of the Biblical Frame-Up: Uncovering the Woman in Genesis 39', in Athalya Brenner (ed.), *Feminist Companion to Genesis* (Feminist Companion to the Bible, 2; Sheffield: Sheffield Academic Press, 1993), pp. 318-42.

Bailey, Randall C., 'When Brothers Dwell Together—The Preeminence of Younger Siblings in the Hebrew Bible: A Review Article', *JBL* 115.1 (1996), pp. 117-18.

Baldwin, Joyce G., *The Message of Genesis 12–50: From Abraham to Joseph* (The Bible Speaks Today; Leicester: Inter-Varsity Press, 1986).

Bar-Efrat, Shimon, *Narrative Art in the Bible* (Bible and Literature Series, 17; Sheffield: Almond Press, 1989).

Barnhouse, Donald Grey, *Genesis: A Devotional Commentary* (Grand Rapids: Zondervan, 1973).

Becking, Bob, 'They Hated Him Even More: Literary Technique in Genesis 37:1-11', *BN* 60 (1991), pp. 40-47.

Berlin, Adele, *Poetics and Interpretation of Biblical Narrative* (Bible and Literature Series, 9; Sheffield: Almond Press, 1983).

Boice, James Montgomery, *Genesis: An Expositional Commentary 37–50*, III (Grand Rapids: Zondervan, 1987).

Bowie, Walter Russell, *Genesis* (IB, 1; Nashville: Abingdon Press, 1952).

Brueggemann, Walter A., *Genesis* (Interpretation; Philadelphia: Westminster Press, 1986).

Bush, George, *Notes on Genesis* (Minneapolis: James Family Christian Publishers, 1979).

Calvin, John, *A Commentary on Genesis*, II (trans. John King; London: Banner of Truth Trust, 1965).

Carmichael, Calum M., 'The Law of the Forgotten Sheaf', in K.R. Richards (ed.), *Society of Biblical Literature 1981 Seminar Papers* (SBLSP, 20; Chico, CA: Scholars Press, 1981), pp. 35-37.

Cassuto, Umberto A., *A Commentary on the Book of Genesis* (trans. Israel Abrahams; 2 vols.; Jerusalem: Magnes Press, 1964).

Chatman, Seymour, *Coming to Terms: The Rhetoric of Narrative in Fiction and Film* (Ithaca, NY: Cornell University Press, 1990).

—*Story and Discourse: Narrative Structure in Fiction and Film* (Ithaca, NY: Cornell University Press, 1978).

Clines, David J.A., 'Deconstructing the Book of Job', in *idem, What Does Eve Do to Help?*, pp. 106-23.

—'God in the Pentateuch: Reading against the Grain', in *idem, Interested Parties,* pp. 187-211.

—'Haggai's Temple, Constructed, Deconstructed and Reconstructed', in *idem, Interested Parties*, pp. 46-75.

—*Interested Parties: The Ideology of Writers and Readers of the Hebrew Bible* (JSOTSup, 205; Sheffield: Sheffield Academic Press, 1995).

—*The Theme of the Pentateuch* (JSOTSup, 10; Sheffield: JSOT Press, 1978).

—*What Does Eve Do to Help? And Other Readerly Questions to the Old Testament* (JSOTSup, 94; Sheffield: JSOT Press, 1990).

Clines, David J.A., and Tamara C. Eskenazi (eds.), *Telling Queen Michal's Story: An Experiment in Comparative Interpretation* (JSOTSup, 119; Sheffield: JSOT Press, 1991).

Clines, David J.A., Stephen E. Fowl and Stanley E. Porter (eds.), *The Bible in Three Dimensions: Essays in Celebration of Forty Years of Biblical Studies in the University of Sheffield* (JSOTSup, 87; Sheffield: JSOT Press, 1990).

Clines, David J.A., David M. Gunn and Alan J. Hauser (eds.), *Art and Meaning: Rhetoric in Biblical Literature* (JSOTSup, 19; Sheffield: JSOT Press, 1982).

Coats, George W., *From Canaan to Egypt: Structural and Theological Context for the Joseph Story* (CBQMS, 4; Washington, DC: The Catholic Biblical Association of America, 1976).

—'The Joseph Story and Ancient Wisdom: A Reappraisal', *CBQ* 35.3 (1973), pp. 285-97.

—'Redactional Unity in Genesis 37–50', *JBL* 53 (1974), pp. 15-21.

—'Strife and Reconciliation: Themes of a Biblical Theology in the Book of Genesis', *HBT* 2 (1980), pp. 15-37.

—'Strife Without Reconciliation: A Narrative Theme in Jacob Traditions', in Rainer Albertz (ed.), *Werden und Wirken des Alten Testaments* (Göttingen: Vandenhoeck & Ruprecht, 1980), pp. 82-106.

Cohn, Robert L., 'Narrative Structure and Canonical Perspective in Genesis', *JSOT* 23 (1983), pp. 3-16.

Collins, Nina L., 'The Figure of Joseph in Post-Biblical Jewish Literature: A Review Article', *NovT* 36.3 (1994), pp. 304-307.

Cooper, Jerrold S., 'Sargon and Joseph: Dreams Come True', in Ann Kort and Scott Morschauser (eds.), *Biblical and Related Studies* (Winona Lake, IN: Eisenbrauns, 1985).

Crüsemann, Frank, 'Domination, Guilt and Reconciliation: The Contribution of the Jacob Narrative in Genesis to Political Ethics', *Semeia* 66 (1994), pp. 67-77.

Crocker, P.T., 'Voluntary Slavery for Food? Was Joseph's Treatment of the Egyptians Politically Correct?', *Buried History* 31 (1995), pp. 56-62.

Culler, Jonathan, *Structuralist Poetics* (Ithaca, NY: Cornell University Press, 1975).

Daube, David, *Studies in Biblical Law* (New York: Ktav, 1969).

Davidson, Robert, *Genesis 12–50* (Cambridge Bible Commentary; Cambridge: Cambridge University Press, 1979).

Davies, Philip R., and David J.A. Clines (eds.), *The World of Genesis: Persons, Places, Perspectives* (JSOTSup, 257; Sheffield: Sheffield Academic Press, 1998).

Day, Linda M., *Three Faces of a Queen: Characterization in the Books of Esther* (JSOTSup, 186; Sheffield: Sheffield Academic Press, 1995).

Delitzsch, Franz, *A New Commentary on Genesis*, II (trans. Sophia Taylor; Minneapolis: Klock & Klock Christian Publishers, 1978).

Derrida, Jacques, *Margins of Philosophy* (trans. Alan Bass; London: Harvester Press, 1982).

—*Of Grammatology* (trans. Gayatri Chakravorty Spivak; Baltimore: The Johns Hopkins University Press, 1976).

—'Plato's Pharmacy', in *idem*, *Dissemination* (trans. Barbara Johnson; Chicago: University of Chicago Press, 1981), pp. 61-172.

—*Positions* (trans. Alan Bass; Chicago: University of Chicago Press, 1981).

—*Speech and Phenomena* (trans. David B. Allison; Evanston: Northwestern University Press, 1973).

—*Writing and Difference* (trans. Alan Bass; Chicago: University of Chicago Press, 1978).

Dochety, Thomas, *Reading (Absent) Character: Toward a Theory of Characterization in Fiction* (Oxford: Charendon Press, 1983).

Donaldson, Laura E., 'Cyborgs, Ciphers, and Sexuality: Re-Theorizing Literary and Biblical Character', *Semeia* 63 (1993), pp. 81-96.

Driver, Samuel R., *The Book of Genesis* (London: Methuen, 10th edn, 1916).

Eagleton, Terry, *Literary Theory* (repr.; Oxford: Basil Blackwell, 1988).

Exum, J. Cheryl, and David J.A. Clines, 'The New Literary Criticism', in J. Cheryl Exum and David J.A. Clines (eds.), *The New Literary Criticism and the Hebrew Bible* (JSOTSup, 143; Sheffield: JSOT Press, 1993), pp. 11-25.

Feldman, Louis H., 'Josephus' Portrait of Joseph [2 Pts]', *RB* 99 (1992), pp. 379-417, 504-28.

Feuer, Lois, 'Happy Families: Repentance and Restoration in *The Tempest* and the Joseph Narrative', *Philological Quarterly* 76.3 (1997), pp. 271-87.

Fewell, Danna N., and David M. Gunn, *Gender, Power, and Promise* (Nashville: Abingdon Press, 1993).

Fisch, Harold, 'Biblical Imitation in *Joseph Andrews*', in David H. Hirsch and Nehama Aschkenasy (ed.), *Biblical Patterns in Modern Literature* (Chico, CA: Scholars Press, 1984), pp. 31-42.

Fish, Stanley E., *Is There a Text in This Class? The Authority of Interpretive Communities* (Cambridge, MA: Harvard University Press, 1980).

Fokkelman, Jan P., *Narrative Art in Genesis* (Amsterdam: Van Gorcum, 1975).

Forster, E.M., *Aspects of the Novel* (Harmondsworth: Penguin Books, 1962).

Fretheim, Terence E., *Genesis* (The New Interpreter's Bible, 1; Nashville: Abingdon Press, 1994), pp. 321-674.

Freund, Elizabeth, *The Return of the Reader* (London: Methuen, 1987).

Frieden, Ken, 'Dream Interpreters in Exile: Joseph, Daniel, and Sigmund (Solomon)', in Vincent Tollers and John Maier (eds.), *Mappings of the Biblical Terrain* (Lewisburg, PA: Bucknell University Press, 1990), pp. 193-203.

Friedman, Richard Elliott, 'Who Breaks the Cycle? Deception for Deception', *BR* 2.1 (1986), pp. 22-31, 68.

Fritsch, Charles T., 'God Was with Him: A Theological Study of the Joseph Narrative [Gen 37–50]', *Int* 9 (1955), pp. 21-34.

Fry, Euan, 'How Was Joseph Taken to Egypt? (Genesis 37.12-36)', *BT* 46 (1995), pp. 445-48.

Garvey, James, 'Characterization in Narrative', *Poetics* 7 (1978), pp. 63-78.

Geller, Barbara, 'Joseph in the Tannaitic Midrashim', in George W. Nickelsburg (ed.), *Studies on the Testament of Joseph* (Septuagint and Cognate Studies, 5; Missoula, MT: Scholars Press, 1975), pp. 139-46.

Getz, Gene A., *Joseph: Overcoming Obstacles Through Faithfulness* (Nashville: Broadman & Holman Publishers, 1996).

Gevirtz, Stanley, 'Of Patriarchs and Puns: Joseph at the Fountain, Jacob at the Ford', *HUCA* 46 (1975), pp. 33-55.

Geyer, John B., 'The Joseph and Moses Narratives: Folk-Tale and History', *JSOT* 15 (1980), pp. 51-56.

Gibson, John C.L., *Genesis* (2 vols.; Edinburgh: Saint Andrew Press, 1981, 1982).

Ginzberg, Louis, *The Legends of the Jews*. II. *Characters From Joseph to Exodus* (Philadelphia: Jewish Publication Society of America, 1946).

—*The Legends of the Jews*. III. *Characters From Exodus to the Death of Moses* (Philadelphia: Jewish Publication Society of America, 1947).

Goldin, Judah, 'Youngest Son or Where Does Genesis 38 Belong?', *JBL* 96 (1977), pp. 27-44.

Goldman, Shalom, *The Wiles of Women/The Wiles of Men: Joseph and Potiphar's Wife in Ancient Near Eastern, Jewish, and Islamic Folklore* (Albany, NY: State University of New York Press, 1995).

Good, Edwin M., *Irony in the Old Testament* (Philadelphia: Westminster Press, 1965).

Goodnick, Benjamin, 'The Character of Joseph: Reconsidered', *Journal of Psychology and Judaism* 12 (1988), pp. 215-29.

Greenspahn, Frederick E., *When Brothers Dwell Together: The Preeminence of Younger Siblings in the Hebrew Bible* (Oxford: Oxford University Press, 1994).

Greenstein, Edward L., 'An Equivocal Reading of the Sale of Joseph', in Kenneth R.R. Gros Louis and James S. Ackerman (eds.), *Literary Interpretations of Biblical Narratives*, II (Nashville: Abingdon Press, 1982), pp. 114-25.

Gros Louis, Kenneth R.R., James S. Ackerman and Thayer S. Warshaw (eds.), *Literary Interpretations of Biblical Narratives*, I (Nashville: Abingdon Press, 1974).

Gunkel, Hermann, *Genesis* (Göttingen: Vandenhoeck & Ruprecht, 1964).

Harris, J.S. Randolph, 'Genesis 44.18-34', *Int* 52.2 (1998), pp. 178-81.

Herbert, Arthur S., *Genesis 12–50* (Torch Bible Commentaries; London: SCM Press, 1962).

Hilgert, Earle, 'The Dual Image of Joseph in Hebrew and Early Jewish Literature', *Journal of the Chicago Society of Biblical Research* 30 (1985), pp. 5-21.

Holbert, John, 'Joseph and the Surprising Choice of God', *P(ST)J* 38 (1985), pp. 33-42.

—*The Storyteller's Companion to the Bible*, I (Nashville: Abingdon Press, 1991).

Hollander, Harm W., 'The Ethical Character of the Patriarch Joseph', in George W. Nickelsburg (ed.), *Studies on the Testament of Joseph* (Septuagint and Cognate Studies, 5; Missoula, MT: Scholars Press, 1975), pp. 47-104.

Holub, Robert, *Reception Theory: A Critical Introduction* (London: Routledge, 1984).

Humphreys, W. Lee, *Joseph and his Family: A Literary Study* (Columbia: University of South Carolina Press, 1988).

Hurowitz, Victor A., 'Joseph's Enslavement of the Egyptians (Genesis 47.13-26) in Light of Famine Texts From Mesopotamia', *RB* 101.3 (1994), pp. 355-62.

Ibn Ezra, *Commentary on the Pentateuch: Genesis (Bereshit)* (trans. and annotated H. Norman Strickman and Arthur M. Silver; New York: Menorah Publishing, 1988).

Iser, Wolfgang, *The Act of Reading: A Theory of Aesthetic Response* (Baltimore: The Johns Hopkins University Press, 1978).

—*The Implied Reader* (Baltimore: The Johns Hopkins University Press, 1974).

Jacobson, Howard, 'Joseph and His Brothers' Beds [*Gen Rabbah* 91-10]', *JQR* 72 (1982), p. 205.

Jacobson, Joe (pseud.), 'The Joseph Syndrome: Handling the Hostility When Call and Kin Collide', *Leadership* 13 (1992), pp. 126-32.

Janzen, J. Gerald, *Genesis 12–50* (ITC; Grand Rapids: Eerdmans, 1993).

Jeansonne, Sharon Pace, 'The Characterization of Lot in Genesis', *BTB* 18.4 (1988), pp. 123-29.

Jobling, David, 'Robert Alter's *The Art of Biblical Narrative*', *JSOT* 27 (1983), pp. 87-99.

—*The Sense of Biblical Narrative: Structural Analyses in the Hebrew Bible*, II (JSOTSup, 39; Sheffield: JSOT Press, 1986).

—'Sociological and Literary Approaches to the Bible: How Shall the Twain Meet?', *JSOT* 38 (1987), pp. 85-93.

Johnson, Barbara, *The Critical Difference: Essays in the Contemporary Rhetoric of Reading* (Baltimore: The Johns Hopkins University Press, 1980).

Jonge, Marinus de, 'Test. Benjamin 3:8 and the Picture of Joseph as "A Good and Holy Man" ', in J.W. van Henten (ed.), *Die Entstehung der jüdischen Martyrologie* (Leiden: E.J. Brill, 1989), pp. 204-14.

Josipovici, Gabriel, 'The Bible in Focus', *JSOT* 48 (1990), pp. 101-22.

—'Joseph and Revelation', in *idem*, *The Book of God: A Response to the Bible* (New Haven: Yale University Press, 1988), pp. 75-89.

Kidner, Derek, *Genesis: An Introduction and Commentary* (TOTC; London: Tyndale Press, 1967).

King, J. Robin, 'The Joseph Story and Divine Politics: A Comparative Study of a Biographic Formula from the Ancient Near East', *JBL* 106 (1987), pp. 577-94.

Kugel, James L., 'The Case against Joseph', in Tzvi Abusch, John Huehnergard and Piotr Steinkeller (eds.), *Lingering Over Words: Studies in Ancient Near Eastern Literature in Honor of William L. Moran* (Atlanta: Scholars Press, 1990), pp. 271-87.

—*In Potiphar's House* (San Francisco: HarperSan Francisco, 1990).

Leach, Edmund, *Genesis as Myth and Other Essays* (London: Jonathan Cape, 1969).

Leitch, Vincent B., *Deconstructive Criticism: An Advanced Introduction* (New York: Columbia University Press, 1983).

Lerner, Berel Dov, 'Joseph the Unrighteous', *Judaism: A Quarterly Journal of Jewish Life and Thought* 38 (1989), pp. 278-81.

Leupold, Herbert C., *Exposition of Genesis 20–50*, II (Grand Rapids: Baker Book House, 22nd edn, 1987).

Licht, Jacob, *Storytelling in the Bible* (Jerusalem: Magnes Press, 1978).

Long, Burke O., *Images of Man and God: Old Testament Short Stories in Literary Focus* (Bible and Literature Series, 1; Sheffield: Almond Press, 1981).

Longacre, Robert E., *Joseph: A Story of Divine Providence* (Winona Lake, IN: Eisenbrauns, 1989).

Lowe, James H. (trans. and annotated), *'Rashi' on the Pentateuch: Genesis* (London: Hebrew Compendium Publishing, 1928).

Lowenthal, Eric I., *The Joseph Narrative in Genesis* (New York: Ktav, 1973).

Luther, Martin, *Lectures on Genesis: Chapters 45–50* (ed. Jaroslav Pelikan; Luther's Works, 8; Saint Louis: Concordia Publishing House, 1966).

MacLaurin, E. Colin B., 'Joseph and Asaph', *VT* 25 (1975), pp. 27-45.

Mann, Thomas W., 'All the Families of the Earth: The Theological Unity of Genesis', *Int* 45.4 (1991), pp. 341-53.

Margolin, Uri, 'Characterization in Narrative: Some Theoretical Prolegomena', *Neophilolous* 67 (1983), pp. 1-14.

—'The Doer and the Deed: Action as a Basis for Characterization in Narrative', *Poetics Today* 7 (1987), pp. 205-25.

—'Introducing and Sustaining Characters in Literary Narrative: A Set of Conditions', *Style* 21.1 (Spring 1987), pp. 107-23.

—'Structuralist Approaches to Character in Narrative: The State of the Art', *Semiotica* 75.1/2 (1989), pp. 1-24.

—'The What, the When, and the How of Being a Character in Literary Narrative', *Style* 24.3 (Fall 1990), pp. 453-68.

Martin, Wallace, *Recent Theories of Narrative* (Ithaca, NY: Cornell University Press, 1986).

Matthews, Victor H., 'The Anthropology of Clothing in the Joseph Narrative', *JSOT* 65 (1995), pp. 25-36.

McGuire, Errol, 'The Joseph Story: A Tale of Son and Father', in Long (ed.), *Images of Man and God*, pp. 9-25.

McKnight, Edgar, *Post-Modern Use of the Bible* (Nashville: Abingdon Press, 1988).

Mir, Mustansir, 'The Quranic Story of Joseph: Plot, Themes, and Characters', *Muslim World* 76.1 (1986), pp. 1-15.

Miscall, Peter D., 'The Jacob and Joseph Stories as Analogies', *JSOT* 6 (1978), pp. 28-40.

—*The Working of Old Testament Narrative* (Philadephia: Fortress Press, 1983).

Moberly, Walter L., *Genesis 12–50* (OTG, 2; Sheffield: JSOT Press, 1992).

Morris, Henry, *The Genesis Record: A Scientific and Devotional Commentary on the Book of Beginnings* (Grand Rapids: Baker Book House, 1976).

Moyers, Bill, *Genesis: A Living Conversation* (New York: Doubleday, 1996).

Nash, Kathleen S., 'Captivity in the Pentateuch', *BToday* 31 (1993), pp. 324-30.

Neufeld, Ernest, 'The Anatomy of the Joseph Cycle', *Jewish Bible Quarterly* 22 (1994), pp. 38-46.

Niditch, Susan, 'The Wronged Woman Righted: An Analysis of Genesis 38', *HTR* 72.1/2 (1979), pp. 142-49.

Niditch, Susan, and Robert Doran, 'The Success Story of the Wise Courtier: A Formal Approach', *JBL* 96.2 (1977), pp. 179-93.

Niehoff, Maren, 'Do Biblical Characters Talk to Themselves? Narrative Modes of Representing Inner Speech in Early Biblical Fiction', *JBL* 111 (1992), pp. 577-95.

—*The Figure of Joseph in Post-Biblical Jewish Literature* (Leiden: E.J. Brill, 1992).

—'The Figure of Joseph in the Targums', *JJS* 39 (1988), pp. 234-50.

Nohrnberg, James, 'Princely Characters [Hebrew Bible]', in Jason P. Rosenblatt and Joseph C. Sitterson (eds.), *Not in Heaven: Coherence and Complexity in Biblical Narrative* (Bloomington: Indiana University Press, 1991), pp. 58-97.

Norris, Christopher, *Deconstruction: Theory and Practice* (repr.; London: Methuen, 1991).

O'Brien, Mark A., 'The Contribution of Judah's Speech, Gen. 44.18-34, to Characterization of Joseph', *CBQ* 59.3 (1997), pp. 429-47.

Payne, Michael (ed.), *A Dictionary of Cultural and Critical Theory* (Oxford: Basil Blackwell, 1996).

Peck, John, 'Note on Gen. 37:2 and Joseph's Character', *ExpTim* 82 (1970/71), pp. 342-43.

Phelan, James, *Reading People, Reading Plots* (Chicago: University of Chicago Press, 1989).

Plaut, W. Gunther (ed.), *The Torah: A Modern Commentary* (New York: Union of American Hebrew Congregations, 1981).

Ploeg, John P. van der, 'Slavery in the Old Testament', in H. Nyberg *et al.* (eds.), *Congress Volume: Uppsala 1971* (VTSup, 22; Leiden: E.J. Brill, 1972), pp. 72-87.

Rad, Gerhard von, *Genesis: A Commentary* (trans. John H. Marks; London: SCM Press, rev. edn, 1972).

—'The Joseph Narrative and Ancient Wisdom', in *idem, The Problem of the Hexateuch and Other Essays* (trans. E.W. Trueman Dicken; Edinburgh: Oliver & Boyd, 1965), pp. 292-300.

Ray, William, *Literary Meaning: From Phenomenology to Deconstruction* (Oxford: Basil Blackwell, 1984).

Redford, Donald B., *A Study of the Biblical Story of Joseph* (VTSup, 20; Leiden: E.J. Brill, 1970).

Reis, Pamela Tamarkin, 'Dead Men Tell No Tales: On the Motivation of Joseph's Brothers', *Conservative Judaism* 44 (1992), pp. 50-60.

Rendsburg, Gary A., 'David and His Circle in Gen. 38', *VT* 36 (1986), pp. 438-46.

—'Literary Structures in the Quranic and Biblical Stories of Joseph', *Muslim World* 78 (1988), pp. 118-20.

—'Redactional Structuring in the Joseph Story: Genesis 37–50', in Vincent Tollers and John Maier (eds.), *Mappings of the Biblical Terrain* (Lewisburg, PA: Bucknell University Press, 1990), pp. 215-32.

Richard, Earl, 'The Polemical Character of the Joseph Episode in Acts 7', *JBL* 98 (1979), pp. 255-67.

Rimmon-Kenan, Shlomith, *Narrative Fiction* (London: Routledge, 1983).

Rogerson, John W., 'Can a Doctrine of Providence Be Based on the Old Testament?', in Lyle M. Eslinger and Glen Taylor (eds.), *Ascribe to the Lord: Biblical and Other Essays in Memory of Peter C. Craigie* (JSOTSup, 67; Sheffield: JSOT Press, 1988), pp. 529-43.

Ross, Allen P., *Creation and Blessing* (Grand Rapids: Baker Book House, 1988).

Ruppert, Lothar, *Die Josephserzählung der Genesis: Ein Beitrag zur Theologie der Pentateuchquellen* (Munich: Kösel, 1965).

Sacks, Robert D., *A Commentary on the Book of Genesis* (Ancient Near Eastern Texts and Studies, 6; Lewiston, NY: Edwin Mellen Press, 1990).

Sailhamer, John H., *Genesis* (The Expositor's Bible Commentary, 2; Grand Rapids: Zondervan, 1990).

—*The Pentateuch as Narrative* (Grand Rapids: Zondervan, 1992).

Samuel, Maurice, 'The True Character of the Biblical Joseph', *BR* 2.1 (1986), pp. 38-51, 68.

Sarna, Nahum M., *Genesis* (The JPS Torah Commentary; Philadephia: Jewish Publication Society of America, 1989).

—*Understanding Genesis* (New York: Schocken Books, 1970).

Savage, Mary, 'Literary Criticism and Biblical Studies: A Rhetorical Analysis of the Joseph Narrative', in Carl D. Evans, William W. Hallo and John B. White (eds.), *Scripture in Context: Essays on the Comparative Method* (Pittsburgh: Pickwick Press, 1980), pp. 79-100.

Savran, George W., *Telling and Retelling: Quotation in Biblical Narrative* (Bloomington: Indiana University Press, 1988).

Schimmel, Sol, 'Joseph and his Brothers: A Paradigm for Repentance', *Judaism: A Quarterly Journal of Jewish Life and Thought* 37 (1988), pp. 60-65.

Schmidt, Ludwig, *Literarische Studien zur Josephsgeschichte* (BZAW, 167; Berlin: W. de Gruyter, 1986).

Schwartz, Regina M., 'Joseph's Bones and the Resurrection of the Text: Remembering in the Bible', in *idem*, *The Book and the Text: The Bible and Literary Theory* (Oxford: Basil Blackwell, 1990), pp. 40-59.

Schweizer, Harald, 'Text Segmentation and Levels of Interpretation—Reading and Rereading the Biblical Story of Joseph', *Semiotica* 107.3/4 (1995), pp. 273-92.

Sedgwick, Colin J., 'Joseph and the Amazing Providence of God [Gen 37-47; Sermon, 16th Sunday After Pentecost]', *ExpTim* 106 (1995), pp. 339-40.

Seebass, Horst, 'The Joseph Story, Genesis 48 and the Canonical Process' (trans. K Engelken), *JSOT* 35 (1986), pp. 29-43.

Seybold, Donald A., 'Paradox and Symmetry in the Joseph Narrative', in Gros Louis, Ackerman and Warshaw (eds.), *Literary Interpretations*, I, pp. 59-73.

Ska, Jean L., 'Proleptic Summaries in Genesis XXVII and in the Recounting of the Story of Joseph', *Bib* 73.4 (1992), pp. 518-27.

Skinner, John, *Genesis* (ICC; Edinburgh: T. & T. Clark, 2nd edn, 1930).

Soggin, J. Alberto, 'Notes on the Joseph Story', in A. Graeme Auld (ed.), *Understanding Poets and Prophets* (JSOTSup, 152; Sheffield: JSOT Press, 1993), pp. 336-49.

Speiser, Ephraim A., *Genesis* (AB, 1; Garden City, NY: Doubleday, 1969).

Steiner, Franz, 'Enslavement and the Early Hebrew Lineage System: An Explanation of Genesis 47.29-31; 48.1-16', in Bernhard Lang (ed.), *Anthropological Approaches to the Old Testament* (Philadelphia: Fortress Press, 1985), pp. 21-25.

Steinmetz, Devora, *From Father to Son* (Louisville, KY: Westminster/John Knox Press, 1991).

Steinsaltz, Adin, *Biblical Images* (New York: Basic Books, 1984).

Stern, Martin S., 'Muhammad and Joseph: A Study of Koranic Narrative [S 12 and Gen 30–50]', *JNES* 44.3 (1985), pp. 193-204.

Sternberg, Meir, *The Poetics of Biblical Narrative: Ideological Literature and the Drama of Reading* (Bloomington: Indiana University Press, 1985).

Stigers, Harold G., *A Commentary on Genesis* (Grand Rapids: Zondervan, 1976).

Taylor, William M., *Joseph the Prime-Minister* (New York: George H. Doran Company, 1914).

Tobin, Thomas H., 'Tradition and Interpretation in Philo's Portrait of the Patriarch Joseph', SBLSP 25 (1986), pp. 271-77.

Tomes, Roger, 'Thomas Mann's *Joseph and His Brothers*', *ExpTim* 89 (1977), pp. 72-75.

Tompkins, Jane P., *Reader-Response Criticism: From Formalism to Post-Structuralism* (Baltimore: The Johns Hopkins University Press, 6th edn, 1988).

Turner, Laurence A., *Announcements of Plot in Genesis* (JSOTSup, 96; Sheffield: JSOT Press, 1990).

Vawter, Bruce, *On Genesis: A New Reading* (New York: Doubleday, 1977).

Victor, P. Hamilton, *The Book of Genesis: Chapters 18–50* (NICOT; Grand Rapids: Eerd-
    mans, 1995).
Vos, Howard F., *Genesis* (Chicago: Moody Press, 1982).
Watt, Trevor, 'Joseph's Dreams', in David L. Miller (ed.), *Jung and the Interpretation of
    the Bible* (New York: Continuum, 1995), pp. 55-70, 121-22.
Wenham, Gordon J., 'The Gap between Law and Ethics in the Bible', *JJS* 48.1 (Spring
    1997), pp. 17-29.
—*Genesis 16–50* (WBC, 2; Dallas: Word Books, 1994).
Wessels, Walter J., 'The Joseph Story as a Wisdom Novellette', in J.A. Loader and J.H. Le
    Roux (eds.), *Old Testament Essays*, II (Pretoria: University of South Africa, 1984),
    pp. 39-60.
West, Gerald, 'Difference and Dialogue: Reading the Joseph Story with Poor and
    Marginalized Communities in South Africa', *BI* 2.2 (1994), pp. 152-70.
Westermann, Claus, *Genesis: A Practical Commentary* (trans. David E. Green; Text and
    Interpretation; Grand Rapids: Eerdmans, 1987).
—*Genesis 37–50: A Commentary* (trans. John J. Scullion; Minneapolis: Augsburg, 1986).
—*Joseph: Studies of the Joseph Stories in Genesis* (trans. Omar Kaste; Edinburgh: T. & T.
    Clark, 1996).
White, Hugh C., 'The Joseph Story: A Narrative Which "Consumes" Its Content', *Semeia*
    31 (1985), pp. 49-69.
—*Narration and Discourse in the Book of Genesis* (New York: Cambridge University
    Press, 1991).
—'Reuben and Judah: Duplicates or Complements?', in James T. Butler, Edgar W. Conrad
    and Ben C. Ollenburger (eds.), *Understanding the Word* (JSOTSup, 37; Sheffield:
    JSOT Press, 1985).
—'Where Do You Come From?', in *idem*, *Narration and Discourse in the Book of
    Genesis*, pp. 232-75.
Whitelam, Keith W., 'The Defence of David', *JSOT* 29 (1984), pp. 61-87.
Whybray, R. Norman, *The Making of the Pentateuch: A Methodological Study* (JSOTSup,
    53; Sheffield: JSOT Press, 1987).
Wildavsky, Aaron, *Assimilation versus Separation: Joseph the Administrator and the Poli-
    tics of Religion in Biblical Israel* (London: Transaction, 1993).
—'Survival Must Not Be Gained through Sin: The Moral of the Joseph Stories Prefigured
    through Judah and Tamar', *JSOT* 62 (1994), pp. 37-48.
Wright, George R.H., 'Joseph's Grave under the Tree by the Omphalos at Shechem', *VT* 22
    (1972), pp. 476-86.
—'The Positioning of Genesis 38', *ZAW* 94.4 (1982), pp. 523-29.
Youngblood, Ronald F., *The Book of Genesis* (Grand Rapids: Baker Book House, 2nd edn,
    1991).
Zornberg, Avivan Gottlieb, *Genesis: The Beginning of Desire* (Philadelphia: Jewish Pub-
    lication Society, 1995).

INDEX OF AUTHORS